Eugene Stock, C. F Warren

Japan and the Janan Mission of the Church Missionary Socielty

Eugene Stock, C. F Warren

Japan and the Janan Mission of the Church Missionary Socielty

ISBN/EAN: 9783337172244

Printed in Europe, USA, Canada, Australia, Japan

Cover: Foto ©Lupo / pixelio.de

More available books at **www.hansebooks.com**

JAPAN

AND THE

JAPAN MISSION

OF THE

Church Missionary Society,

BY

EUGENE STOCK,

Editorial Secretary of the Society.

SECOND EDITION,

REVISED, IN PART RE-WRITTEN, AND CONTINUED TO DATE, BY THE

REV. C. F. WARREN,

Formerly Missionary of the Society at Osaka, and Secretary of the Japan Mission.

WITH A MAP AND ILLUSTRATIONS.

"The mighty God, even the Lord, hath spoken, and called the earth from the rising of the sun unto the going down thereof."—Ps. l. 1.

> Land of the East, awake,
> Soon shall your sons be free;
> The sleep of ages break,
> And rise to liberty.
> On your far hills, long cold and gray,
> Has dawned the everlasting day.

London :

CHURCH MISSIONARY HOUSE, Salisbury Square.
SEELEY, JACKSON, & HALLIDAY, 54, Fleet Street.

1887.

CONTENTS.

CHAPTER				PAGE
I. The Land of the Rising Sun				1
II. The People of Japan				16
III. Japan in Past Times				26
IV. The Two Religions of Japan				34
V. The Jesuit Missions				51
VI. The Locking and the Unlocking				60
VII. The Revolution				71
VIII. New Japan				79
IX. Protestant Missions in Japan				89
X. The Church Missionary Society's Mission :—				
			(I.) Introduction	111
XI.	,,	,,	(II.) Nagasaki	120
XII.	,,	,,	(III.) Kiushiu Out-stations	140
XIII.	,,	,,	(IV.) Osaka	167
XIV.	,,	,,	(V.) Osaka Out-stations	202
XV.	,,	,,	(VI.) Tokio	221
XVI.	,,	,,	(VII.) Hakodate	246
XVII.	,,	,,	(VIII.) Aino Mission	260
XVIII. Conclusion				271

NOTE.

THE First Edition of this book was published in 1879. It has been for some time out of print. I am greatly indebted to the Rev. C. F. Warren for his kindness in revising it, and continuing the history of Japan and its Missions, and particularly of the C.M.S. Mission, down to the present time. More than half of the present work is entirely new, and is contributed by Mr. Warren.

E. S.

CHURCH MISSIONARY HOUSE,
December, 1887.

PREFACE TO THE SECOND EDITION.

IN preparing this Edition the original plan of the work has been preserved. Several of the earlier chapters have needed very little revision, but considerable additions and modifications have been introduced in others. The additional matter in the New Edition of *The Mikado's Empire* has been consulted, and in revising the Chapters on the People and Religions of Japan, I have been much indebted to the valuable Papers and Translations of E. Satow, Esq., J. Troup, Esq., and B. H. Chamberlain, Esq., published in the *Transactions of the Asiatic Society of Japan*, and also to a Paper by the latter gentleman, published by the Imperial University of Tokio. The later Chapters, from Chapter IX., have been almost entirely re-written, and the history of the Mission has been brought down to the latest possible date.

I have to thank the Rev. E. W. Syle, D.D., and several other friends, for valuable suggestions and help in various ways.

C. F. W.

2, GROVE ROAD,
   NEW SOUTHGATE, N.
     August 4th, 1887.

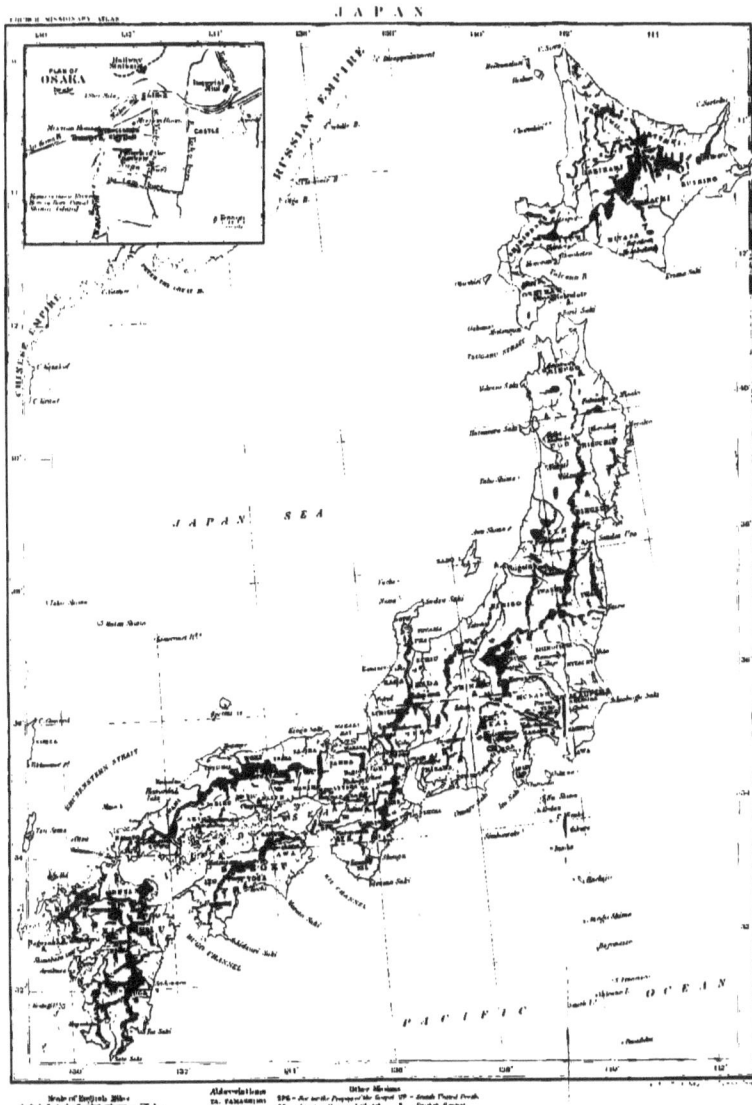

JAPAN AND THE JAPAN MISSION.

I.

THE LAND OF THE RISING SUN.

"He maketh His sun to rise on the evil and on the good."—*Matt.* v. 45.

JAPAN is the Great Britain of Asia. The British Isles are the western outpost of Europe in the Atlantic. The Japanese Isles are the eastern outpost of Asia in the Pacific. Instead of two large islands, however, like Great Britain and Ireland, there are four, viz., Hondo,* Kiushiu, Shikoku, and Yezo, with innumerable smaller islets. The total area of the British archipelago is 122,550 square miles; of the Japanese, about 147,000. The British population in 1881 was 34,884,848; the Japanese, by the census of 1882, was 37,041,368. The four principal islands lie between the thirty-first and forty-sixth parallel of North

---

* The name Nippôn, or Nihon, by which the largest island is known to English Geographers, is not applied to it by the Japanese. They had no name for it apart from its satellite islands until lately. Their modern maps call it Hondo, or Honshiu="Main roads" (*do*) or "principal provinces" (*shiu*). Nippôn, or Dai Nippôn (Great Japan), is the name of the whole empire. Nippôn is the colloquial and Nihon the classical form. "Japan" is our foreign corruption of the Chinese form of Nippôn, *Ji-pun*.

A

latitude, their united length being about 1,200 miles, and the breadth of the main island varying generally from 100 to 175 miles. They are all but continuous, the Straits between the main island and its two southern satellites—Shikoku and Kiushiu—being extremely narrow. Besides the principal islands and the numerous smaller ones immediately contiguous to them, the Japanese Empire also includes the Kurile Islands, stretching away some 600 miles in a north-easterly direction

WESTERN ENTRANCE TO THE INLAND SEA OF JAPAN.

from Yezo, towards the icy coast of Kamschatka ; the Loochoo Islands, extending some 500 miles in a south-westerly direction from Kiushiu to a little east of Formosa ; and the chain of islands commencing with Vries, near the Gulf of Yedo, and terminating in the Bonin group, some 500 miles to the south.

The distance between the principal islands—with which we are at present exclusively concerned—and Korea, may be roughly given as 100 miles, but the westernmost outpost of the Japanese Empire—the large island of Tsushima—in the Korea Channel, is within twenty-five miles of the continent of Asia.

Japan is the crest of a submarine mountain chain. From its shores the land plunges down abruptly into deep water. The islands are everywhere exceedingly mountainous. The more lofty mountains are from 4,000 to 9,000 feet high, and Mount Fuji, a beautiful cone, towering in solitary grandeur thousands of feet above the highest mountains in its vicinity, rises to an elevation of some 13,000 feet above the sea level, its summit being covered with snow the greater part of the year. It is no wonder that the unique form of this "matchless mountain" has inspired the poets and artists of Japan. It is frequently the central object in the background of Japanese ideal and allegorical pictures. It is painted at the bottom of the delicate china cup from which he sips his tea, and on the bowl from which he eats his rice. It appears on his fan, on the back of his metal looking-glass, and on the skirts of his garments.

Many of the peaks of the mountain chains are volcanoes, mostly extinct or quiescent, and "even the superb Fuji owes its matchless form to volcanic action, being clothed by a garment of lava on a throne of granite" (Griffis). Some of the volcanoes are still active. Asama-yama, N.W. of Tokio, "puffs off continual jets of steam," and so does the volcano on Vries Island; and, as late as 1874, the volcano of Taromai in Yezo, whose crater had long since congealed, exploded, blowing its rocky cap far into the air, and scattering a shower of ashes as far as the sea-shore many miles distant. Shocks of earthquake are frequently felt, and they have sometimes been attended with disastrous results, but for the most part they are harmless. Of late years they have been more numerous in the neighbourhood of the capital than in the other parts of Japan where Europeans reside. Hot springs are found in all parts of the country, and many of them, owing to their medicinal properties, are much resorted to by persons suffering from various ailments.

Japan is not a country of large rivers, yet several of the principal streams form important water-ways, and are navigated by boats and small steamers of light draught. Many of the rivers, for a great part of the year, are nothing more than torrent beds, with very narrow streams of water, and some of them are all but dry, except in the spring or after heavy rain. Mountain streams are, however, numerous and perennial, and their water is utilised to irrigate the terraced rice-fields in the narrow valleys between the hills and in the plains below. There are many waterfalls in different parts of the country—the Japanese enumerate upwards of 600—the largest of which is that of Nachi in the province of Ki-i, south of Osaka, which is said to be upwards of 800 feet high and 100 feet broad; but they are generally more remarkable for beauty than for grandeur. The Minō Fall, twelve miles from Osaka, though a comparatively small stream with a fall of about 100 feet, is one of the prettiest. Its situation and surroundings are extremely lovely. It stands at the head of a valley, with rocky but well wooded hills rising on either side; and when seen in the autumn, just as the maples are changing colour, and their crimson foliage of various shades is mingled with that of numerous evergreens, and the yellow and many-coloured leaves of deciduous plants, presents such a picture as baffles both pen and pencil.

The lakes, which are said to be more than 200 in number, are for the most part small; but many of them, standing in silent grandeur among the mountains—like the Hakone lake, near the celebrated Hakone Pass on the Tokaido, west of Tokio—or nestling in luxuriant beauty amidst the foliage of surrounding hills—like Chiuseuji, several miles above

Nikko—are extremely pretty. There are some larger ones, and Biwa, a few miles east of Kioto, which is the largest, is a magnificent sheet of water, with a coast-line of about 180 miles.

Japan is not devoid of mineral wealth. Gold and silver are found, and in the sixteenth century the Portuguese and Dutch exported considerable quantities of both these precious metals, but the present output is limited. Of the useful metals copper has now become an important article of export.

IN THE INLAND SEA OF JAPAN.

Lead, tin, and iron are also found. The coal-fields are extensive, but the coal is inferior; mines are being worked both in Kiushiu and Yezo. But the true wealth of the country consists in its agricultural resources. The soil is fertile, and in some places, as in the Osaka plain, yields two crops annually; but owing to the mountainous character of the country only a limited portion is under cultivation. Rapeseed, which is grown for its oil, wheat, barley, peas, and beans are among the crops harvested in early summer. Rice, which is the principal grain crop, cotton, sweet potatoes, &c., are grown later in the year. Tobacco and tea are cultivated for home use as well as for the foreign market. The wax-tree and camphor-tree also produce important articles of commerce; and the mulberry-tree is cultivated to provide food for silkworms.

Animal life is not so abundant in Japan as in some other countries. Mr. Griffis says: "The poverty of the *fauna* strikes the traveller with surprise." "Bird song must be omitted from the catalogue of natural glories." Yet it must not be supposed that Japan is deficient in birds, or that among the 325 species enumerated by two naturalists in 1880,* there are none remarkable for either beauty or song. Some of the Flycatchers, and especially the Long-tailed Flycatcher (Tchitrea Princeps), which, when alive, "rivals in beauty any denizen of the tropics"; "two species of Pheasants peculiar to the country," "the Mandarin Duck," "the Falcated Teal," and, when flying in the sunlight, "the Japanese Ibis," are birds of noteworthy plumage. The song of the Skylark, and the sweet, though not much varied notes of the Japanese Nightingale, frequently remind the Englishman of two of his favourite songsters. "Three species of Thrushes, all good songsters, abound on Fuji-san. Two of the Flycatchers . . . sing sweetly, and the chorus of birds there in the early morning is delightful."†

The seas of Japan are scarcely equalled in the world for the abundance, variety, and excellence of their fish, and fishing is an important industry all along the extensive coast line of the islands.

---

* *Catalogue of the Birds of Japan*, by T. Blakiston and H. Pryer. Vide *Transactions of the Asiatic Society of Japan*, vol. viii., p. 172.
† *Ibid.*, pp. 174, 175.

The climate of Japan is mainly governed by monsoons. The south-west monsoon, which blows from May to August, and is accompanied by heavy rains, produces a hot and damp summer; and the north-east monsoon, which lasts from October to February, makes the winter cold; but the extremes in either case are not so great as are experienced on the neighbouring continent. In winter, changes of temperature are great and sudden, and severe night frosts are common after warm and sunny days. Heavy falls of snow are not uncommon even in Southern Japan, and the mountain ranges are covered with it for weeks together. The climate varies very considerably in different parts of the country, owing to the extent of latitude covered and the influence of ocean currents. At Sapporo, in Yezo, the average temperature for the whole year is less than 46°; at Tokio it is 57°; and at Nagasaki it is nearly 62°. Kiushiu, the south coast of which is struck by a warm current, called the Kuroshiwo, or "Black Stream," is in the latitude of Egypt, and the heat in summer is almost tropical. Yezo, on the other hand, with a cold current from the sea of Okhotsk passing its eastern coast, though in the latitude of northern Spain, has a climate in winter more severe than our own.

The scenery is fine everywhere and highly diversified. Bamboo thickets and pine groves are important features in almost every landscape. The mountains in many places are clothed with fine timber. Most of the trees, and many of the plants, are evergreen, keeping Japan in perpetual verdure. The very broken coast-line gives a continuous succession of bays and gulfs; and the far-famed Inland Sea, between the main island and its two southern satellites, studded with numerous small islands in some of its narrowest parts, presents some of the loveliest views in the world.

The cities and towns are numerous, and many of them

have large populations. Tokio (formerly called Yedo), Kioto, and Osaka, are *fu* or first-class cities.

The treaty-ports are Tokio, Yokohama, Osaka, Hiogo, (Kobé), and Niigata in the main island; Nagasaki in Kiushiu; and Hakodate in Yezo.

KIOTO, the once sacred capital, where the Mikados resided for upwards of a thousand years—from A.D. 794 to 1868—is by far the most interesting city in the country. Since the revolution in 1868 it has been called Saikio,* or "Western Capital," in contradistinction to Tokio, the "Eastern Capital." It is in the heart of Japan, a few miles west of Lake Biwa. Except to the south, the plain in which it stands is encircled by mountains, and on its eastern side— parallel to the river Kamo, which flows through and divides the city—a range of hills several hundred feet high, quite distinct from the higher mountain range beyond it, adds much to the beauty of its situation. The Kamo is spanned by several long bridges, but it is not navigable even for small boats, being little more than a dry shingly bed, except when swollen by heavy rains. The river bed is quite a marked feature of the city. It is utilised for bleaching linen, scores of lengths of which may be seen spread on it on any fine day. In the summer evenings some portions of it are alive with multitudes of citizens, their families and friends, who occupy booths and "cooling stages," sipping tea or wine, eating ices and fruit, smoking their tiny pipes, using their fans, chatting and otherwise refreshing and amusing themselves. The city is well built and the streets are broad and clean. Most of the residences formerly occupied by nobles and court officers have been demolished, but the Imperial Palace still

---

* In early works on Japan, Kioto is called Miaco, which is the Japanese word for capital, and of which Kio and Kioto are the Chinese equivalents.

remains, and it was occupied by the Emperor for some months during the Satsuma Rebellion in 1877. Though shorn of its former dignity and glory by the removal of the Court to Tokio, the industries and trade of Kioto still flourish, and its population is probably upwards of 300,000.

Kioto has for centuries been the principal centre of the nation's religious life, and both Buddhist and Shinto temples and shrines are numerous. It wears the aspect of a city wholly given to idolatry. In the city, among the many, the chief temples of the great Shin sect are conspicuous, and Tera-machi, "Temple Street," as its name implies, is full of temples. In the suburbs, and all along the hill which forms the background of the city on its eastern side, temples abound everywhere; and the grounds of many of them, especially those which include woods and thickets on the hill-sides, are both extensive and beautiful. Some are like parks, some are laid out as gardens—admirable specimens of Japanese landscape gardening—and in all of them the people, who are great lovers of nature, find abundant pleasure and delight.

TOKIO, formerly called Yedo, is a comparatively modern city. Until the beginning of the seventeenth century it was a place of no importance. Then it was that Tokugawa Iyeyasu, who had just succeeded to the Shogunate, as the founder of a new dynasty, by erecting his castle, and establishing his government there, laid the foundation of its future greatness. It is now the largest city in the Empire, and has a population of about a million. When the Shogûnate was abolished in 1868, Yedo received its new name Tokio, and became the seat of the Mikado's Government. The city stands at the head of what is called by foreigners the Gulf of Yedo, and at the mouth of the Sumida river, which divides its eastern suburb. The first C.M.S. missionary at Tokio, the

Rev. J. Piper, thus wrote of it in 1874, the year of hi arrival :—

Although it cannot boast of such a beautiful structure as the Taj in Agra, nor possesses ruins at all equal to those in Lucknow or Delhi, yet it far surpasses those cities in extent, and certainly surpasses them in the arrangement, width, and nature of its streets; and, as compared with the great cities of China, which I have visited, viz., Canton, Fuh-Chow, and Ning-po, it exceeds them as much as the Strand does Lower Thames Street, or as the western half of London does the eastern. It is about eight miles from north to south, and nearly the same distance from east to west. The main street, a part of the famous *Tokaido* (*i.e.*, Eastern Ocean Road), divides the city into two unequal parts. In the western are the Imperial domain and extensive grounds, and most of the old residences of the nobility; in the eastern part the buildings are mostly warehouses, shops, and dwellings for the poorer classes; Shinto and Buddhist temples are to be found in abundance. These temples are beautifully situated, and cover many acres of ground. Many of them are, nevertheless, in a state of ruin, since the Buddhistic faith has been practically set aside by the Government. Some of the mansions formerly occupied by the nobility are now used by the government for offices and barracks. Some are in ruins, whilst others have entirely disappeared; and hence there are acres of ground now covered with long grass.

The main street is a remarkably good one; it has a row of trees newly planted on either side, between which and the shops is a brick causeway which would be a credit to any city. Most of the other streets are straight and wide, and they are kept in good order. The large number of canals running through the city give occasion for a still larger number of bridges, which I think benefit as well as beautify the metropolis. The houses are seldom more than two storeys high—many of them only one.

Originally built as a military stronghold, its principal feature was the Shogûns' Castle, the walls and moats of which still remain. The moats and other canals are connected and communicate either with the Sumida river or the bay; and it is over one of these, which crosses the main street of the city, that the famous Bridge of Japan—Nihon Bashi—is built; from which all distances in the Empire are measured. But the bridge "of cedarwood, with highly ornamental balustrades," or, as described by another, the "humpbacked structure, a crazy mass of old firewood," of former days, has given place to a well-built bridge of stone, almost level, and well adapted for the passage of the continuous stream of tramcars, waggonettes, and *jinrikisha*, which were unknown in Tokio twenty years ago. The city is becoming more and more Europeanised every year. Not only have many public buildings been erected in European style, but the houses in the western half of the city, many of which a few years ago were slightly-built structures of wood with shingle roofs, and were burnt down by tens of thousands, have been replaced by more substantial edifices, constructed with a view to resisting fire, and divided into blocks to minimise the danger from that source.

YOKOHAMA is situated on a bay in the Gulf of Yedo: the important town of Kanagawa, which gives the official name to the port, being on one side of the bay, and Yokohama, "the cross-strand," just opposite. It is eighteen miles from Tokio, with which it is connected by railway, and is the principal treaty-port and the head-quarters of the principal mercantile firms established in the country. Before the opening of the ports in 1859, it was a miserable fishing village on the edge of a swamp. It is now a large and flourishing town of 80,000 inhabitants, with European and native quarters; and has some fine buildings in European style, including the Custom House, Post Office, Town Hall, and Court House. The European commerical quarter is substantially built, but some of the streets are narrow. Many of the foreigners reside on the Bluffs, a range of low hills, extending from the shore of the bay inland, on which there are numerous pleasantly situated villas, with gardens well screened from the roads by evergreen hedges and shrubberies. The regular foreign residents in 1884, were 1,229, besides visitors and sailors in harbour, and exclusive of 2,471 Chinese, many of whom are merchants, store-keepers, brokers, money-changers, and clerks, others being working carpenters, painters, tailors, shoemakers, and domestic servants in European houses. The resident Europeans support an English chaplain and have their own church, which is not, however, an imposing edifice. Services connected with other denominations are held in the "Union Church," a neat and substantial building, which is also the regular meeting place of a Japanese congregation.

OSAKA stands in the delta of the River Yodo, about two miles from the sea and thirty from Kioto. This river is formed in the plain south of Kioto, by the union of the waters of its four principal affluents—one issuing from Lake Biwa, another flowing across the Kioto plain to the west of the city, another passing through the city itself, and the fourth draining the country to the south and south-east—and thence flows towards the Gulf of Osaka, into which it falls by several channels. Having lost a portion of its water above Osaka it enters the city at its north-eastern extremity, and is thence divided. Its several streams, together with the numerous canals cut at right angles to each other, completely intersect the city. These are spanned by scores of bridges—chiefly of wood, but with a few modern ones resting on iron piles—and on this account Osaka has been frequently called the "Venice of the East." The city is well built, but the streets are narrow, except where advantage has been taken of the destruction of buildings by fire to make them wider. The Shogûn's Castle, with its massive granite walls and broad moats, still stands at the north-east corner of the city, and is now the head-quarters of the Osaka garrison. The public buildings include the Imperial Mint and Arsenal, the Railway Station, and the Government Offices of the *Fu*, all of which are substantially built in European style. The population is upwards of 300,000. As a port of foreign trade it has been eclipsed by Kobe, twenty miles distant, but it retains its supremacy as the centre of native trade in Southern and Western Japan. Not only is it in constant communication with numerous ports on the inland sea and on the outside coasts, but it is connected with Kobe on the one hand, and with Kioto, the Lake Biwa district, and beyond, on the other, by railway. It is also the seat of local government for the Osaka Fu, the most populous prefecture in the country, with nearly 1,600,000 inhabitants. In 1884 the European residents were 98, and the Chinese 97.

HIOGO is an old and important town in the Gulf of Osaka, which, though giving the treaty-port its official name—just as in the case of Kanagawa already noticed—has no direct connection with its foreign trade. This is exclusively carried on at KOBE, where there is a small but well-built and well-ordered settlement, with its own municipal government, and adjoining it, chiefly to the west, a large and flourishing Japanese town of more than 50,000 inhabitants. Kobe is pleasantly situated on the edge of the gulf. Behind it the ground gradually rises for more than half a mile, and beyond this is a mountain range of considerable elevation. The port not only has the advantage of a fine anchorage, but it is in direct railway communication with Osaka, Kioto, and the south-western shore of Lake Biwa, whence steamers run across the lake to its north-eastern shore, where two other sections of railway are in operation, the one terminating at Tsuruga on the west coast, and the other running eastward, in the line of the great central road of the country called Nakasendo, where its construction is being continued. Kobe has a much smaller European community than Yokohama. In 1884 it numbered 385, including children. There is a "Union Protestant

Church," in which Church of England services are held by English and American Church missionaries, but the building is also used by other denominations. In 1884 there were 528 Chinese residents. As a port Kobe is steadily rising in importance.

NAGASAKI is the treaty-port in the Island of Kiushiu, the southernmost of the four principal islands of the Japanese group, and so called from its division into "nine provinces." It stands near the head of a lovely bay, which, with its rocky coasts and surrounding hills, makes it by far the prettiest of the treaty-ports. The town has a population of some 33,000, exclusive of the suburbs, and it is the seat of government for the prefecture, now called the Nagasaki *Ken*. It is historically interesting as one of the places connected with the final struggle between Romish Christianity and the Secular power in 1637, when many, faithful unto death, were hurled from the top of the small rocky island of Pappenberg, at the mouth of the bay, a little south of the town ; and further, as having been the place of the Dutch trading settlement of Deshima, the only point of contact between Japan and the outside world for 230 years, after the expulsion of foreigners in 1624. In 1884 there were 248 European and 603 Chinese residents.

HAKODATE is the treaty-port in Yezo, the northernmost of the four large islands. This island consists mainly of impenetrable jungles, inaccessible mountains, and impassable swamps, and has some volcanoes, several of which are still in full activity. Its area is considerably larger than that of Ireland, but its population is sparse, numbering about 150,000, and consists chiefly of colonists from the central and southern islands, many of whom are actively engaged in bringing available land under cultivation in and near the south-west coast. Hakodate is by far the largest and most flourishing town in the island. In 1859, when it was first opened to foreigners, it had a population of about 6,000, and was only resorted to by whalers. It is now an important commercial centre, with a population of some 40,000, and is in direct steam communication with Yokohama, Kobe, and other ports. The town is pleasantly situated on the slope of a hill, and the shore-line of a land-locked bay which forms a deep, commodious and safe harbour. In 1884 the European residents were 40, and the Chinese 41.

NIIGATA is on the west coast, at the mouth of the Shinano-gawa, the largest river in Japan. It is the capital of one of the richest provinces in the Empire, but it has not been successful as a treaty-port. Very few foreigners have ever settled there, and direct foreign trade has not developed as at the other ports. The important island of Sado, noted for its gold mines, is off Niigata.

Such, in a few words, is the Land of the Rising Sun, as the Japanese themselves delight to designate their country. They sail out into the East, but find nothing save the broad expanse of the Pacific; a stretch of four thousand miles to the opposite coast of North America; and their national flag represents the morning sun rising out of the sea.

II.

THE PEOPLE OF JAPAN.

"And hath made of one blood all nations of men for to dwell on all the face of the earth, and hath determined the times before appointed, and the bounds of their habitation."—*Acts* xvii. 26.

"WO distinctly marked types of feature are found among the people of Japan. Among the upper classes, the fine, long, oval face, with prominent, well-chiselled features, deep-sunken eye-sockets, oblique eyes, long drooping eyelids, elevated and arched eyebrows, high and narrow forehead, rounded nose, bud-like mouth, pointed chin, small hands and feet, contrast strikingly with the round, flattened face, less oblique eyes almost level with the face, and straight noses, expanded and upturned at the roots. The one type prevails among the higher classes, the nobility and gentry; the other among the agricultural and labouring classes. The former is the southern, or Yamato type, the latter the Aino, or northern type." (Griffis.)

These two types of face represent probably two distinct immigrations. The northern horn of the crescent-shaped chain of Japanese islands almost touches the mainland of Siberia. The separating channel is but five miles across, and so shallow that, after certain winds, it is occasionally dry; and in the winter it is frozen over. Across this narrow strait probably came the Aino immigration. Again, the southern shores of Japan are washed by one of the great equatorial currents of the Pacific, the Kuroshiwo, or Black Stream, up which many a boat has drifted from the Malay archipelago ; and in this way, and also by immigration from Korea, the coast of which is distant but a day's sail in a junk, were peopled the southern islands of Kiushiu and Shikoku. Gradually the southern immigrants conquered the northern, and in the course of ages the races were fused together, and formed the present Japanese people ; the original distinction, however, being still visible in the two types of countenance. Such at least is the theory of Mr. Griffis, to which also Dickson and others incline.

In the island of Yezo, however, the Ainos long maintained their independence, and their purity of race ; and a remnant of them, some 15,000 in number, still survive, though subject for centuries past to the Japanese. "As the Aino of to-day is and lives, so Japanese art and traditions depict him in the dawn of history : of low stature, thick-set, full-bearded, bushy hair of a true black, eyes set nearly at right angles with the nose, which is short and thick, muscular in frame and limbs, with big hands and feet. His language, religion, dress, and general manner of life are the same as of old. He has no alphabet, no writing, no numbers above a thousand. . . . In character and morals they are stupid, good-natured, brave, honest, faithful, peaceable, gentle." (Griffis.)*

The general account of their origin, as given in their own traditions, is that they are the offspring of a breed between man and beast, their remote ancestor on one side having been a large white dog or wolf. The term Aino—more correctly Ainu—is their common word for "man," and notwithstanding its close resemblance in sound with the Japanese words *inu*, "a dog," and *ai-no-ko*, "cross-breed," its derivation from these

---

* An account of the Ainos, with fac-similes of Japanese pictures of them, appeared in the *C. M. Gleaner* of May, 1877.

words, as suggested by some Japanese scholars, appears to be altogether fanciful. In the older Japanese literature they are called *ebisu*, "savages."

The Aino and Japanese languages, although at first striking the student as having "a great apparent resemblance," are in reality wholly different. The similarity "vanishes as soon as the two languages are more carefully compared. The paradox of two races so strongly contrasted speaking related languages has no foundation in fact."* Such is Mr. Chamberlain's verdict, after a scholarly comparison of Aino with Japanese and its related languages. He inclines to accept Von Schrenck's assertion, "that Aino is to be regarded as a language altogether isolated at the present day." If this be so, it is a strong proof that there was no ancient connection between the two peoples.

The Japanese appear to be the true progenitors of the North American Indians, and of the Mexicans and Californians, or at all events a branch of the same stock. When Cortes arrived in Mexico he was received by Montezuma and his sages as a long-expected messenger from their ancestors *in the far distant west*. Photographs of Colorado and Nebraska Indians have been taken by Japanese for their own countrymen. "Some affirmed that they were acquainted with the persons represented." "Scanty or no beard, colour of skin, hair, and eyes, were alike." There are said to be some remarkable correspondences in the Japanese and Red Indian languages; but this branch of inquiry has not yet been followed out.

How would the Japanese reach North America? They would be drifted thither by the great current, the Black

---

* Memoirs of the Literature College, Imperial University of Japan, No. I. *The Language, Mythology, and Geographical Nomenclature of Japan, viewed in the Light of Aino Studies*, by B. H. Chamberlain, Esq., p. 4.

Stream, already mentioned. It flows up past Japan and the Kurile Islands to the coast of Alaska, and thence southwards towards California. This is not speculation. Forty-seven Japanese junks were wrecked or met with on American shores between 1782 and 1876, some of which had been eighteen months adrift.

If this view be correct, tribes related to both Japanese and Ainos may be found in North America, and the likeness between the Ainos and Esquimaux which some have traced may prove to be a real one.

THE JAPANESE JINRIKISHA. (*From an Original Sketch by an Officer of H.M.S. Challenger.*)

The Japanese are very small in stature, the average height of the men being not much over five feet ; but they are not lacking in endurance and activity. The *jin-riki-sha* men will run with the little carriage and its occupant thirty miles at the rate of six miles an hour.*

---

* Twelve years ago there was no such thing as a wheeled carriage in Japan. *Kago*, a kind of sedan, but altogether unlike those in use in China, were to be had ; or the traveller could ride on horseback, or walk. An ingenious English-

"In moral character," says Griffis, "the average Japanese is frank, honest, faithful, kind, gentle, courteous, confiding, affectionate, filial, loyal. Love of truth for its own sake, chastity, temperance, are not characteristic virtues." "The merchants are mean, and in moral character low." "In reverence to elders and to antiquity, obedience to parents, gentle manners, and universal courtesy and generous impulses, the Japanese are the peers of any, and superior to many, peoples of Christendom."

The Japanese cannot be called a moral people, if we judge them by our Christian standard; but they are certainly no worse than other heathen nations. Much of their evil reputation in this respect arises from their disregard of what we consider the ordinary decencies of life, as shown by their bathing in public, &c.; but they are manifestly quite unconscious of any impropriety in these habits. Nations differ in their views of such matters. The Mohammedan lady in the East conceals her face; the Brahmin lady in India sees, and is seen by, no man but her husband; and both consider English customs highly improper. The Japanese has only one legal wife, but secondary wives are allowed, if he can

---

man had an arm-chair fixed upon wheels, and hired a Japanese to drag him about. The idea took; and with the rapidity which is so extraordinary a feature of the progress of civilisation in Japan, the *jinrikisha* became the national vehicle. *Jin-riki-sha* means "man-power carriage," or as a Yankee phrased it, "*Pull-man-car.*" It is a two-wheeled carriage, not unlike a Bath chair without the small wheel in front. There is generally a hood of woollen cloth to keep the sun off, and in wet weather this is covered with oiled paper such as rain-coats are made of. It is drawn by a single man, running between the shafts, and sometimes assisted by a second pushing behind, or pulling in front tandem fashion. They will trot along all day at a good pace. The ordinary rate is six miles an hour, at 2*d.* per mile. Mr. Warren says the travelling would be fairly comfortable but for the bad roads, which cause incessant jolting. "The coolies, however, are very good-natured, and by their pulling, twisting, and groaning, progress is made."

support them. Mr. Griffis affirms, however, that not five per cent. of the population avail themselves of this conventional licence. In some other matters, the immorality of Japan is very marked; yet it is to be feared that the Japanese are not

JAPANESE PEASANT AND WIFE.

without excuse when they say that some foreigners are worse than themselves. Certainly vice is most rampant in the treaty-ports. On leaving Yokohama and Tokio for an inland city, Mr. Griffis (not a missionary be it remembered, but a professor of physical science) wrote these sad words :—" I had seen how long contact with heathen life and circumstances slowly disintegrate the granite principles of eternal right once held by men in a more bracing moral atmosphere. I met scores of white men, from Old and New England, who had long since forgotten the difference between right and wrong." Two illustrations will suffice : (1) One merchant at a treaty-port had ten Japanese wives; (2) The form of agreement which the Government required white gentlemen engaged for educational purposes to sign contained an undertaking that they would not get drunk!*

The position of woman in Japan is much better than it is in most other Asiatic countries. This is all the more creditable to the people, seeing that Buddhism accords her a very low place, and tells her that her only hope of "salvation" is to be re-born as a man. In the history and literature of Japan women occupy an honourable place. Nine of its 123 sovereigns, and those not the least famous, have been women. Mr. Aston, of the British Legation, says: "I believe no parallel is to be found in the history of European letters to the remarkable fact that a very large proportion of the best writings of the best age of Japanese literature was the work of women." And Mr. Griffis, in his more grandiose style: "Moses established the Hebrew, Alfred the Saxon, and Luther the German tongue in permanent form ; but in Japan, the mobile forms of speech crystallised into perennial beauty under the touch of woman's hand." The latter writer speaks highly of the Japanese ladies. " No ladies excel them in innate love of beauty, order, neatness, household adornment

---

* The moral tone of the Treaty-Ports, though still far below what it should be, has much improved of late years, since the communities of foreign residents have become more settled, and their social life has been purified by the advent of numerous European ladies.

and management." "In maternal affection and tenderness, the mothers need fear no comparison with those of other climes. As educators of their children they are peers to the mothers of any civilisation." "The three fundamental duties of woman, which include all others, are almost universally fulfilled with-

JAPANESE FISHERMEN, ISLAND OF YEZO.

out murmurings or hesitation, viz., (1) obedience to her father when a child, (2) obedience to her husband when a wife, (3) obedience (at least formal) to her eldest son when a widow.' "The biography of a good woman is written in one word—obedience."

The people of Japan are (or rather were, for since 1868 a levelling process has been going on) divided into four principal classes :—(1) The Samurai, or military and literary class— the sword and the pen being united as in no other country ; (2) the farmers and agriculturists; (3) the artizan class ; (4) the merchants and shop-keepers, who have always been regarded as the lowest in social rank in Japan. Below these again, outside the pale of humanity, were the pariahs of Japan, the *eta*, generally living in separate villages, and following the occupation of skinners, tanners, leather-dressers, grave-diggers, &c.,—and the *hinin*, beggars. These were enfranchised in 1871. Since then Samurai, farmer, artizan, trader and *eta* have been on an equal footing before the law. At the head of the Samurai were the Daimio, the great feudal chiefs, 268 in number; and above them again in rank, though not in wealth and power, were the Kugé, or court nobles of Kioto, numbering 150 families, all branches, more or less distant, of the Imperial house.

The Samurai, or "two-sworded men," who had the right, until March 1876, to wear two swords,* are called by Mr. Griffis "the brightest type of the Japanese man." For centuries they "monopolised arms, learning, patriotism, and intellect." "The Samurai is the soul of the nation." On the other hand, of the farmer he says, "Like the wheat that for successive ages is planted as wheat, sprouts, beards, and fills as wheat, the peasant, with his horizon bounded by his rice-fields, his water-courses, or the timbered hills, his intellect laid

---

* Dickson, writing in 1869, says, "All Japan is divided into two classes— those who have a right to wear two swords, and those who have no such right. The swordless man pays rent for his ground, house, and shop. The two-sworded man pays no rent and no taxes, because he is not allowed to trade." He translates *Samurai* "an officer and a gentleman." (*Japan*, p. 138.) All these distinctions are now abolished.

away for safe keeping in the priest's hands, is the son of the soil; caring little who rules him, unless he is taxed beyond the power of flesh and blood to bear—then he rises as a rebel."*

The happy brightness of child-life in Japan has struck all who have visited the country. Sir R. Alcock has nicknamed it "a Paradise of babies." Mr. Griffis has an entertaining chapter on the games and sports of Japanese children, which he regards as, "in general, natural, sensible, and in every sense beneficial." Some, he says, teach history or geography, good sentiments or language; some inculcate reverence and obedience to the elder brother or sister, to parents, or to the Mikado, or "stimulate the manly virtues of courage and contempt for pain." And he concludes with these words: "The character of the games has much to do with that frankness, affection, and obedience on the side of the children, and that kindness and sympathy on the side of the parents, which are so noticeable among the good points of Japanese life and character."

---

* All classes of the population are now rising in the social scale, and the Samurai, shorn of their special privileges as a military caste, no longer enjoy a monopoly of political influence. With the advance of education and the spread of knowledge, even the intelligent country villager joins with other classes in discussing the many questions that affect the welfare of the country.

III.

JAPAN IN PAST TIMES.

"And the times of this ignorance God winked at; but now commandeth all men everywhere to repent."—*Acts* xvii. 30.

HE present Mikado* or Emperor of Japan, Mutsuhito, claims to be the 123rd sovereign in direct succession. Remembering that Queen Victoria is only the thirtieth from William the Conqueror, we can form an idea of the alleged antiquity of Japanese annals.

Japan boasts of a voluminous historical literature. The oldest works extant are the *Kojiki*, or "Records of Ancient Matters," and the *Nihongi*, or "Chronicles of Japan," the former completed in 712 A.D. and the latter in 720. "The scope of the two histories is the same; but the language of the latter and its manner of treating the national traditions stand in notable contrast to the unpretending simplicity of the elder work." "The subject matter is touched up, re-arranged and polished as to make the work resemble a Chinese history as far as possible" (Chamberlain). Many commentaries have been written upon them. They contain the

---

* The meaning of "Mikado" is doubtful. The Chinese characters used to express the term mean "Honourable Gate," a phrase similar to "Sublime Porte." The Emperor is never spoken of by his personal name, but as *Ten-shi* ="Son of Heaven." The name by which he will be known to posterity will be conferred on him after his death. See the following note.

cosmogony, the mythology, and the early history of the nation. Much of the contents is fabulous on the face of it. The first Mikado, Jimmu Tenno,* whose date corresponds with 660 B.C., and who would be contemporary with Manasseh King of Judah and Assurbanipal King of Assyria, is said to have had a goddess for his mother, and to have come from heaven in a boat. He is worshipped as a god at thousands of shrines ; and on the 7th of April, the traditional day of his accession, salutes are fired in his honour by the Krupp and Armstrong guns of modern Japanese ironclads.

Authentic history does not begin till the seventh century A.D. ; but from that time to the present the records are complete and trustworthy.† The chief authority is the *Dai Nihon Shi*, or History of Great Japan, a really great work, published in 1715. It is written in pure Chinese, which is to Japanese what Latin is to the languages of modern Europe, and fills 243 volumes. The people are enthusiastically fond of the history of their country ; and local records (like our county histories), diaries, official guide-books, &c., abound. There are hundreds of children's histories ; and the national annals hold a prominent place in the education of the young.

This is not the place to attempt any summary of Japanese history, but a few notes may be added. The earliest traditions of the Empire, embodied in the "Records of Ancient

---

* *Jim-mu*="divine valour" is the posthumous or canonical name of *Kamu-yamato-ihare-biko.* Until the eighth century A.D. such canonical names were not given, and those of the preceding monarchs, from Jimmu 660 B.C. to Ko-niu 781 A.D., were all invented by a scholar, after the latter date, at the command of the Emperor Kuwan-mu. *Ten-no*="heavenly king," the ruler by divine right, is the official title.

† Speaking of the "Records" and "Chronicles" Mr. Chamberlain says :—
" So far as clear native documentary evidence reaches, 400 A.D. is approximately the highest limit of reliable Japanese history." *Transactions Asiatic Society of Japan*, vol. x., Supplement, p. lxiv.

Matters" and the "Chronicles of Japan" are of the scantiest kind possible. From the beginning of the reign of Jimmu's successor there is "a blank of (according to the accepted chronology) four hundred years, during which absolutely nothing is told us excepting dreary genealogies, the place where each sovereign dwelt, and where he was buried, and the age to which he lived."* But the later traditions have their heroes : Sujin, the civiliser, who with the aid of his generals subdued various turbulent districts in the first century B.C. ; Yamato-Daké, of the imperial family, a great conqueror ; and the Emperor Sei-mu, who divided the Empire into provinces, districts, cities, towns, &c., in the second century A.D. ; and, in particular, the Empress Jingu (*i.e.*, "godlike exploit"), one of the nine queens already alluded to, who after her husband's death took the reins of power, and subsequently assisted her son, who was born after her return from Korea, in the government of the Empire. She flourished in the third century A.D., and is renowned for her "beauty, piety, intelligence, energy, and martial valour." She conquered Korea (now part of the Chinese empire); and through the communication thus established with the mainland, Japan received from China during the next three centuries its philosophy, letters, jurisprudence, ethics, art, and science—in short a new civilisation. From China came also a new religion—of which more hereafter.

In the fourth century A.D. lived Nintoku—the sage emperor —a man of simple tastes and habits, whose benign rule was characterised by paternal consideration for the poorer classes of his subjects. He remitted all taxation for three years, and it is said that during his reign there was no criminal trial. In the seventh century A.D. the custom of attaching special

---

* *Transactions Asiatic Society of Japan*, vol. x., Supplement, p. xlix.

names to successive periods of years, as in China, was introduced by the Emperor Kotoku,* who also, among other reforms, appointed governors over the provinces, established postal stations, and enrolled an army for defensive purposes. In the same century the reign of Tenji, which was characterised by the introduction of water-wheels, the first manufacture of iron-ware, and the foundation of schools, is considered the most prosperous one of the middle ages. In the next century the Chinese calendar † was introduced, and in its latter half Keiki, better known by his canonical name, Kōbō-Daishi, the inventor of the Japanese syllabary, was born.

From the earliest times down to the twelfth century A.D., the government of Japan was imperialism. The Mikado not only reigned, but ruled. Gradually, however, the feudal system arose.‡ The great nobles, or Daimios, in their fortified castles, became more and more powerful and independent. Their armed retainers formed the military caste of Samurai, or "two-sworded men," already noticed. For many centuries, coming down to our own day, Japan was in much the same condition as Scotland is pictured to us in the pages of Sir Walter Scott, parcelled out among great clans, the chiefs of which professed unbounded loyalty to the king while keeping much of the real power in their own hands. The Daimios

---

* Since that time Japanese history has been divided into 228 periods, commencing with Dai-kuwa, the Era of "Great Glory," and ending with Mei-ji, the current period, the Era of "Illustrious Rule."

† This continued in use until 1872, when it was superseded by the Gregorian calendar.

‡ Mr. Chamberlain, whose knowledge of ancient Japanese literature gives his opinion considerable weight, whilst denying that anything like the organized feudalism which prevailed from the twelfth century A.D. down to 1868, existed in ancient times, yet thinks it indisputable that "beyond the immediate limits of the Imperial domain the government *resembled* feudalism rather than centralization."—*Transactions Asiatic Society*, vol. x., Supplement, p. lxii.

were the Macduffs and the Macdonalds, the Campbells and the Douglases of Japan.

Towards the close of the twelfth century A.D., Yoritomo, who belonged to the Minamoto clan, one of the two rival military families of the time, and who after his father's defeat had been exiled as a boy, succeeded in concert with other members of the family in completely destroying the power of the rival house. Thus becoming military master of the

JAPANESE KAGO.

country, he ended by himself usurping all the executive authority of the state, while still acknowledging the Mikado as his liege lord. He subsequently received the title of Shogûn* (general), and laid the foundation of the dual form of government which lasted till 1868, more than 700 years. He made Kamakura his capital, and there the power of the Shogûns was chiefly centred until Iyeyasu transferred it to

---

* The Shogûn has generally been called Tycoon, or Taikûn, by Europeans (*e.g.*, Sir R. Alcock's book, *The Capital of the Tycoon*); but this name is not known to the Japanese people. It was invented for the American treaty of 1854 (p. 65). The full title conferred on Yoritomo was *Sei-i-dai-Shogun*="Barbarian Subjugating Great General."

Yedo in the seventeenth century.* The Mikado held his court at the sacred capital Kioto, rarely appearing before his subjects, but worshipped by them almost as a god; while the Shogûn resided generally at Kamakura, or later at Yedo, and virtually governed the country. It was not, as has been supposed, that the Mikado was spiritual and the Shogûn temporal head. The Shogûn only ruled in the Mikado's name. "The soldier who would begin revolution, or who lusted for power, would make the Mikado his tool; but however transcendent his genius, he never attempted to write himself Mikado. No Japanese Cæsar ever had his Brutus, nor Charles his Cromwell, nor George his Washington. Not even, as in China, did one dynasty of alien blood overthrow another and reign in the stead of a destroyed family." "Though individual Mikados have been dethroned the prestige of the line has never suffered. The loyalty or allegiance of the people has never swerved." (Griffis.) The dynasty is one of the oldest in the world.

The greatest of the Shogûns was Hideyoshi, better known as Taiko Sama (Taiko being a title he received, and Sama, "honourable," answering to "his highness"), who was contemporary with our Queen Elizabeth. His name is still a household word among the people, and he is everywhere worshipped as a god under the name of Toyokuni. It was he who banished the Jesuit missionaries—of whom more presently. On his death in 1598, one of his generals, Iyeyasu, of the Tokugawa clan, usurped power, and after a severe struggle, which is interesting on account of the part taken in it by the Romish Christian Japanese, totally defeated his rivals at the battle of Sekigahara, some miles to the east of Lake Biwa, on the

---

* Kamakura is a few miles west of Yokohama. Its glory has departed. It is now a small village, but its former greatness is attested by the colossal statue of Buddha, and the temple of Hachiman, where many relics of Yoritomo are preserved. The great warrior's grave is on the hill-side.

great central road called Naka-sendo. "This battle decided the condition of Japan for over two centuries, the settlement of the Tokugawa family in hereditary succession to the Shogûnate, the fate of Christianity, the isolation of Japan from the world, the fixing into permanency of the dual system and of feudalism, the glory and greatness of Yedo as the Shogûn's capital." The last of the Shogûns, who was deposed in 1868, belonged to the Tokugawa family, and was the fifteenth in the direct succession from Iyeyasu.

Thus the Shogûnate continued unchanged down to our own day; and with it continued all the characteristic features of mediæval feudalism. Even in externals the resemblance between the Samurai of less than twenty years ago and the knights of the age of chivalry in Europe was most remarkable. Every trooper, and his horse, wore a complete suit of armour, specimens of which have been sent over to our International Exhibitions; every clan had its banner emblazoned with its lord's arms; every Daimio had his well-known and much-prized crest, and Japanese heraldry was as elaborate as European. The crest of the Mikado was the Chrysanthemum flower, which is still represented heraldically on the government seal. One of the mediæval civil wars, in which the contending factions had respectively red and white flags bearing this device, has been happily called, in imitation of a familiar episode of English history, the War of the Chrysanthemums.*

One of the most characteristic institutions of Japanese "chivalry" was the *hara-kiri*, or suicide by ripping up the

---

* Three of these crests are represented on the cover of this book, on the front, at the bottom. To the left is that of the Tokugawa clan, who held the Shogûnate from 1603 to 1868, representing three hollyhock leaves pointing inward. In the centre is that of the Mikado, representing the sixteen petals of the chrysanthemum. To the right is that of the Shimadzu clan of Satsuma (see p. 68), the ring of a horse's bridle-bit.

body. A defeated warrior or a deposed official who had any regard for his own honour destroyed himself in this horrible manner. Hence arose, about the fifteenth century, the fashion of wearing two swords, the shorter one being reserved for the wearer's own body.* Under the Tokugawa Shogûns the practice was introduced of using *hara-kiri* as a judicial punishment for the Samuri class, condemning a man to commit suicide. In few countries is human life less valued than in Japan. One of the national proverbs is, " If you hate a man, let him live."

---

* Some curious accounts of *hara-kiri* occur in Bp. Smith's *Ten Weeks in Japan*, pp. 131—142, and Mr. Mitford in his *Tales of Old Japan* gives a detailed account of a case of which he was an official witness. It was considered an honourable kind of execution, and did not carry with it the disgrace attached to other modes of capital punishment.

IV.

THE TWO RELIGIONS OF JAPAN.

"Having no hope, and without God in the world."—*Eph.* ii. 12.

HE ancient religion of the Japanese is called *Kami no michi*, "the way of the gods." The Chinese equivalent of the name, *Shin-to*, is the one commonly used; whence this religion is called by English writers Shintoism.

Mr. Kodera describes it as "simply a remnant of the primitive worship long prevalent among the rude tribes of the islands of Japan, and subsequently developed and shaped according to the degree of civilisation to which they attained;" "a mixture of that nature worship which is so common among uncivilised races, and the worship of ancestors, especially of some chiefs or heroes."* Shintoism is founded on the mythologies and traditions preserved in the *Kojiki*,† the bible of the Shintoists, where it appears as "a bundle of miscellaneous superstitions, rather than a co-ordinate system."‡

---

* Paper on "Shintoism," *C. M. Intelligencer*, 1884 (p. 477).

† Valuable as the *Kojiki* is, as embodying "more faithfully than any other book, the mythology, the manners, the language, and the traditional history of Ancient Japan," it must be remembered that it contains much that is unedifying, and some narratives characterised by "shocking obscenity in word and deed."—Chamberlain, Vid. *Transactions of the Asiatic Society of Japan*, vol. x., Supplement, p. xlii.

‡ *Ibid.*, p. lv.

Commencing in atheism, it represents the first deities as coming into existence when heaven and earth spontaneously began. Five single deities and seven pairs, called the Seven Divine Generations, successively appear, whilst the earth still continues in a state of chaos, and the land is like floating oil and drifts about like a jelly-fish. Then Izanagi and Izanami, the last of these divine pairs, receive commandment from the heavenly deities to consolidate and give form to the drifting land. They "are united in marriage and give birth to the various islands of the Japanese archipelago. When they have finished producing islands they proceed to the production of a large number of gods and goddesses, many of whom correspond with what we should call personifications of the powers of nature."* Subsequently Izanami dies in childbirth and goes to the land of Hades. Izanagi visits her there, and on his return "purifies himself by bathing in a stream, and, as he does so, fresh deities are born from each article of clothing that he throws down on the river-bank, and from each part of his person. One of these deities was the Sun-goddess, who was born from his left eye,"* and to whom he gave the charge to rule the Plain of High Heaven.

This late-born child of Izanagi is the supreme deity of Shintoism, and her supremacy rests not only on the fact that the sun is "the greatest visible sign of the powers of Nature," but on the belief that the Sun-goddess is the ancestress of the ruling family of Japan. Each successive emperor, according to the orthodox Shinto view, is directly descended from her, and her sole representative on earth. This is, indeed, the fundamental belief of Shintoism, and out of it grows the duty of absolute obedience to the Mikado, which is one of the main

---

* *Transactions of the Asiatic Society of Japan*, vol. x., Supplement, pp. xlv., xlvi.

characteristic features of the system. According to Motoöri, as summarised by Mr. Ernest Satow, he "is the immovable ruler who must endure to the end of time, as long as the sun and moon continue to shine. In ancient language the Mikado was called a god, and that is his real character. Duty therefore consists in obeying him implicitly without questioning his acts."* This explains the statement of Mr. Griffis that the united verdict given him by native scholars was, "Shinto is not a religion ; it is a system of Government regulations, very good to keep alive patriotism among the people." This, too, is the reason why Mr. Satow speaks of Shintoism, as expounded by Motoöri, as "nothing else than an engine for reducing the people to a condition of mental slavery," and why Shintoism was made the state religion and placed under a department of State after the revolution of 1868, which subsequently put forth the following commandments as embodying its essential principles :—

1. Thou shalt honour the gods, and love thy country.
2. Thou shalt clearly understand the principles of heaven and the duty of man.
3. Thou shalt revere the Mikado as thy sovereign, and obey the will of his court.†

But, with regard to the second of these commandments, it should be observed that Shinto has no moral code. The *Kojiki*, or Records of Ancient Matters, already alluded to, contains only mythological and heroic narratives. "It lays down no precepts, teaches no morals or doctrines, prescribes no ritual." Motoöri, whom Griffis calls "the great

---

* *Transactions of the Asiatic Society of Japan*, vol. iii., Pt. I., Appendix, p. 27.
† A curious account of the official sermons preached on the occasion of the proclamation of these commandments appeared in the *C. M. Intelligencer* of Jan., 1873.

JAPANESE SHINTO PRIESTS WORSHIPPING THE RISING SUN.

modern revivalist of Shinto,"* taught that "morals were invented by the Chinese because they were an immoral people; but in Japan there was no necessity for any system of morals, as every Japanese acted aright if he only consulted his own heart."

Together with the Sun-goddess numerous other deities, commonly spoken of as "the eight hundred myriads of gods," are worshipped. These include "not only the Imperial ancestors and those divine personages who lived in the mythological age, but numerous poets, scholars, warriors, statesmen, and patriots,"† who have been successively deified in both ancient and modern times, by Imperial decree, it being a part of the prerogative of the representative of the Sun-goddess thus to create gods to be honoured by the nation. These multitudinous deities govern all things. "They direct the changes of the seasons, the wind and the rain, the good and bad fortune of states and individual men"; hence the occasions for seeking their protection and deliverance are manifold. Their worship is very general. In most houses, even those of Buddhists of some sects, the "god's shelf" is found, and shows that one or more Shinto deities are reverenced by the family. Every village, town, or division of a town has its patron deity and common temple, and the inhabitants of the district are called the children of the god, and bring their infant children to be dedicated to him. When the local festivals are held business is often suspended, and each householder hangs a large lantern at his door in honour of the god.

The most sacred shrines in the country are those of the

---

* For an able account by E. M. Satow of the Revival of Pure Shinto, see Appendix to vol. iii. (Pt. I.) of the *Transactions of the Asiatic Society of Japan*, 1875.

† Shintoism. See *C. M. Intelligencer*, vol. ix., p. 476, August, 1884.

Sun-goddess and the Goddess of Food in the province of Ise, which are near each other, and are known as the "Two Great Divine Palaces." They are annually visited by thousands of pilgrims from all parts of the Empire.

Great simplicity characterises the architecture of Shinto temples. During the ascendency of Buddhism elaborately decorated and highly ornamented temples were erected with *torii* (gateways) of bronze or granite; but the pure Shinto shrine, like that of the sun-goddess, is built of plain, uncoloured wood, thatched with straw or covered with shingles, and its *torii*,* three in number, are made of trunks of fir, with the bark removed.

Shintoism has no images, but every temple contains some object, generally within the closed doors of the actual shrine, in which the spirit of the deity is supposed to reside. In the temple of the Sun-goddess this object is the mirror which, according to the tradition, was given by the goddess to her grandson Ninigi when he was sent down to subdue the earth, and with reference to which she said, "Look upon this mirror as my spirit, keep it in the same house and on the same floor with yourself, and worship it as if you were worshipping my actual presence." All the mirrors in Shinto temples are imitations of this one, but they are not exposed to view except in temples that have been under Buddhist influence. The *go-hei*†—"a slender wand of unpainted wood, from which depend two long pieces of paper, notched alternately on opposite sides"—may be seen wherever the gods are

---

* The *torii* (bird-rest) was originally what its name denotes, a perch for fowls kept at Shinto shrines, but not for purposes of sacrifice. It is now simply a gateway, and marks the entrance to the grounds of a Shinto temple, or the beginning of a road leading to one.

† "*Go-hei* is compounded of two Chinese words, meaning 'august,' or 'imperial,' and 'presents.'" (Satow.)

worshipped. Originally offerings of rough and fine white cloth, which from its preciousness was supposed to attract the gods, "they came in later times to be considered as the seats of the gods, and even the gods themselves." Shintoism has its married priesthood, its virgin priestesses who dance before the shrine on festival and ceremonial occasions, its services, prayers and purifications, and its offerings of wine, water, salt, fruit, vegetables, and other articles of food. It lays much stress on bodily purification. Not only must the priest bathe before officiating and place a piece of paper over his mouth when presenting offerings, but every worshipper before he approaches the god must wash his hands and rinse his mouth with water from the laver at the entrance of the temple. No peculiar sanctity is supposed to attach to the water, for it is frequently conveyed from mountain streams through bamboo pipes, and pilgrims at the shrine of the Sun-goddess perform their ablutions in a running stream close by.

However imperfect the conception of sin may be, the recognition of national and individual guilt, and of the need of cleansing, with a view to deliverance from divine judgments, is a marked feature of Shintoism. Twice every year, in the sixth and twelfth months, festivals are held at Ise, which are supposed to purify the nation from the sins of the previous half-year. In individual prayers, too, the correction of faults and the removal of guilt are sought.

But Shintoism, whatever its influence upon the individual, social, and political life of the Japanese, and however closely interwoven with their customs and institutions, has been to a large extent superseded by Buddhism. For although Shinto is the religion of the government, the religion of the people is BUDDHISM.

Buddhism does not, as has been supposed, surpass every other religion in the number of its votaries. Sir M. Monier

Williams puts it fifth, after Christianity, Hinduism, Confucianism, and Mohammedanism. Still, it cannot but be regarded from a Christian point of view with deep and painful interest. This is not the place, however, to discuss its history, principles, and influence. We have only to do with its relation to Japan.

Buddhism had run its course of a thousand years in India, and been finally overthrown and banished by the Brahmins, before it spread to Japan. It was then no longer a "pure atheistic humanitarianism," with its lofty moral code, and its melancholy view of life as a delusion, and of absorption into the infinite (*nirvana*) as the only goal of existence. It had developed into a popular religion, with an elaborate array of ceremonial and priest-craft, monks and nuns, shrines and relics, images and altars, vestments and candles, fastings and indulgences, pilgrimages and hermits. "The bare and bald original doctrines of Buddha were by that time glorious in the apparel with which Asiatic imagination and priestly necessity had clothed and adorned them. The Buddhist missionaries entered Japan having a mechanism perfectly fitted to play upon the fears and hopes of an ignorant people, and to bring them into obedience to the new and aggressive faith." (Griffis.)

Nevertheless, Buddhism won its way but slowly among the Japanese. Introduced into the Empire towards the close of the sixth century A.D., it was quickly adopted by the nobles; but not until the ninth century, when a priest named Kukai, better known by his posthumous name of Kōbō Daishi, who had travelled in China, tried to combine the two religions by teaching that the Shinto gods and heroes were manifestations of Buddha, did it spread further among the people. Its great triumphs were achieved in the thirteenth century by the proselytising zeal of two famous preachers, Shinran and Nichiren, since which time it has been the prevailing religion.

JAPANESE PRIESTS.

The Buddhists of Japan must not be thought of as a homogeneous body. They are divided into some fourteen sects (*shiu*) as much opposed to each other as those of Christendom. Of these, the two most important were founded by the two leaders just mentioned, Shinran and Nichiren. "The Nichirenites,"* says Mr. Griffis, "excel all others in polemic bitterness, sectarian bigotry, and intolerant arrogance." "They excel in the number of pilgrims, and in the use of charms, spells, and amulets. Their priests are celibates, and must abstain from wine, fish, and all flesh. A 'revival-meeting' in one of their temples is a scene that often beggars description. What with prayers incessantly repeated, drums beaten unceasingly, the shouting of devotees who work themselves into an excitement that often ends in insanity, and sometimes in death, and the frantic exhortations of the priests, the wildest excesses that seek the mantle of religion in other lands are by them equalled, if not excelled." "Christianity in Japan will find its most vigorous and persistent opposers among this sect."

The other chief sect, Jō-do-Shin-shiu—commonly called the Shin-shiu or True Sect—is, as its name implies, a split from the Jō-do, and claims to be the true (*shin*) Jō-do sect. When Genku Daishi established the Jō-do sect, the regent, Prince Kamezane, became his great benefactor, and Shinran his chief disciple. On one occasion, referring to the discrepancy between his own life as a layman and that of his teacher who, as a member of the priesthood, abstained from wine and marriage, the regent asked, "Is there no distinction of excellent and base in this?" Genku replied, "All equally call Buddha to remembrance; what fault is there in this?" Whereupon the regent, wishing all doubt to be removed,

---

* The sect is called *Nichiren-shiu*.

proposed that his own daughter should be married to Shinran. This was at length arranged, and the marriage resulted in the founding of the Shin sect.*

One peculiarity about the sect is that its chief-priesthood is hereditary in the family of Shinran, the present primate of the sect being his actual descendant in the twenty-second generation.

Mr. Griffis calls the Shin-shiuists the Protestants of Japan. " Shinran taught that marriage was honourable, and celibacy an invention of the priests. Penance, fasting, prescribed diet, pilgrimages, the hermitage and the cloister, and generally amulets and charms, are all tabooed by this sect. The family takes the place of monkish seclusion. Devout prayer, purity and earnestness of life, and trust in Buddha himself as the only worker of perfect righteousness, are insisted upon." The sacred writings of other sects are written in Chinese, which only the learned can read; those of the Shin-shiuists are in the vernacular. They plant their temples in the great centres of population, and are untiring in their efforts to win adherents. For good or for evil, they wield vast influence over the people.

The unique position of this, the most influential and popular of all the Buddhist sects in Japan, will be better understood from the following brief account of its teaching, chiefly summarised from a paper by James Troup, Esq., Her Majesty's Consul at Kobe.† According to Buddhism the "unenlightened," who have not attained to Buddhahood, are "subject to the evil of birth and death," "sinking and floating in the sea

---

* Several years ago the present emperor conferred posthumous honours upon Shinran, by creating him a *Dai-shi* (="Great Teacher") with the new name, Ken-shin (="seeing or perceiving truth"), and he is now honoured by the sect as Ken-shin Dai-shi.

† *Transactions of the Asiatic Society of Japan*, vol. xiv., Part I.

of existence" through ages measured by millions of years ; and the aim of all its sects is to obtain "deliverance from the cycle of birth and death, in other words, to reach Nirvâna." Thus far agreed, they differ in regard to the means of attaining this end. Those sects which follow what is called the "Holy Path" seek deliverance "by the practice of the moral and religious precepts and prohibitions of Buddhism," that is to say, by good works and virtuous actions. On the other hand those of the Pure Land*—the Jō-do sect, and its offshoot the Jō-do Shin-shiu—look upon this way of salvation as utterly impossible for men in the present age of the world, this being, according to Buddhist doctrine, the "Period of the Latter Days of the Law,† when "the inferior capacities of men are dark, and they cannot tread the Holy Path and rise to perfection." They consequently seek deliverance by birth into the Pure Land of Amida Buddha, resting their faith and hope on the "Original Vows,"‡ which this imaginary being of bygone Kalpas is said to have made "in respect of his determination to attain the rank of Buddha." The eighteenth of these vows, which embodies the conditions in which deliverance may be obtained, is as follows: "If when I attain Buddhahood, any of the living beings in the ten regions, who with sincerity having faith and joy, and an ardent desire to be born into My Country call [My Name] to remembrance ten times, should not [then] be born there, I shall not accept

---

* The original of this is *Jo-do*, and hence the name of the sects.

† Supposed to commence 1,500 years after the death of Sakyamuni, since whom no Buddha has appeared.

‡ Of the forty-eight vows of Amida three are called *Hon-guwan*=original vows, and of these again the eighteenth is called so *par excellence*. The expression also gives the name to the principal temples of the two main divisions of the sect at Kioto and in other places. They are called *Hon-guwan-ji*=" Temples of the Original Vow."

A JAPANESE BUDDHIST PRIEST.

enlightenment. But from this the five classes of reprobates* and revilers of the Right Law are excluded." This is interpreted by the "True Sect" to mean that men of all classes and conditions and in all ages of the world—whether priests or laymen, merchants or husbandmen—whether married or single, with or without families—whether abstaining from flesh and wine or not—"if they only put forth the Believing Heart and invoke Amida Buddha," after this life "they will be born in Heaven, they will reach Nirvâna."

In connection with this way of salvation three points of Shin-Shiu teaching must be noted: (1) They believe in, call to remembrance, and invoke, Amida Buddha *alone*—"as a faithful servant does not serve two masters." (2) The Believing Heart is not, as the original Jōdo sect teaches, "faith by one's own power," "faith excited and kept alive by means of religious observances," but "faith by the power of another"—a Believing Heart conferred by the Power of Amida Buddha. The former, they say, "is not strong; speedily it changes. It is like a picture drawn on water. But the Believing Heart by the Power of another—this recedes not from its strength; it is like the diamond." (3) The invocation of Amida—"the action of calling to remembrance with the living voice" his sacred name—results from the possession of a Believing Heart; that its object is not to obtain salvation as a reward, but to express gratitude for the "boundless great compassion" of Amida, and for the certainty of deliverance by being born into His Pure Land. Such in a few words is the teaching of this remarkable sect in regard to salvation in the other world. But, if in this matter it ignores Prohibitions and Rules, it is not unmindful of the importance of social

---

* These are "parricides, matricides, those who incite the priesthood to quarrel, they who shed the blood of a Buddha, they who put to death an Arhat."

and relative duties. In the " Greater Sutra," one of the three Sutras that constitute the Scriptures of the sect, it is said : " For a servant to betray his lord, for a child to deceive his father, for brothers and sisters, husbands and wives, wise or unwise (priesthood or laity) to fail in their duty to each other, these are the actions violating the relations of life, which the venerated Shiaka (*Sakya*) has denounced."

The census of 1875 returned 207,669 "religious" (to use the Romish phrase), *i.e.*, priests, monks, nuns, &c., of all grades. " In Japanese as in European history, romance, drama, and art, the monk and nun are staple characters." And as in the West, so in the East, their character and reputation vary greatly. As in mediæval Europe, so in mediæval Japan, the monks were not seldom the sole possessors of scholarship and the most civilising agency in the community. The sciences of astronomy and mathematics, the arts of painting and sculpture, were cultivated in the monasteries. The copying of sacred writings was as regular an occupation at Kioto as at Clairvaux.

Among the most prominent objects of Japanese mediæval art were images of Buddha, and bells. Some of the templebells are magnificent. " Few sounds," says Mr. Griffis, " are more solemnly sweet than their mellow music. On a still night a circumference of twenty miles was flooded by the melody of the great bell of Zozoji."* These bells have no clapper ; they are struck from the outside by a piece of timber suspended by ropes. The casting of a bell was always an occasion of public rejoicing, and the description of the festivities reminds one of Schiller's famous poem.†

---
* The great temple of Zozoji was destroyed by fire on the night of Dec. 31st, 1873. It had been sequestrated by the Government, and was to be turned into a Shinto shrine; but a fanatic Buddhist incendiary saved the great bell from being used in the service of the rival religion.

† There is a picture of the great bell at the temple of Daibuts at Kioto in the *C. M. Gleaner* of Dec., 1877.

Of the colossal images, the figures of Dai Butsu (sometimes printed Daiboots), or "Great Buddha," at Kamakura and Nara, are the most celebrated. The former is a mass of copper 44 feet high, and a work of high art. The latter, which was first erected in the eighth century, destroyed during the civil wars, and recast about 700 years ago, is $53\frac{1}{2}$ feet high; its face is 16 feet long, and $9\frac{1}{2}$ feet wide. The width of its shoulders is $28\frac{7}{10}$ feet. Its head is adorned with 966 curls, and encircled by a halo 78 feet in diameter, on which are 16 images, each 8 feet long, The metal is said to weigh 450 tons.*

Buddhist temples† are numerous in all parts of the country. In most large towns there is a street of temples, which is called Tera Machi, answering to our familiar "Church Street."

The position of both Buddhism and Shintoism has been seriously affected by the revolution of 1868 and the changes consequent upon it. The cause of Buddhism had been for centuries identified with that of the Shogûns, and the revolution was a severe blow to its power and prestige, as it was then deprived of State patronage and support. On the other hand Shintoism, so closely connected with the semi-divine person of the Mikado, and the basis of his authority, gained a triumph. Under the new *régime* both religions remained under the control of the Government. In 1877 the "Department of Religion" was abolished as a separate office and made a branch of the Home Office; and at the same time the

---

* Mr. Clark, an American gentleman who was engaged in educational work under the Japanese Government, writes: "After studying the Daibuts at Nara as a work of art, I climbed up into his capacious lap, and sat upon one of his thumbs, which are placed together in a devout attitude. Here I began to sing the Doxology, to the astonishment of the priest standing below." (*Life and Adventure in Japan*, p. 20.)

† A Buddhist temple is called *tera;* a Shinto shrine *miya*.

Shinto priests, in lieu of such of their revenues as were derived from the State, were awarded pensions, to cease after twenty years. A few of them "commuted" and went into trade, but the bulk continued to exercise the priestly office. The changes thus far were the beginning of the end, and prepared the way for the more decided step taken in 1884, when the connection of both Buddhism and Shintoism with a department of State was severed, and each sect was enjoined to make provision for its internal government and administration. But although disestablished, and deprived of State support, both religions continue to exist, and under the new order of things Buddhism especially has manifested fresh energy. In January, 1879, some ten years after the Revolution, the Rev. C. F. Warren thus wrote :—

Buddhism, at least in one of its branches—the Monto or Shin sect—shows remarkable signs of vigour. It has recently established a mission in China, which is reported to be flourishing; it is making strenuous efforts to get a footing in Satsuma, from which province it has hitherto been excluded; and it has just completed a large college at Kioto for the accommodation of 600 students, who will be selected from their schools in the provinces.

Still it cannot be doubted that the action of the Government has done much to prepare the way for Christianity, as the Rev. J. Piper wrote nearly ten years ago :—" This gradual withdrawal of State aid will not dry up the torrent of heathenism in the country, yet it must necessarily reduce the stream to such a moderate depth that Christianity will be able more easily to stop its course. May God hasten such a happy result!"

V.

THE JESUIT MISSIONS.

"The fire shall try every man's work of what sort it is."—1 *Cor.* iii. 13.

"IPANGU," says Marco Polo, "is an Island towards the East, in the high seas, 1,500 miles distant from the Continent, and a very great island it is. The people are white, civilised, and well-favoured. They are idolaters, and they are dependent on nobody, and I can tell you the quantity of gold they have is endless."

These words, written by the old Venetian traveller nearly six centuries ago, however inaccurate, first revealed to Europe the existence of Japan. Marco Polo spent seventeen years, 1275—1292, at the court of Kublai Khan; and there he heard of the Land of the Rising Sun, which the great Tartar chieftain had tried in vain to conquer: his fleet, like another armada sent to annex another island empire, being utterly destroyed by the winds and waves.

Marco Polo's book appeared in 1298. Two hundred years later it found an ardent student in Christopher Columbus; and there is now little doubt that when the discoverer of America sailed out into the West, it was Japan that he was in search of. But not until 1542 did any European reach Japan, and then not across the Atlantic, but round the Cape; and not a Spaniard, but a Portuguese, Mendez Pinto, whose vessel was driven thither by stress of weather. Japanese historians note that year as the date of the first appearance of foreigners, Christianity, and fire-arms. "To many a native," sadly writes Mr. Griffis, "these are still members of a trinity of terrors, and one is a synonym of the other."

The confiding Japanese received the traders, Portuguese, Spanish, and Dutch, who now poured in, with open arms. And the traders were not alone. Seven years after Mendez Pinto came Francis Xavier. A Japanese named Anjiro wandered to India in one of the Portuguese vessels, and at Goa met with the great Jesuit missionary, learned Portuguese, and embraced the new religion. Xavier asked him what prospects Christianity would have in Japan, and thus records his reply:—"His people, he said, would not immediately assent to what might be said to them, but they would investigate my religion by a multitude of questions, and, above all, by observing whether my conduct agreed with my words. This done, the Daimios, the nobility, and the people would flock to Christ, being a nation which always follows reason as a guide." "These words," observes Mr. Griffis, "seem fresh, pertinent, and to have been uttered but yesterday, so true are they still."

In August, 1549, Xavier landed at Cangoxima (Kagoshima), a port in the southern island of Kiushiu,* and subsequently proceeded to the main island, and made his way to Kioto. "There is something heroic in the simple story of his privations and difficulties, as in the depth of winter, thinly clad and barefoot, he made his two months' journey to the capital, through snow drifts and mountain torrents."† His reception,

---

* On May 1st, 1879, the first C.M.S. converts at Kagoshima were baptized by the Rev. H. Maundrell. See a later chapter.
† Bp. Pakenham Walsh, *Heroes of the Mission Field*, p. 178.

however, was not encouraging, and after about two years' labours he left the country.* But his successors reaped an extraordinary harvest; and of the Romish Mission as a whole, it may well be said, in the words of the Roman general, that they came, they saw, they conquered. Within five years, Christian communities were rising in every direction. Within thirty years the converts numbered 150,000, and the churches 200. The Japanese themselves give two millions as the figure ultimately reached, but the Jesuits do not claim that, and perhaps half a million may be nearer the mark. This was however a great success; to what is it to be attributed?

The answer is not far to seek. Shinto, which is now a power, politically at least, was then a myth unknown to the people. Buddhism, with all its external splendour, had lost what little life it had once possessed. The Jesuit priests gave the Japanese all that the Buddhist priests had given them—gorgeous altars, imposing processions, dazzling vestments, and all the scenic display of a sensuous worship—but added to these a freshness and fervour that quickly captivated the imaginative and impressionable people. The Buddhist preacher—unless of the Shin sect—promised heavenly rest, such as it was, only after many transmigrations involving many weary lives. The Jesuit preacher promised immediate entrance into paradise after death to all who received baptism. And there was little in the Buddhistic paraphernalia that needed to be changed, much less abandoned. The images of Buddha, with a slight application of the chisel, served for images of Christ. Each Buddhist saint found his counterpart in Romish Christianity; and the roadside shrines of Kuwan-on,†

---

* See Venn's *Life of Xavier*, pp. 167—213.
† This is the Japanese pronunciation of the Chinese characters read *Kwan-yin* in Pekinese, and *Kun-yam* in Cantonese.

the goddess of mercy, became centres of Mariolatry.* Temples, altars, bells, holy-water vessels, censers, rosaries, all were ready, and were merely transferred from one religion to the other. It is a strange spectacle. And those who have seen both rituals marvel whether Buddhism is a child of Romanism, or Romanism of Buddhism, or whether both must not have some common origin.

There was also a political cause for the success of the Jesuits. The Shogûn of that day, Nobunaga, hated the Buddhists, and openly favoured the missionaries, thinking to make them a tool for his own designs. In 1583, four nobles were sent by the Christian Daimios of Kiushiu to Europe as an embassy to Pope Gregory XIII., to declare themselves vassals of the Holy See; and at the same time the subjects of these same Daimios were ordered to embrace Christianity or go into exile. The decree was carried out with great cruelty. The spirit of the Inquisition was introduced into Japan. Buddhist priests were put to death, and their monasteries burnt to the ground. The details are given, with full approval, by the Jesuit Charlevoix in his *Histoire du Christianisme au Japon*. Take one passage as a specimen:—" In 1577, the lord of the island of Amakusa issued his proclamation, by which his subjects—whether bonzes [priests] or gentlemen, merchants or tradesmen—were required either to turn Christians, or to leave the country the very next day. They almost all submitted, and received baptism, so that in a short

---

* Xavier himself thus relates the first presentation of Christianity to the Japanese:—" Paul [the converted Japanese, Anjiro] showed a beautiful picture he had brought from India, of the Blessed Mary and the child Jesus sitting in her lap. When the governor looked upon it, he was overwhelmed with emotion, and falling on his knees, he very devoutly worshipped it, and commanded all present to do the same."—Xavier's Journals, quoted in Venn's *Life of Xavier*, p. 180.

time there were more than twenty churches in the kingdom. God wrought miracles to confirm the faithful in their belief."*

Rome in Japan took the sword—and perished with the sword. European national antipathies were carried into the far east ; and the Dutch traders bitterly opposed the Spaniards and Portuguese. The different religious orders also quarrelled amongst themselves ; and Jesuits, Franciscans, and Dominicans illustrated by their mutual hatred the hollowness of Rome's boasted unity. Nobunaga's successor, the famous Taiko Sama or Hideyoshi, found the Jesuits, true to their traditions, plotting against his throne ; and in 1587 he issued a decree of expulsion against them.

They were not so easily got rid of. Closing their churches, they withdrew from public notice for a while, but secretly continued their work as actively as ever. Then persecution began ; and then a religious civil war. Taiko Sama died in 1598, and in the struggle for power that followed, the Christian nobles took the side of his young son ; but the battle of Sekigahara, as already noticed, decided the conflict in favour of Iyeyasu, who at once set to work to put down the foreign religion. Plots, revolts, and fighting, however, continued. At length, in 1615, the son of Taiko Sama was besieged in Osaka, where he was entertaining some Jesuit priests. The city was taken, and a terrible massacre ensued ; and Sir R. Alcock justly emphasises the fact that this final blow fell in the very year in which a few Puritan pilgrims landed at New Plymouth, and laid the foundation of Protestant America—to which, in our own day, is due the re-introduction of Christianity into Japan.†

Iyeyasu's triumph was complete ; and under him and his

---

* A fuller account of the Jesuit Missions will be found in the *C. M. Intelligencer* of March, 1872.

† Alcock's *Capital of the Tycoon*, vol. i., p. 60.

immediate successors fire and sword were now freely used to extirpate Christianity.* The unhappy victims met torture and death with a fortitude that compels our admiration; and it is impossible to doubt that, little as they knew of the pure Gospel of Christ, there were true martyrs for His name among the thousands that perished. They were crucified, burnt at the stake, buried alive, torn limb from limb, put to unspeakable torments; and historians on both sides agree that but few apostatised. One Jesuit priest, Christopher Ferreyra, after enduring horrible tortures, was at last hung by his feet in such a way that his head was in a hole in the ground from which light and air were excluded. His right hand was left loose, that with it he might make the prescribed sign of recantation. He hung for four hours, and then made the sign. He was at once released, and compelled to become a Japanese inquisitor, and to consign Christians to torture and death.

At length, in 1637, the Christians struck a last desperate blow for freedom. They rose in Kiushiu, fortified an old castle at Shimabara, and raised the flag of revolt; but after a two months' siege they were compelled to surrender, and thirty-seven thousand were massacred, great numbers being hurled from the rock of Pappenberg, near the harbour of Nagasaki.

This was their expiring effort. The Christianity which Rome had presented to the Japanese was finally banished. What did it leave behind?

It did not leave the Bible behind. If it had, Japan might perhaps have been another Madagascar. Persecution as bitter fell upon the Malagasy Christians under Queen Ranavalona,

---

* In the castle grounds of Iyeyasu at Shidzuoka, 260 years after his death, an American Christian gentleman taught a purer Christianity to Japanese students. See Clark's *Life and Adventures in Japan*, p. 70.

and the door into Madagascar was as fast closed. But when it opened again, a true and living and indigenous Church stood revealed to the astonished gaze of Christendom. Not so with Romanism in Japan.

It left a name of infamy, a memory of horror. The name of Christ, writes Mr. Griffis, was regarded as "the synonym of sorcery, sedition, and all that was hostile to the purity of the home and the peace of society. . . Christianity was remembered only as an awful scar on the national annals. No vestiges were supposed to be left of it, and no knowledge of its tenets was held, save by a very few scholars in Yedo, trained experts, who were kept, as a sort of spiritual bloodhounds, to scent out the adherents of the accursed creed."

A special police commission was organised, called "The Christian Inquiry," and every year the Buddhist priest had to report to the commissioners on the orthodoxy of their parishioners, if we may call them so. High rewards were offered to informers. Suspected persons were compelled to trample on pictures or images of Christ; and sometimes the whole population of a town would be tried by this test. Now and then a stray Christian would be detected; and as late as 1829, six men and an old woman are said to have been crucified at Osaka. Was all this a leaf taken out of the book of the Spanish Inquisition?

Notwithstanding, a small and obscure community of adherents did remain in Kiushiu, who have been recognised by modern Roman Catholic missionaries as the descendants of the Jesuit converts. How they were regarded in their own land may be guessed from the fact that an image of the Virgin Mary and infant Christ was found a few years ago in a cave, where it was held sacred by the country people, who supposed it to be an image of Buddha and his mother, and believed that it healed diseases.

In the year following the Revolution of 1868 (page 71), persecution was revived against this remnant. Three thousand Romish Christians, who apparently formed the entire population of the village of Urakami, near Nagasaki, were torn away from their homes, and banished, some to the interior of the country and others to the Goto Islands. Horrible accounts of the cruelties inflicted on them were circulated by the Propaganda, but on Sir Harry Parkes, the British Minister, interposing on their behalf, the Japanese authorities were able to show that these statements were almost entirely without foundation, and affirmed that the deportation itself was rendered necessary by the disloyalty of the Christians. In their reply to Sir H. Parkes, these significant words occur:—

> The Japanese Government has been obliged to take this course from a conviction of its necessity, and particularly in consequence of a growing pressure of public opinion, which arose from the memory of the deplorable events connected with the introduction of Christianity by Roman Catholic missionaries some centuries ago. Public opinion even now demands that the same seeds of discord should be removed which at that period so nearly succeeded in overthrowing the government, and endangering the independence of this country.

We have no means of knowing on what grounds the charge of disloyalty was brought against the villagers of Urakami. Most of them were ignorant and probably inoffensive peasants, and unless they were being manipulated by foreign intriguers, they could scarcely have been very dangerous; and in 1873 they were restored to their homes. But under any circumstances, the official apology is a melancholy commentary on the history of the Jesuit Missions in Japan.

Still more melancholy is the inscription which, for two hundred and thirty years, appeared on the public notice-boards along with prohibitions against crimes and breaches of the law, at every roadside, at every city gate, in every village throughout the empire :—

"*So long as the sun shall warm the earth, let no Christian be so bold as to come to Japan; and let all know that the King of Spain himself, or the Christians' God, or the Great God of all, if he violate this command, shall pay for it with his head.*"

Who is "the Christians' God," so curiously distinguished in these shocking words from "the great God of all"? Is it Christ? Or is it the Pope? One of the letters carried to Pope Gregory XIII. by the four Japanese nobles (p. 54) was thus addressed—" A celui qui doit être adoré, et qui tient la place du Roi du Ciel, le grand et Très-Saint Pape"; and another began thus—"J'adore le Très-Saint Pape, qui tient la place de Dieu sur la terre."

We can honour the zeal and self-denial of the Jesuit missionaries. We can believe that among their converts there were some who, in much ignorance, did trust their souls to the Saviour. But the responsibility for the blasphemous proclamation which for two centuries and more shut out Christianity from Japan must lie at the door of Rome.

VI.

THE LOCKING AND THE UNLOCKING.

"I have set before thee an open door, and no man can shut it."—*Rev.* iii. 8.

OR two hundred and thirty years Japan was closed to the outer world. By the century of intercourse with European nations she had gained the knowledge of gunpowder and firearms, and of tobacco smoking; the enrichment of her language by a few foreign words; some additions to her familiar forms of disease; and an inveterate hatred of Christianity. Content with these acquirements, and desiring no more, she retired from public gaze. "The curious cabinet which had so suddenly opened, and into the secret drawers of which the eyes of Portuguese, Spaniards, English, and Dutch, had so eagerly pryed, was as suddenly locked, and the key hid carefully away for upwards of two centuries." (*C.M. Intelligencer*, December, 1861.)

In 1624 all foreigners except Dutch and Chinese were banished from Japan. At the same time, the Japanese were forbidden to leave the country, and all vessels above a very small size were ordered to be destroyed. It is manifest that these edicts were directed especially against communication with Roman Catholic nations. The English were not in question. Their share in the trade had been small. The first Englishman to enter the country, Will Adams,* did not land until fifty years after Xavier; the first English ship only reached Japan twelve years before the decree of expulsion; and before that decree was issued the English traders had left the country—"with an unstained reputation," says the American Dr. Hawks.† And the Dutch were specially exempted.

Even the Dutch had to submit to very humiliating terms.‡ They were confined to a little artificial islet, 600 feet by 200, in Nagasaki harbour, called Deshima (*de*, out; *shima*, island; *i.e.*, "exit island"); and a strong Japanese guard always held the small bridge connecting it with the mainland. One ship only was allowed to come to this settlement once in six months; and when it arrived, two water-gates were opened for its admission, which remained closed at all other times. Once in four years the Dutch Commissioner had to go to Yedo, bearing the costly gifts required as tribute from the foreigners. The Chinese were also allowed to live in Nagasaki, but at no other port.

Why were the Dutch exempted? In the first place, to them the Government owed the discovery of the Jesuit plots. One of their vessels intercepted a letter to the King of Portugal, asking for troops to overthrow the Mikado; and they eagerly seized the opportunity to discredit their Portuguese rivals.

---

* Will Adams was a remarkable man. From being the English pilot of a Dutch fleet he rose by his ability and integrity to be the trusted adviser of the great Shogún Iyeyasu. The street in Yedo where he lived is still called *Anjin Cho*, "The Pilot's Street," and the dwellers in that street hold an annual festival in his honour on the 15th of June. His grave, with a stone monument erected by the Japanese, was discovered in 1872.

† A treaty had been concluded between the Mikado and James I., which is printed in the *C. M. Intelligencer* of July, 1859.

‡ Some curious details are given in Bp. Smith's *Ten Weeks in Japan*, pp. 18—24.

THE ISLET OF DESHIMA, NAGASAKI, JAPAN.

In the second place, they carefully abstained from all profession of Christianity, as is acknowledged by their own historian Kaempfer. One of them, being taxed with his belief, replied, " No, I am not a Christian, I am a Dutchman."

At long intervals efforts were made to open the closed cabinet, but in vain. Charles II. sent a vessel to Japan, but it was not allowed to trade because the Dutch had informed the Japanese authorities that Charles had married the daughter of the King of Portugal. In 1695, a Chinese junk was sent away from Nagasaki because a Chinese book on board was found to contain a description of the Romish cathedral at Peking. In 1709 an Italian priest, the Abbé Sidotti, persuaded the captain of a ship to put him on shore. He was seized, and kept a prisoner for several years until his death. A Japanese book has been found which gives a full account of him. Russia made efforts to get into Japan at the beginning of this century, but without success ;* after which she seized the Kurile Islands,† which had been part of the Japanese empire.

It was reserved for the United States to take a key and unlock the cabinet, and for England to lift the lid. In seeking to open negotiations with the Japanese, the American Government sought to secure proper treatment for shipwrecked sailors, and to obtain the opening of ports to facilitate the coaling and provisioning of her trans-Pacific steamers, the running of which between San Francisco and Hong-Kong

---

* Captain Golownin, of the Russian Navy, has given a detailed account of the seizure and imprisonment of himself and his officers, when they ventured to land on the Island of Yezo to obtain provisions, in a work entitled *Narrative of My Captivity in Japan* (London, 1818).

† These now form part of the Empire of Japan, Russia having transferred all her authority over and interest in them to Japan, in exchange for a similar transfer of all the rights of Japan over a portion of Saghalien. This was done by treaty in 1875.

was contemplated. But the aggression of Russia was the immediate occasion of the opening. The American Government took alarm, and resolved to forestall her further advances by sending a naval expedition to Japan.

On July 8th, 1853, the American squadron, commanded by Commodore Perry, anchored off Uraga, at the mouth of the Gulf of Yedo. A Japanese official went off to the flagship, but the Commodore was determined to negotiate only with authorities of the highest rank, and the official was informed that the President of the United States had sent a letter for the Emperor of Japan, but that it could only be delivered, with due ceremony, to a functionary properly qualified to receive it. He replied that the laws of Japan prohibited any communication with foreigners except at the port of Nagasaki, and that the squadron must go there. This was exactly what Commodore Perry did not mean to do. To go away hundreds of miles from Yedo, and humbly knock at the little wicket-gate at which so many indignities had been inflicted on the Dutch, would entirely defeat his purpose. Ultimately the quiet but resolute courtesy of the commodore prevailed, and a noble of high rank was sent to receive the letter. Some sentences of it are worth recording:

I have directed Commodore Perry to assure your Imperial Majesty that I entertain the kindest feelings towards your Majesty's person and Government, and that I have no other object in sending him to Japan but to propose that the United States and Japan should live in friendship, and have commercial intercourse with each other. . . . We know that the ancient laws of your Imperial Majesty's Government do not allow of foreign trade except with the Chinese and the Dutch; but as the state of the world changes, and new governments are formed, it seems to be wise from time to time to make new laws. . . . The United States constitution and laws forbid all interference with the religious or political concerns of other nations. I have particularly charged Commodore Perry to abstain from every act which could possibly disturb the tranquillity of your Imperial Majesty's dominions.

The commodore was content to take one step at a time; and having delivered this letter with all possible ceremony, he sailed away from Japan. Eight months afterwards he came back again with a more powerful squadron than before, to conclude a formal treaty. Lengthened negotiations followed; the Japanese strove hard to confine their new friends to Nagasaki; but nothing would move the commodore from his purpose, and on March 31st, 1854, a treaty was duly signed and sealed, which opened two ports, viz., Shimoda, 100 miles south of Yedo, and Hakodate, in the northern island of Yezo, to American trade. Shimoda was soon afterwards destroyed by an earthquake, and by the treaty of 1858, Yokohama, which is now the most important centre of foreign trade, was opened instead.

Other nations were not slow to claim similar advantages; but it was only under much pressure that the Japanese granted them. Russia succeeded in getting a treaty signed, and Holland in procuring the withdrawal of some of the restrictions under which her merchants had laboured at Deshima. A treaty was also negotiated by a representative of Great Britain, but it was never ratified. But all concessions were refused to France and Portugal, obviously because they were Roman Catholic nations. Of course in after years they acquired the same liberty as others.

Thus the "curious cabinet" was unlocked. But it could scarcely be said to be opened yet. That was the work of England.

On August 12th, 1858, Lord Elgin, fresh from his triumphs in China, where the Treaty of Tientsin had been signed six weeks before, entered the Gulf of Yedo. Taking advantage of the fact that he had with him a small steam yacht sent by the Queen as a present to "the Emperor of Japan," he determined to sail right up to the capital. Shimoda was passed;

JAPANESE PEASANT IN WINTER COSTUME.

Uraga was passed; Yokohama itself was passed. Japanese guard-boats in vain tried to arrest the progress of the squadron; two-sworded officials in vain waved it back with their fans. Vouchsafing no answer, and perceiving by the presence of some large vessels purchased by the Japanese* that the channel (yet unsurveyed) was safe for his frigates, Lord Elgin steamed on until he cast anchor opposite Yedo, to the consternation of the authorities.

They were shrewd enough, however, to see that their old policy of isolation could no longer be maintained; and they gave the British ambassador very little trouble. Within a fortnight, on the 26th of August, Prince Albert's birthday, the Treaty of Yedo was signed. It was a much more comprehensive document than Commodore Perry's. Hakodate, Kanagawa (Yokohama), and Nagasaki, were to be opened to British subjects at once, and Hiogo, Osaka, and Niigata at a given date; consuls were to be stationed at all these ports; a diplomatic agent was to reside at Yedo, with liberty to travel all over the realm; and other important concessions were granted. Since that time the Treaty has been supplemented by various Conventions and Articles of Arrangement affecting the conduct of foreign trade, Customs duties, the opening of the later ports and Tokio to foreign trade and residence; but it is still the basis of our relations with Japan.†

Thus a bloodless victory seemed to have been gained; but

---

* An amusing incident occurred when the Japanese received the first of these ships from the Americans. The engines being once set going, the native crew knew not how to stop them, and, to prevent the vessel running ashore, she had to be steered round and round the bay till the steam was expended.

† Whilst these pages were being revised (1887), negotiations for a new treaty were being conducted in Tokio, which seemed likely to open the entire country to foreign residence, and otherwise materially modify our relations with Japan; but they fell through.

not without bloodshed were the fruits reaped. Sir Rutherford (then Mr.) Alcock took up his abode at Yedo as the first British Minister to Japan; merchants hastened to establish themselves at the open ports; and the Japanese, both rulers and people, appeared eager for friendly and mutually profitable intercourse. But the turbulent Samurai resented the admission of strangers on to their sacred soil, and a succession of outrages kept the foreign communities in a state of alarm for several years. In particular, the American Secretary of Legation was assassinated in 1861; in the same year a desperate assault was made on the house occupied by the British Legation, some members of which were badly wounded; in 1862 an English gentleman, Mr. Richardson, was murdered on the high road; in 1863 some new buildings for the British Minister were blown up; and in 1864 two English officers were assassinated at Kamakura. The parties concerned in these outrages were in some cases punished by the Shogûn's government, and indemnities paid; but for Mr. Richardson's death they disclaimed responsibility, as the murderers belonged to the powerful Satsuma clan, the head of which, Shimadzu,* refused reparation, and set the Shogûn at defiance. The British fleet accordingly sailed to the south end of Kiushiu, and bombarded the chief Satsuma city, Kagoshima (the place where Xavier had landed (see p. 52). And in the following year, the guns of another great feudal prince, the prince of Choshiu (Nagato), which commanded the narrow strait at the western entrance to the Inland Sea, having fired on an American ship, the allied squadrons of England, France, Holland, and the United States, proceeded to bombard his forts likewise. These two actions, though they did not escape animadversion at home, made a lively impression

---

* Respecting Shimadzu and the Satsuma clan, see p. 85.

on the Daimios and their followers, and no further fighting of the kind has since occurred.

Up to this time the Shogûn had been supposed to be the real ruler of Japan, and English writers called him the "Temporal Emperor," regarding the mysterious Mikado, of whom they could get very little information, as the "Spiritual Emperor." The Shogûn had concluded the treaties on his own authority, in which he was styled the Tai-kûn; and Sir R. Alcock, who was Her Majesty's minister at Yedo for several years, gave to the book he published on his return home the name of *The Capital of the Tycoon*. Gradually, however, it became apparent that the Shogûn was not the sovereign ruler of the empire even in things temporal; that he had no right to make the treaties at all; that the Mikado had not sanctioned what had been done; and that the great Daimios were much enraged at having been ignored in the matter. At first they objected to the admission of foreigners; then, when they saw the advantages of extended trade, they objected equally because the Shogûn had (naturally enough) only opened ports over which he had direct control—ports which did not belong to the feudal lords, and from the opening of which they received no profit. The first thing that Sir Harry Parkes, the new British Minister, did, on reaching Japan in 1865, was to obtain the formal ratification of the Treaty of Yedo by the Mikado himself; though he did not then see the Mikado, nor even approach his old sacred capital, Kioto. He paid, however, a state visit to Shimadzu, the great Daimio of Satsuma, at Kagoshima, the scene of the bombardment.

All this time the forces were at work which led to the extraordinary Revolution described in the next chapter; and in 1868 the final overthrow of the Shogûn and his *régime* caused some anxiety as to the maintenance of the treaties.

But the young Mikado who had ascended the throne the year before, and who was now *de facto* as well as *de jure* ruler, proved most friendly; and on April 26th, 1868, Sir Harry Parkes stood face to face with the sovereign whose predecessors had been invisible to, and unapproachable by, even their own subjects for hundreds of years. This was at Osaka. Towards the close of the year, the Mikado removed to his new capital, the Shogûn's old capital, Yedo—thenceforth called Tokio; and on January 5th, 1869, he gave his first state audience to the Foreign Ministers. The date is worth noting; for it was only a few days after, on January 23rd, that the first English missionary, the Rev. G. Ensor, landed in Japan.

VII.

THE REVOLUTION.

"God is the Judge : He putteth down one, and setteth up another."—*Ps.* lxxv. 7.

THE year 1868 in Japan was the year of one of the most astonishing revolutions in the history of the world.

What was this Revolution? It was, (1) the abolition of the Shogûnate after it had lasted 700 years; (2) the resumption by the Mikado of the reins of government; (3) the voluntary surrender by the Daimio of their feudal powers and privileges into the hands of the central government; (4) the adoption of the European system of departments of State, with a responsible Minister at the head of each. It was a radical and thorough change, from feudalism to personal rule—indeed to constitutional government in theory, but this is hardly attained yet. In addition, the Revolution (5) was meant to effect the suppression of Buddhism—but it failed in that; and (6) it actually resulted in that which it was designed to prevent, the adoption by Japan of Western civilisation.

This Revolution, though to outsiders it appeared sudden, and seemed to be an immediate consequence of the opening of Japan to foreign nations, was in reality the crisis and consummation of a long period of silent preparation for change.

For a century and more the jealousy of the Daimios at the

exclusive power wielded by the Shogûn, who was properly only one of themselves, had been growing more and more restive; and at the same time an important intellectual movement was fashioning the political views of the educated classes. A revival of Chinese learning, which sprang up at the end of the seventeenth century, imbued the Japanese mind with the ethics of Confucius, from which they derived lofty ideas of the reverence due to the sovereign. The publication of the *Dai Nihon Shi*, the great history already mentioned, in 1715, the central purpose of which was to exalt the sole authority of the Mikado, powerfully stimulated the development of these ideas; and when at last the spirit of loyalty burst forth like a volcanic eruption and swept the Shogûnate away, the rallying cry of the imperial party was "King and Subject!" A revival of Shintoism helped the movement. The study of the old Shinto books showed that the Mikado had always been revered as the representative of the gods (see chap. iv.); and when the Revolution came a cry arose for the abolition of Buddhism, which was identified with the Shogûnate. But although Shinto became the State religion, and the Buddhist temples were deprived of State support, and in many cases used for barracks, hospitals, schools, &c., Buddhism has proved to be too closely bound up with the life of the people to be thus easily thrust aside, and it still remains, as we have before seen, the popular religion of Japan.

The detailed history of the Revolution itself cannot be given here. The foreign treaties were undoubtedly the immediate occasion of it. The Shogûn who signed them died shortly after under suspicious circumstances. The heir being a minor, a regent was appointed, who was soon assassinated, and his head exhibited with a placard inscribed with these words—"This is the head of a traitor who has violated the most sacred law of Japan"; and then anarchy prevailed, the

Bakufu (Shogûn's council) continuing to conduct foreign affairs, but being set at defiance at home by the Daimios. The young Shogûn died in 1866, but not before he had at last obtained the Mikado's acceptance of the treaties, and the withdrawal of the ancient edict prohibiting Japanese from leaving the country ; for the Daimios, as intimated in the preceding chapter, were beginning to see that Japan would gain and not lose by foreign intercourse, and the most powerful of them all, Shimadzu of Satsuma, had already, despite the edict, sent the most promising of his young men to visit Europe and America. The new Shogûn, Keiki (sometimes called by one of his titles, Yoshi Hisa), entered into intrigues with the envoys of Napoleon III., hoping to make France his ally in the impending struggle, and sent a handsome consignment of Japanese products to the Paris Exhibition of 1867.

Thus both parties were now seeking foreign intercourse, and the Revolution, which began with the cry of, "Expel the barbarians," ended by admitting them more freely than the old *régime* had ventured to do. The Satsuma men who had visited Europe returned, with open eyes and high hopes, just in time to guide the empire at the crisis of its change, which was now imminent.

The new Shogûn had scarcely assumed power when the Mikado died, February 3rd, 1867. His successor, Mutsuhito, being a young man, the party of progress seized the opportunity to push their designs. They persuaded Keiki, a timid and vacillating man, to resign the Shogûnate ; and then, to ensure complete success, on January 3rd, 1868, they seized the palace at Kioto, and proceeded to administer the government in the name of the Mikado. Civil war ensued ; but in a desperate battle fought at Fushimi,* a place between Kioto

* Fushimi is a few miles south of Kioto, on the Uji river ; the river through which the water of Lake Biwa flows into the Yodo. See Chap. i.

and Osaka, which lasted three days, January 27th to 30th, the Shogûn's army was totally defeated ; and although the northern clans continued the contest on their own ground, the imperial forces were everywhere victorious, and within a few months the young Mikado was the undisputed ruler of all Japan. Keiki himself submitted at once, and was allowed to live in retirement; and the last of the Shogûns became a quiet and loyal country gentleman. Equal clemency was shown even to the leaders who held out longer ; and the very last to lay down his arms, a noble named Enomoto, afterwards became Japanese envoy at the court of St. Petersburg.

Some of these men were scholars and authors, who had themselves also been sent to Europe and America by the Shogûn's government, and, like their opponents of the southern clans, had come back fired with a new patriotic ambition. One, Fukuzawa, wrote a book on "Western Manners and Customs," which had an enormous circulation. Another, a schoolmaster named Nakamura, translated English books like Smiles's *Self-Help*, &c.

The young Mikado now came forth from behind the screen of ages, and took his place as head of the State. He proclaimed that "the uncivilised customs of former times should be broken through, and the impartiality and justice displayed in the workings of Nature adopted as a basis of action ; and that intellect and learning should be sought for throughout the world in order to establish the foundations of empire."

In the eye of the people the outward and visible sign of the change was the transfer of the capital from Kioto to Yedo. For nearly three centuries Yedo had been the seat of the executive government; but Kioto was the sacred imperial city, and during the progress of the revolution, Yedo, being identified with the falling cause, became much discredited, and the population was rapidly diminishing. For the Mikado,

THE MIKADO OF JAPAN IN 1878.

after 700 years' seclusion at Kioto, to come forth and set up his throne at Yedo before the world, was a token indeed that a new era had begun. To emphasise the change, the name of the new capital was changed to Tokio; and the emperor entered it in state on November 26th, 1868, being then eighteen years of age. Six months afterwards he entered it a second time with a young empress at his side.

Then followed a still more remarkable phase of the revolution. It became clear to the victorious Daimios, under the influence of the men who had seen Western civilisation, that the weak point in the Japanese polity was their own feudal power; that semi-independent principalities were an anachronism; and that if the Mikado was to reign over a mighty and united empire, a centralised government was essential. In the enthusiastic tide of patriotism personal interests were swept aside; and with a self-abnegation scarcely to be paralleled in history, the leading Daimios, to enable their country (so said their public manifesto) "to take its place side by side with the other countries of the world," voluntarily surrendered the whole of their feudal rights, lands, and revenues into the hands of the imperial government, and took the position of private gentlemen. Their retainers were exhorted to give their entire allegiance directly to the Mikado; and the clans became absorbed in the nation. In the very same year that the petty kings and princes of Germany crowned King William of Prussia Emperor at Versailles, the princes and nobles of Japan assembled in solemn council at Tokio, and bowed their heads in submission to the Mikado, as his new Prime Minister read out the imperial decree abolishing feudalism.

Truly it is a wonderful spectacle. Some writers, however, have rather overdrawn the picture. Of course the Daimio, in rank and in public estimation, were Daimio still; in many cases they became governors, under the imperial government, of the provinces formerly their feudal domains; and life pensions were granted to them and their retainers out of the national funds—which has helped not a little to cripple the finances of the country. Still, for a great territorial aristocracy to become pensioners of the state, however exalted, and for a proud and warlike historic caste to merge its peculiar privileges in ordinary citizenship, was, after all deductions, an event of the highest significance.

A deeply interesting account is given by Mr. Griffis of the farewell gathering of the great Echizen clan on the occasion of the retirement under this decree of their wealthy feudal chief, on Oct. 1st, 1871. "I count," he says, "among the most impressive of all my life's experiences that scene in the immense castle hall of Fukui, when the Daimio of Echizen bid farewell to his three thousand two-sworded retainers, and amidst the tears and smiles and loving farewells of the city's populace, left behind him lands, revenue, and obedient followers, and retired to live as a private gentleman in Tokio. . . . He adjured them all to transfer their allegiance wholly to the Mikado and the Imperial House. Then, wishing them all success and prosperity in their new relations, and in their persons, their families, and their estates, in chaste and fitting language he bid them solemn farewell. . . . To them it was more than a farewell to their feudal lord. It was the solemn burial of the institutions under which their fathers had lived for seven hundred years. Each face seemed to wear a far-away expression, as if their eyes were looking into the past, or striving to probe an uncertain future."

This lord of Echizen was one of the most liberal and far-seeing of the Daimios. Six years before this he had presented a memorial to the Mikado and the Shogûn, advocating a more enlightened policy. Some extracts are given in Mossman's *New Japan*. "Western foreigners of the present day," he said, "differ greatly from those of former times; and while they are united in bonds of friendly commerce, Japan, standing apart in her solitude, has not known the changes in Heaven's course, and has lost the friendship of the world at large. Hence to shut up this country and drive out foreigners were a positive evil. . . . The so-called corrupt religion of the Western nations is a different thing from the Christianity of former times. Were Japan to adopt and practise it, I am of opinion that no sects would arise to ruin or damage the country."

VIII.

NEW JAPAN.

"Yet lackest thou one thing."—*Luke* xviii. 22.

F the impressive scene just referred to was a token of the passing away of the old order of things, the presence, in a distant city in the interior of Japan, of the clever American gentleman who describes it, was a sign of the coming in of the new.

Immediately after the assumption of power by the Mikado, the new government had begun to invite foreigners to Japan to fill high administrative offices. Englishmen and Americans had been appointed Comptrollers of the Navy and Public Works, Inspectors of Mines, &c., &c.; and most comprehensive educational machinery had been set on foot, with foreign professors of languages and science in some of the great cities. Mr. Griffis was in 1871 scientific lecturer in a school of 800 students at Fukui, the capital of the Echizen province; hence his presence at the Daimio's farewell.

But after the abolition of feudalism, the advance of civilisation proceeded at a greatly accelerated rate; and the year 1872 is memorable in the annals of New Japan as a year of extraordinary progress. The Army, Navy, and Civil Service were entirely reconstructed; the Imperial Mint at Osaka was opened, and a new coinage introduced; the Educational Department established in 1871 largely extended its operations under an enlightened minister of state, and a University was established at Tokio ; the Post Office was organised, runners being employed who by connections could cover 125 miles a day ; an Industrial Exhibition was held at the sacred city of Kioto ; on June 12th, the first railway in Japan was opened, from Tokio to Yokohama, a distance of eighteen miles ; and, perhaps most wonderful of all, on June 28th, the young Mikado set out on a tour of inspection through his dominions. On New Year's Day of 1873 the Calendar of the civilised world was adopted : the years, however, being reckoned from the traditional accession of the first Mikado, or from the new period inaugurated at the revolution called *Meiji*, so that 1873 was the year 2333 of the Empire, and the 6th of *Meiji*.*

Nor were the changes all material in character. Many moral reforms were carried out. The *eta*, the pariahs of Japan, were admitted to citizenship ; the "two-sworded men" lost their exclusive privileges, and the two swords were soon laid aside ; important regulations were framed to promote the sacredness of marriage and to raise the condition of women ; and above all, a move was made towards the toleration of Christianity, of which more hereafter.

In the meanwhile, Japan ratified her entrance into the comity of nations by sending an embassy of nobles and ministers of high rank, headed by Iwakura, the Minister of Foreign Affairs, and one of the most enlightened men of the progressive party, to the courts of America and Europe. This was the first Imperial embassy ever sent to the west by Japan. On the 4th of December, 1872, the ambassadors were received by Queen Victoria at Windsor Castle.

The last fifteen years have been a period of great and con-

---

* A succinct narrative of the adoption of these various reforms is given in Mossman's *New Japan*, down to 1873. Mr. Griffis gives less detail, but brings the story of progress down to 1886, in the New Edition of his book.

tinuous progress. A decided advance has been made towards the establishment of representative institutions. Under the Mikado's government as established after the revolution of 1868, the supreme legislative and executive power of the empire was vested in the Privy Council, which besides the Emperor consisted of three chief Ministers of State and a number of Privy Councillors; and affairs concerning the general administration of the empire were usually conducted in accordance with the decision of the Emperor, by and with the advice and assistance of the First Minister, and after deliberation by the other two ministers and the Privy Council. Immediately subordinated to the Privy Council were the Ministries or Departments of State. This was only a transition government, for when the Mikado assumed the reins of power he solemnly promised "that a deliberative assembly should be formed," and "all measures decided by public opinion." The first steps in this direction were taken in 1875 by creating a deliberative assembly composed of the Governors of Provinces, who were to consult and advise on measures relating to administrative matters of general application, and by establishing a House of Senators to discuss and decide upon measures of new legislation, or for the revision of existing laws. There was a still more decidedly onward movement in 1877 when Provincial Representative Assemblies were called into existence for Local Government purposes. The discussion of questions of local taxation, and of matters of local interest to be pressed upon the attention of the Central Government, has done much to make the people conscious of their power, and to show them the value of representative government, and to educate them for it.* The

---

* It is worthy of note that a voter must be able to read and write, and that it is necessary in recording his vote to write his own name and that of the candidate for whom he votes on the ballot paper.

press, platform, and debating club, both before and since, have contributed towards forming public opinion on the subject, and in December, 1881, the Emperor, yielding to its pressure, definitely promised to establish a representative Parliament in 1890, when constitutional government in Japan will become an actuality. In 1884 the system of nobility was modified to suit the altered circumstances of the country, and hundreds who have rendered distinguished services to the Empire have been admitted to its orders, and now figure among ourselves as marquises, viscounts, barons, &c. Thus the way is being prepared for the formation of a Second Chamber when the popular assembly is elected in 1890. In anticipation of the same great change the Government was reorganised in December, 1885. This was no mere redistribution of offices, but a complete reconstruction of the government fabric. Not only were men of the old court party removed from office and young men educated abroad called to fill the highest posts, but "the triple Premiership, Privy Council, and Ministries as then constituted were abolished," and a Cabinet, formed after European models, established in their place; but it has yet to be decided whether under the new constitution the Ministers will be responsible to the Emperor or the Parliament. The change, too, besides bringing the Emperor and his subjects closer together, was one greatly in the interests of economy, for by it the services of some eight thousand officials were dispensed with.

The Government of the Restoration entered on its arduous task with very heavy financial responsibilities, but it has met them with complete success. In 1877 a scheme of commutation was promulgated, which provided for the extinction of hereditary and life pensions created by the abolition of the feudal system. This enormously increased the national debt, which still amounts to nearly 250 million dollars, and necessitates an annual expenditure of 20 millions. At the same time the land tax—the principal source of revenue—has been reduced one-sixth, involving an annual loss to the Treasury of some 8 million dollars; and yet the national income, amounting to nearly 75 million dollars, fully covers the expenditure.

Tokens of progress are to be seen in every direction. The newspaper press has gone on developing in intelligence and power, in spite of the check it received in 1876, when the state of the country rendered stringent regulations necessary, and numerous editors and writers suffered imprisonment for violating them. A dozen daily newspapers are now published in Tokio, three in Osaka, and more in other large towns, whilst many more are published once, twice, or three times a week in all parts of the country. Education is making rapid strides. Of the 53,000 primary schools contemplated, nearly 30,000 have been built, and are in active operation. They are taught by teachers trained in normal schools, and are attended by three million children, of whom about a million are girls. The English language has been included among the subjects taught, and is being more widely studied than ever. Higher education is attracting more attention, and that of women is now *the* question to the front. The writing of Japanese with Roman letters is being strongly urged in some quarters, and a new society called the *Romaji Kai* or Roman Letter Association, was formed in 1884 to promote it. Should the system be adopted it will greatly facilitate the work of education. The Post Office has developed into a most important institution, with its Money Order and Savings' Bank business. In 1880 nearly thirty-three million letters, seventeen million postcards, and fourteen million newspapers passed through the post-offices of the Empire, and in 1885 nearly one hundred million letters and packages were forwarded.* Japan is now a member of the Postal Union, and regularly receives and despatches foreign mails. The telegraph, first introduced in 1869, now runs from end to end of the Empire. In 1885 there were nearly six thousand miles open, with fifteen thousand miles of wire; and nearly three million messages were transmitted. Cables connect the island Empire with the continent of Asia and the whole of the civilised world. The telephone is also in use in the large cities. Railway construction is being pushed forward. The first little railway — that between Tokio and Yokohama — was opened in 1872. In 1885 "there were 265 miles open, 271 miles in course of construction, and 543 miles in contemplation." The work of surveying and engineering was formerly done by Europeans; it is now in the hands of Natives. Japanese packet and war steamers are to be met with thousands of miles from Dai Nippon. The Japan Mail Shipping Company has a large fleet of steamers, and those regularly running between Shanghai and Yokohama, calling at Nagasaki and Kobe, belong to this company. Lighthouses stand on the principal promontories, and on some of the outlying islands along the coast where they are required to facilitate navigation. Machinery has been introduced, and manufactories of all kinds are in operation.

One of the most remarkable instances of Japanese imitation of the customs of Christendom is the official adoption of Sunday as a day of rest. There was formerly a national holiday every fifth day,† viz., the 1st, 6th, 11th, 16th, 21st,

---

* Even eleven or twelve years ago the Rev. J. Piper, travelling in the heart of the country, found a letter-box in almost every village, with in most places the English words, "Post Office." The number is now much greater, and pillar and wall-boxes are common in both town and country.

† Called *Ichi-roku*=one-six.

and 26th of each month. On the 1st of April, 1876, these were abolished, and the first day of each seven substituted. As the many Europeans engaged in various departments refused (from whatever motives) to work on Sundays, the inconvenience of the old system was manifest, and as the Saturday half-holiday has been introduced as well as the Sunday rest, officials have lost nothing by the change.

But this progress, though continuous, has not been always uninterrupted. Disaffection repeatedly showed itself among the Samurai after they were dispossessed of their privileges and wealth, and more than once open insurrection broke out. The Satsuma Rebellion of 1877, especially, was a most serious affair, and demands a brief notice.

Satsuma is (or rather was) a principality at the southern end of Kiushiu. The Daimio of the Satsuma clan was the most powerful, and almost the richest, of the Japanese nobles, and certainly the most independent. The then *de facto* chief, Shimadzu Saburo, who had acted for his son, the nominal head of the clan (but a minor), since 1858, played a leading part in the Revolution. It was he whose retainers killed Mr. Richardson in 1862; it was he whose city, Kagoshima, was bombarded, and who afterwards entertained Sir H. Parkes; it was he who led the attack on the Shogûnate. Among his leading Samurai were Saigo and Okubo, who, under the revived government of the Mikado, became respectively Commander-in-chief and Minister of Finance.

Within a year after the Revolution, divergences of opinion began to appear in the Cabinet. The Prime Minister and Vice-Prime Minister, Sanjo and Iwakura, headed the progressive party, and were supported by Okubo and other Satsuma men; while Shimadzu (who held no post, but had great influence) and Saigo were unwilling to go further than they had already gone, and exhibited reactionary tendencies.

In particular, the two latter advocated the old rights of the Samurai, and endeavoured in 1873 to force Japan into a war with Korea, hoping that by gaining military glory the two-sworded men would recover their former pre-eminence. Iwakura and Okubo, having been in Europe and America, had learned the advantages of peace, and their views prevailed in the Government, although, as a kind of sop to the discontented Satsuma Samurai, an expedition was undertaken in 1874 to Formosa, to punish the people of that island for some outrages on shipwrecked Japanese. Saigo retired from the ministry, and Shimadzu presented to the Mikado a solemn protest against twenty specified innovations contrary to national usage, one of which was "the engagement of foreigners for the service of the State and the adoption of their ideas," and another, "the non-prohibition of the extension of evil doctrines" (*i.e.*, Christianity). No attention was paid to this memorial; and when in March, 1876, the final abolition of the "two-swords" was decreed, it was to Shimadzu "the knell of all his hopes and dreams of a return to the old order of things." "He acknowledged the impossibility of realising his dream, and retired from the political arena."*

Saigo was not so easily overcome. In view of a possible contest, he and the Satsuma Samurai carried on the manufacture of arms at Kagoshima on their own account, and gradually perfected a military organisation for the overthrow of the Government, all being done nominally in the name of the Mikado, though in avowed opposition to his ministers. At length in February, 1877, civil war broke out. A desperate conflict ensued, which desolated Kiushiu for seven months,

---

* The notification of March, 1876 was:—" No individual will henceforth be permitted to wear a sword unless he be in Court dress, a member of the military or naval forces, or a police officer," when it appeared there were very few of the *Samurai* who were wearing swords except on special occasions.

and cost Japan 35,000 men and eight millions of money. But it ended in the total defeat of Saigo. On September 24th he and the remnant of his personal followers were surrounded and overpowered. He was one of the first to fall wounded to the ground, when one of his lieutenants, true to the ancient custom of Japan, cut off his chief's head with a single blow of his heavy sword, and then slew himself by *hara-kiri*. The head was discovered and recognised by the victors, and " Admiral Kawamura, the senior officer present, reverently washed it with his own hands as a mark of respect for his former friend and companion in arms."*

The suppression of the rebellion greatly strengthened the Government. But it did not give universal satisfaction. Thousands of the people of Satsuma have since visited the grave of Saigo; and the popular belief at the time of his death was that his spirit had taken up its abode in the planet Mars, while those of his followers inhabited a new race of frogs which was said to have appeared in Kiushiu.

A great calamity fell upon the Cabinet and the country in the following year. Iwakura had been assaulted and severely wounded by disaffected Samurai in 1873 ; and now his able colleague Okubo met a violent death at their hands, being assassinated in Tokio itself on May 14th, 1878. In him Japan lost a great man, and one of her most enlightened and judicious leaders.

But the progress, if checked, has never been stopped. Iwakura continued to serve his country for four years, and then passed away in July, 1883. Sanjo, his former chief, still lives, though the active duties of government have passed into younger hands. But the tide of progress still flows. The

---

* This brief notice of Saigo's revolt and the circumstances that led to it is based upon a most interesting book, Mounsey's *Satsuma Rebellion* (Murray, 1879). See also an article in the *C. M. Intelligencer* of July, 1879.

Europeanising process is going on more rapidly than ever. Politically, socially, and religiously old things have passed away and all things have become, or are becoming, new. In England, the Revolution of the seventeenth century followed on the Reformation of the sixteenth, and was, as far as the State was concerned, its crown and completion. Japan has had its Revolution, not indeed, as we have seen, independent of all connection with religion, but untouched at all events by any faith that can exercise a chastening and an elevating influence on the people. Will that Revolution have its crown and completion in a true Reformation—in the adoption of the *Yesu-no-michi*, the Way of Jesus? Some of the following pages may help us to answer the question, or at least to form an opinion as to the way it is likely to be answered in the not very distant future.

IX.

PROTESTANT MISSIONS IN JAPAN.

" Arise, shine ; for thy light is come, and the glory of the Lord is risen upon thee."—*Isa.* lx. 1.

NGLAND was mainly instrumental in opening the door for the Gospel to enter Japan, and the American Churches were foremost in carrying it in. Under Commodore Perry's limited treaty several American missionaries, connected with China, paid brief visits to Japan, to ascertain what were the prospects of commencing missionary work; but nothing further could be done until Lord Elgin's Treaty of 1858, and the similar treaties concluded between Japan and other Western nations, secured liberty for foreigners to reside at certain specified ports. When these came into operation in July, 1859, the Rev. J. Liggins, and the Rev. C. M. (now Bishop) Williams, of the Protestant Episcopal Church of the United States, were already at Nagasaki, and in the following October Dr. Hepburn of the American Presbyterian Board arrived at Kanagawa. These were followed in November by two clerical and one medical missionary connected with the Dutch Reformed Church of America, and in the following April by a missionary of the American Baptist Free Mission Society. Thus, within a year from the opening of the treaty-ports to foreign residence, four American societies were represented by five ordained and two medical missionaries.

The Civil War in the United States, of 1860—4, sadly crippled American missionary effort generally for the time ; and in 1861, some of the Episcopal missionaries who were compelled to retire from Japan for lack of support from home wrote to England, and appealed to the Church Missionary Society to take up the work they had begun. The means for this, however, were not forthcoming; and on the restoration of peace in America, the Churches there were enabled to strengthen their missions.

It was just at that epoch, 1864, that a remarkable event occurred which more than anything else was instrumental in awakening Christian people in the United States to their responsibilities. A young Japanese of good family named Neesima, had been struck by a book on geography in the Chinese language, published by an American missionary. It began, " In the beginning God created the heavens and the earth."* What could this mean ? Who was that God ? Certainly He did not live in Japan ; perhaps He might live in America, whence the author of the book came. So reasoned the young man, and determined to go to America and seek for God. He left Japan secretly, and at the peril of his life (for the old law forbidding Japanese to leave their country was still in force), made his way to China in a trading vessel, and thence obtained a passage to Boston. There he found himself more perplexed than ever. "I came all the way to Boston," he said to the captain of the ship that had brought him, " to find God, and there is no one to tell me." The captain took him to the owner of the vessel, a well-known Christian merchant, Mr. A. Hardy. The merchant took him home, treated him as a son, and sent him to college. He

---

* " An excellent introduction," says a missionary who tells the story, the Rev. J. H. Ballagh, "to a system of geography. It would hardly be tolerated in this Christian land, but in a heathen land it might pass."

soon found the God he had been seeking, and with his whole heart embraced the faith of Christ. In 1875 he returned to Japan as a missionary at the charges of his benefactor and in connection with the American Board, and became president of a Christian college at Kioto, which was then founded, and where in 1884—5 there were 172 students pursuing the ordinary collegiate course, and 48 theological students preparing to labour among their countrymen. But the deep interest which his case excited at the time gave a great impetus to American missionary zeal on behalf of Japan.

The pioneer missionaries were in circumstances of no little discouragement and difficulty for several years after they entered upon their work. The Government viewed them with suspicion ; the people, though by no means hostile, were distant and timid ; and all classes dreaded Christianity as a pestilential creed, the introduction of which would bring manifold evils upon the country. Official spies were frequently sent to the missionaries ostensibly to make friends with them, but really to discover what object these unofficial and non-trading foreigners had in coming to Japan. Even in private the greatest caution was necessary in dealing with visitors, for so much were the consequences of being suspected of favouring Christianity feared, that whenever the subject was mentioned to a Japanese he would involuntarily put his hand to his throat as a token of the danger to which the introduction of such a subject exposed him. Some young men who in these early days came to a missionary to learn a little English, purchased copies of a book called *The Christian Reader*, and at once erased the word " Christian " from the title page and cover, for fear it should be noticed by others and bring them into trouble.

But even then, when open missionary work was an impossibility, and any attempt to engage in it would have invited disaster, the personal influence of the missionaries was making itself felt, and the disposal by them of numerous copies of the Holy Scriptures and other books in Chinese, which were imported for circulation among the educated classes—who studied and read Chinese as a classical language —carried the light of Christian truth to places far away from the treaty-ports. Almost from the first there were a few earnest, though timid seekers after truth, and every year their number increased. This was especially the case after three or four years, when, owing to the change in official and popular feeling, larger numbers came to the missionaries for instruction in English; and the improvement was still more marked when a little later Government schools were established in Yokohama and Nagasaki, for the teaching of English, and placed in charge of missionaries. It was chiefly in this way that the Gospel was first brought in contact with the people. "From 1859 to 1872 there was no preaching worthy of mention. The missionaries were all engaged in teaching. God led our missionaries into the schools, and the Kingdom of Christ entered Japan through the schools."*

In January, 1866, "a little band of believers of various nationalities" residing in Yokohama, who had been observing the Week of Universal Prayer, issued "an address to God's people throughout the world, asking their prayers in a special manner for Japan." It mentioned some favourable changes in the circumstances of the missions; that the Government no longer sent spies to watch the missionaries, but began to repose confidence in them by employing them as school teachers; that in the schoolrooms and in the houses of the missionaries the intelligent young men who came to learn English manifested a readiness to talk about Christianity, and

* Report of the General Conference on Foreign Missions, held at Mildmay, Oct., 1878. Paper by Rev. Dr. Ferris, on "Missions in Japan."

no longer uttered the name of Jesus with bated breath; and that some of them went daily to the missionaries' houses "in groups of from two or three to six or seven to read the English Bible, preferring this to the study of school-books."

In June, 1869, the C.M. Society's experienced missionary in China, the Rev. W. A. (afterwards Bishop) Russell, visited Japan, and in his report to the Society he laid especial stress upon the fact that while "against Christianity in a Roman Catholic garb, from what took place in the past, there no doubt existed a very bitter feeling, no hostility was manifested against Protestant Christianity," which the Japanese were already beginning to discern to be a very different thing. He found visitors to the missionaries speaking with reserve about religion till they ascertained them to be Protestants, "and then religious conversation was prosecuted without hesitation." This probably arose from a growing conviction that Protestantism was politically less harmful than either Roman Catholicism or the system of the Russo-Greek Church, but it nevertheless betokened the advance of knowledge among intelligent and discriminating men, for during the earlier years no such distinctions were made.

But whatever change of opinion may have been discernible in some quarters the law against Christianity was still unrepealed, and the Mikado's Government seemed bent on maintaining it in its integrity. Soon after the Revolution in 1868, the laws of the Shogûn's Government, which had been posted on the notice-boards in every town and village, were replaced by those of the new Imperial Government. Among the new enactments were the following:—

The evil sect, called Christian, is strictly prohibited. Suspicious persons should be reported to the proper officers, and rewards will be given.

Human beings must carefully practise the principles of the five social relations. Charity must be shown to widowers, widows, orphans, the childless, and sick. There must be no such crimes as murder, arson, or robbery.

And a few months later a further decree appeared :—

With respect to the Christian sect, the existing prohibition must be strictly observed. Evil sects are strictly prohibited.

But notwithstanding these hostile notifications some relaxation could not long be delayed. Already Christian men and Christian missionaries were residing in the country, and "allowed the free exercise of their religion," and had "the right to erect suitable places of worship," under treaties. Already, too, the law that made it criminal for a Japanese to leave the country, or having left to return to it, which was enacted at the same time as the laws against Christianity, had fallen into abeyance, and these were soon destined to be similarly disregarded. In 1873 all the new Imperial notifications just quoted were withdrawn from the notice-boards. This action of the Government was equivocal. It did not repeal the law against Christianity ; but just as the laws respecting " murder, arson, and robbery " remained in force, notwithstanding the removal of the particular prohibitions respecting them, so was it with the prohibition of " the evil sect." Indeed, officers were appointed to warn the people against supposing that the law was changed because the notices were no longer exhibited as formerly. But, in spite of these explanations, the people soon began to regard what had been done as equivalent to a repeal of the obnoxious edicts ; and the Government, who were undoubtedly anxious to avoid offending the Christian sentiment of Western nations, were not averse to such a construction being put upon their action, and were better able to ignore breaches of the law when its existence was less conspicuous.

But whilst the central Government every year pursued a

more liberal and enlightened policy, local officials were in many cases slow to follow. Ostensibly acting in the interests of public order, they had numerous opportunities—of which they sometimes took advantage—of throwing obstacles in the way of the open propagation of Christianity, and of intimidating and oppressing those who favoured or embraced it. But eventually the views of the party of progress triumphed, all official opposition ceased, and toleration became virtually complete. Buildings were set apart for Christian worship, not only for foreigners but for natives, not only at the treaty-ports but in towns and villages far removed from them. No obstacles were placed in the way of the evangelistic work of either natives or foreigners. No difficulty was experienced in holding public meetings in theatres and other large buildings. Christian literature was everywhere exposed for sale and openly circulated by booksellers, and by colporteurs employed for the purpose. In 1884—less than twelve years after the removal of the edicts from the notice-boards—the final step was taken, and the topstone of the edifice of religious toleration laid by the issue of notifications in regard to registration and burial. Until that time every citizen was registered as a Buddhist or Shintoist, and difficulties were sometimes experienced by Christians in getting their names transferred from the register in one place to that in another. A still greater difficulty was sometimes experienced in burying the Christian dead. In some places where public cemeteries had been established—as at Osaka—there was no such difficulty, as the cemeteries were open to all, of whatever sect or creed, and the employment of a Buddhist or Shinto priest was optional. But in other places it was quite different. Thus in 1875 the Rev. Mr. Thompson, an American missionary at Tokio, having buried a convert with Christian rites, two Japanese who took part in the funeral were summoned before one of the courts, severely reprimanded, and threatened with a fine for breaking the law which required every burial to be according to Buddhist or Shinto rites. As most of the burial-grounds were connected with Buddhist temples and under the control of the priesthood, the difficulty was increased by the tenacity with which the priests very naturally clung to their prescriptive rights and dues. In process of time Christian burials were allowed to take place in some of the Buddhist burial-grounds with the consent of the priest in charge. Even so lately as 1884, one of the C.M.S. Christians was thus buried in Tokio. The priest received the customary fee, and to accommodate those concerned went out for the day, leaving the Christians free to bury the remains of their departed sister with Christian rites. By the notifications just referred to, all religious distinctions in registration and burial were abolished, and provision was made for the establishment of public cemeteries to be open to all, so as not to interfere with the prescriptive rights of the priesthood. Thus thirty years after the negotiation of Commodore Perry's treaty, and twenty-five after the opening of the ports, the last obstacles to Christian liberty were removed, and perfect religious equality was established ; and that without any such reference to Christianity by name as would have marked it out for opposition from those interested in maintaining the old religions of the country.

This happy result has been achieved by a variety of means. Christianity was not recognised by the treaties with Japan as a religion inculcating virtue, nor did Western nations stipulate that liberty should be given to propagate it ; yet Christian diplomacy has done much to promote the cause of religious freedom in Japan. It must not be forgotten that the withdrawal of the anti-Christian edict in 1873 happened at the very time the first Imperial embassy visited Europe and

America, and that the still more decided and altogether unequivocal action of the Government in 1884 followed closely upon the return from Germany of Mr. Ito, a member of the Privy Council, who is said to have learnt from conversations with Prince Bismarck and the Emperor William that Christianity was "not a mere human device for the maintenance of influence and power," but "a reality in the hearts of men," exerting an "influence of untold value to the individual and the nation," and to have recommended the Mikado to study it and to promote its introduction.

In the early days of cautious and tentative effort much good was also effected by the influence of able and devoted Christian laymen, chiefly from the United States, who engaged in educational work under the Government; and unquestionably the toleration that so soon obtained was largely due to the spread, by their instrumentality, among the governing and literary class—the very class they came in contact with in the colleges and schools—of correct views of the high character of the Christian religion. One of these gentlemen, Mr. E. Warren Clark, in his pleasant little book *Life and Adventures in Japan*,* gives incidentally some interesting glimpses of the exercise of this kind of Christian influence. He was engaged as a teacher of science at the city of Shidzuoka. When he reached Japan from America, he found in the agreement he was to sign a clause forbidding him to teach Christianity, and binding him to silence for three years. "It was a great dilemma," he says; "for I had spent all my money in coming to Japan and getting ready to go into the interior." Some of his friends urged him to accept the condition; and his Japanese interpreter recommended him to sign the agreement and then disregard it. But he felt a great principle was at stake,

---
* Published in England by J. Nisbet & Co.

and he stood firm. Unless the clause was struck out, he informed the Government, he must decline to go on. " It is impossible," he added, " for a Christian to dwell three years in the midst of a Pagan people, and yet keep entire silence on the subject nearest his heart." His firmness triumphed ; the clause was struck out ; and the Japanese, he says, respected his "pluck," and were more friendly than ever. He began the very first Sunday he was at Shidzuoka, and conducted a Bible-class the whole time he was there; and when he was transferred to the Imperial College at Tokio, he resolved to hold three every Sunday, for the convenience of different classes of students. Unusual difficulties arose here, but he persevered. "I confess," he wrote, "that when the feeling floods upon me, that *these* are souls for whom Christ died, and *mine* is the privilege to make the fact known unto them, it breaks through all bounds of mere expediency, and forces me to speak the truth at all risks. There is a solemnity beyond expression in the attempt to bring before these young men the words of eternal life."

Another American gentleman, Captain Janes, who was for some time engaged as a school-teacher at Kumamoto, in Kiushiu, was the means of leading a fine body of young men to Christ, of whom more than thirty joined the Christian College at Kioto at once, in 1876, and were subsequently received into the Christian Church in that city. About a dozen of this number completed their theological course— extending over three years—in 1879, and are now engaged in educational, pastoral, evangelistic and literary work.

What would have been the result, not only in Japan but in every part of the world, if English and American Christians had always thus reflected the light of Christ in word and deed! The Japanese, like other intelligent races, were not slow to notice the marked difference between the Christianity preached by the missionaries and the Christianity exhibited in the lives of too many who came from Christian countries, and to infer that the religion of Christ had no more living power than the religion of Buddha. This is illustrated by the following passage from an essay by a young Japanese, quoted in Lanman's *Japanese in America* :—

> The conduct of foreigners, excepting some of the better class of missionaries and a few laymen, is a very shame to the name of Christianity and civilisation, and retards the progress of both. . . . It is in vain that some really good Christians try to persuade the natives that Christianity is the true religion of God while they are beset on all sides by these splendid specimens of nominal Christians. . . . A traitor is worse than an enemy; yet these nominal Christians are such. . . . Woe to the betrayer of their Master! If He should appear in this world at this time He could scarcely recognise His own people.

The open discussion of Christianity and the advocacy of its toleration in the numerous daily and weekly newspapers published in the capital and the provinces, also tended to help forward change in this direction. An extract or two from articles which appeared in 1875 may be quoted :—

> The faith of people can only be formed by their hearts, and it seems therefore improper for the Government to dictate to them which form of faith is right or wrong, and what they shall do and what not do on this subject. It would be better for the Government to permit the people to worship God as they please, provided that in doing so they do not violate the laws of their country. . . . This, therefore, is a thing to which our rulers ought to give the greatest consideration. Ye statesmen, what are your views?
>
> A religion is established by the number of those who believe it. . . . An athlete, however strong, could not by the force of his muscles, wrench the belief of another from his mind, nor could an eloquent man by his eloquence. A Government ought, therefore, to leave religion to the free consciences of men, and it has no right to say, "We insist on this belief and prohibit the other belief," for a Government itself is composed only of men.
>
> The entrance of Christianity is the natural outcome of time. There is

nothing better than Christianity to aid in the advancement of the world, but there are sects which are injurious, as well as sects that are beneficial. The best mode, therefore, of advancing our country is to introduce the most free and enlightened form of Christianity and have it diffused among the people.

These and many similar utterances of the native press were read and discussed in all parts of the country. If they provoked opposition in some quarters, they enlightened the popular mind, and emboldened multitudes to study Christianity.

The presence of Missionaries, domiciled in the country for the avowed object of propagating the faith of Christ in the face of anti-Christian edicts, opened the conflict, and their quiet but persistent, and, in due time under God's blessing, successful efforts to win individuals to Christ intensified it. Then it was that the widespread manifestation of Christian truth and its exemplification in Christian lives, the influence of Christian Governments, the zeal of enlightened journalists, and the action of far-seeing statesmen, combined to secure for the people of Japan perfect liberty of conscience in matters of religion. Surely in all this the Church may hear the voice of her living Lord, the King of nations, saying, " Behold I have set before thee an open door, and no man can shut it."

Until 1869 only the four American societies which entered the field in 1859 and 1860 had representatives in the country. Then two new Missions were established, that of the C.M.S. at Nagasaki, and the American Board Mission, whose first missionary reached Yokohama in November, and removed to Kobe in the following spring (1870). In 1871 three agents of the Woman's Union Missionary Society of America arrived at Yokohama, and in the year following they established the " American Mission Home," an important female educational institution, which has been " the spiritual birthplace of many," and which still continues to be an important centre of female missionary work. In 1873-74 the older Missions were considerably strengthened and their operations extended, and several new ones were commenced. In the former year the American Baptist Missionary Union took the place of the Baptist Free Mission Society, and three other new Missions entered the field—those of the American Methodist Episcopal Church, the Methodist Church of Canada, and the English Society for the Propagation of the Gospel; and in the latter year the Edinburgh Medical Mission was started, and the United Presbyterian Church of Scotland sent out its first missionaries. Since then eleven other smaller missions have commenced work, and the Edinburgh Medical Mission has withdrawn from the field, and transferred its work at Niigata to the American Board. At the close of 1886 there were, therefore, 22 Protestant Missionary Societies represented in Japan, viz., 14 American, 1 German-Swiss, and 7 British— the British being 1 Scotch, 1 Canadian, and 5 English—but nine of the entire number had fewer than five missionaries each, and two of them had only one missionary each.

The total number of male missionaries at that time was 128, and of single lady missionaries 87. Of the former 92 were American, 1 German-Swiss, and 35 British—3 being Scotch, 8 Canadian, and 24 English—and the lady workers were made up of 75 American and 13 British—5 being Canadian and 8 English. Thus it will be seen that American missionaries, who were first to enter Japan in 1859, and who were doing useful pioneer work nearly ten years before the arrival of the first British missionary, still continue to take the lead.

Most of the missionaries have hitherto resided at one or other of the seven treaty-ports, but some of them have from time to time resided at other places, as *employés* of Japanese, generally in the capacity of school-teachers, with, in some cases, no little advantage to the work. Thirteen such places were occupied during 1886 by one or more missionary workers, viz., Fuku-oka and Kumamoto in Kiushiu, Kochi in Shikoku, Nemuro and Sapporo in Yezo, and in the main island Naka-no-Seki in Choshiu in the west, Okayama in Bizen (opposite the island of Shikoku), Wakayama in Kii, south of Osaka, Kioto the old capital, where the American Board has had a strong staff in connection with Mr. Neesima's Christian College for more than ten years, Shidzuoka on the Tokaido, west of Tokio, Kanazawa in Kaga on the west coast, Kubota in the Akita *ken* in the extreme north-west, and Sendai on the north-east coast. Of the twenty places just mentioned including the treaty-ports, thirteen were in each case occupied by one society only, but at the remaining seven two or more societies were working side by side. Thus at Tokio, the head-quarters of so many missions, fourteen societies were represented, at Yokohama eight, at Osaka six, at Sendai four, at Nagasaki and Kobe three, and at Hakodate two. But while the ingathering at these chief centres has been large, much work has been done in numerous other places, both by missionaries travelling under Government passports, and by stationary and itinerant native evangelists.

The first Japanese convert to receive Christian baptism from a Protestant missionary was Yano Riu, who had been a teacher of the language to one of the missionaries since 1860. He was baptized at his own house in Yokohama in the presence of his family, and with their full consent, in October, 1864, and died shortly afterwards in the assurance that he was about to be with Jesus. The next were two brothers who held official positions in Kiushiu under the Prince of Hizen. An English pocket Testament, which had been accidentally dropped overboard from one of the ships of the English fleet which visited Japan in 1854, came into the hands of the elder, Wakasa by name, and on learning that there was a Chinese translation of it, he procured a copy and began to study it. This eventually resulted in his younger brother and three others becoming interested in Christianity. When they sought instruction from Mr. (now Dr.) Verbeck, who was then living at Nagasaki, they were residing at Saga, where the C.M.S. now has an outstation. Being unable to visit their instructor, owing to official duties, they were plentifully supplied with Chinese Christian books, and two messengers were employed going regularly to and fro between teacher and pupils—a two days' journey each way—with questions from the latter and explanations in reply to them from the former. In May, 1866, Wakasa and his brother visited Nagasaki, and on Whit-Sunday they were secretly baptized. Wakasa fell asleep in Jesus in 1872, and happy fruit gathered in 1880 bore witness to his continuance in the faith, and to his earnest and faithful efforts to win his children, friends, and servants to Christ.

Other isolated converts were gathered from time to time, but up to the spring of 1872, a period of nearly thirteen years since the arrival of the first Protestant missionaries, only ten Japanese had received baptism at their hands, the last being Mr. Nimura, who was baptized by Mr. Ensor at Nagasaki in 1871.

The first native Japanese Church was organised at Yokohama on March 10th, 1872, nearly a year before the withdrawal of the edicts against Christianity. Its first membership embraced nine young men, who then received baptism, and two who had been baptised previously, one of them being Mr. Ensor's first convert just mentioned. It was called "The Church of Christ in Japan," and its constitution consisted of a simple evangelical Creed, and some rules which placed the government of it in the hands of the pastor and elders, with the consent of the members. It is now one of the numerous congregations connected with the body called "The United Church of Christ in Japan," which, as will presently be seen, was organised in October, 1877, and embraces all the Christians gathered in connection with the American Presbyterian and Dutch Reformed and Scottish U. P. Missions.

The ingathering, so slow at first, has been rapid during the last few years; so that at the close of 1886—less than fifteen years after the first church was organised—there were 193 "organised churches" or congregations, and the ten Christians baptized during the more than twelve years ending with the close of 1871, had grown into a body of 14,710. During the year 1886 there were 4,115 baptisms, and the net increase in the three years ending December, 1886, was 8,112, or 123 per cent. One of the most marked evidences of the reality of this work and of the vigour of Japanese Christianity, is the spirit of independence and self-support which characterises the Native churches. Thus of the 193 organised churches reported to be in existence in 1886, no fewer than 64 were wholly self-supporting, and 119 partially, and their united contributions amounted to nearly $26,866, which, at the par rate of 4s., is equal to £5,373, or more than 7s. for each baptized church member.

The relations between the several missions have been, as a rule, most cordial and friendly, and in spite of national, denominational, and individual differences, substantial unity has prevailed, and, in some important matters of common interest, united action has been secured. This has been the case in the work of translating the Old and New Testament Scriptures. A committee for the translation of the New Testament, to "consist of one member from each mission desirous of cooperating in this work," was appointed by a united conference of Protestant missionaries held at Yokohama in September, 1872, and arrangements were made for translating the Old Testament, by a similar but larger representative conference held in Tokio in 1878. Not to mention the older translations of Doctors Gutzlaff, Bettleheim, and S. W. Williams, "the early existence of which," says Dr. Verbeck, "testifies to the Christian zeal and industry of those worthy men," previous to the formation of the New Testament committee in 1872, the early missionaries had prepared and published the Gospels of St. Matthew, St. Mark, and St. John, and a second translation of St. Matthew was published in the following year. The committee commenced to meet for joint work in June, 1874, and the revision of the last book of the translation was completed on November 3rd, 1879. The first editions of the several books were printed from wooden blocks, and published as they were prepared : St. Luke, the first joint production of the committee having appeared in August, 1875, and several Epistles and the Revelation, the last portions, in April, 1880 ; and the completion of the work was celebrated by a united meeting for thanksgiving, held at Tokio on April 19th, which was attended by representatives of fourteen American and English Missionary Societies, and of the Japanese churches in the neighbourhood of the capital. In preparing the translation the first place of honour belongs to J. C. Hepburn, M.D., LL.D., by whom the greater portion of the draft translations were made, and to whose indefatigable labours the work owed its early completion. He was ably seconded by his two principal colleagues, the Rev. S. R. Brown, D.D., and the Rev. D. C. Greene, D.D., who were associated with him throughout.*

The translation of the Old Testament has now been com-

---

* Osaka Conference Report, 1883, p. 41.

pleted. Many of the books have already been published, and the rest soon will be. Dr. Hepburn has taken an active part in the work, and the Rev. P. K. Fyson, of the C.M.S. Mission, has been wholly engaged in it since 1882 (with the exception of a few months spent in England in 1884), under an arrangement with the British and Foreign Bible Society. A desire having been expressed by the Japanese Churches for a responsible share in the work, in 1884 an arrangement was made to include as their representatives in the committee of translators three Christian Japanese scholars, their expenses being in part paid from a fund raised for the purpose by the native Christians of all denominations. A uniform translation of the Scriptures—whether that just now completed, or some subsequent revision of it—appealed to by all the Native churches, will, it is hoped, long bear witness to their substantial unity in all that is essential.

The printing and circulation of the separate portions of the Bible, and of the completed New Testament in Japanese— including editions printed from metal type, and the justly popular New Testament, with 12,000 references, prepared by the Rev. J. Piper, of the C.M.S.*—has been the work of the British and Foreign, the Scotch National, and the American Bible Societies. They have also had prepared by competent scholars special editions of the Chinese Scriptures, with marks for Japanese readers. These editions of the Holy Scriptures, in both Chinese and Japanese, are being widely circulated in all parts of the empire. In 1886 the colporteurs of the Scotch Bible Society alone sold 611 Bibles, 10,437 Testaments, and 45,288 portions; and the agent of the American Bible Society

---

* A pocket edition of this valuable work has recently been issued, and thousands of copies have been sold. Some years ago a Romanized edition of the New Testament was published. A second has now been issued to meet a demand.

states in his last report that during the past fifteen years about half a million Bibles, Testaments, and portions have been circulated in the country.

The preparation of Japanese Christian literature is being proceeded with. Since Dr. Hepburn published his first religious tract in 1867 many more have been prepared by different missionaries, and sent forth by tens of thousands every year, by the Religious Tract Society and its sister the American Tract Society. Numerous other larger works have also been prepared and published. During 1886 the Religious Tract Society alone printed 174,824 publications with 2,700,000 pages, and put into circulation 156,000. The *Pilgrim's Progress* is in circulation, the first edition of 2,000 copies having been almost entirely sold out. Year by year thousands of copies of Dr. Martin's *Evidences of Christianity* (first published in China for the Chinese) are issued. Thus not only tracts but books of various sizes, some suited to the general reader and some intended for theological students, are being prepared and circulated. It shows marvellous progress that a tract which twenty-five years ago no Japanese dared to print—the first edition having been printed in China—is now circulated by thousands every year, and that an edition in Roman letters has just been published, as books in the Roman character are in great demand.

In April, 1883, a General Conference of Protestant Missionaries was held at Osaka, which was attended by 106 representatives of nineteen missionary and the three Bible societies, including the wives of missionaries. Apart from its value to the missionaries as affording an opportunity for the interchange of views on a variety of subjects affecting the welfare of their common work, and as a means of promoting mutual edification and brotherly love, it had a marked influence on the native Christians in their relations to each other. The native brethren, revived by the "showers of blessing" which God graciously granted in different parts of the country in that year, were more closely knit together in sympathy and love, their fellowship became more real, and they received fresh power to witness for their Lord before the world. That year was a fresh starting point to the infant Churches, and the remarkable ingathering of the three subsequent years shows that they went forward.

Young Men's Christian Associations have been formed in some places. That in Osaka, in addition to promoting Christian edification, has been the means of uniting the native Churches of the city in common evangelistic efforts in theatres and public halls; and now having been able, with the aid of sums sent from England, America, and Australia, to erect a suitable building for united work on the principles of the Y.M.C.A., these efforts have become more regular and systematic.* A Scripture Union, too, has been formed, and at the close of 1886 had a membership of about 4,800.

The several missions have organised their converts in congregations and churches mainly according to the systems they represent. This, if inevitable in the present divided state of Protestant Christendom, should certainly only be temporary, and in working Church systems and adapting them to the circumstances of a new race being won to Christ, the utmost liberty should be accorded to native Christians; free and informal intercourse in united gatherings, if not organic union, should be fostered; the ultimate establishment of a really native Church, embracing within its pale the bulk, if not all, of the native Christians connected with the several missions, should be steadily kept in view; and any action in

---

* Their new hall was opened on the Mikado's birthday, November 3, 1886. It will accommodate more than a thousand.

the least calculated to frustrate this desirable end should be avoided. This has been the view of at least a majority of the Protestant missionaries in Japan. As early as 1872, when some of the earlier missionaries met in conference at Yokohama, they agreed to use their influence to secure as far as possible identity of name and organisation in the native Churches, in the formation of which they might be called to assist. This decision did not, however, result in any organic union of the kind some contemplated. But in 1876 the three Presbyterian missions then established in the country agreed on a basis of union, and in October, 1877, the " United Church of Christ in Japan" held its first official assembly. This body, which embraces all the Christians gathered in connection with the American Presbyterian, Dutch Reformed, and Scottish U.P. Missions, increased from eight churches with 623 members in 1877 to 55 churches with 5,472 members in 1886. This is now the largest organised Protestant Church body in Japan, and it is especially strong at the capital, and its membership may be augmented at any time by the admission to the union of the congregations connected with three more recently established Presbyterian Missions. The church body next in importance in point of numbers is that comprising the Congregational Missions, which are located for the most part in Central Japan, and are 35 in number with an aggregate membership of 4,231. Overtures have recently been made with a view to amalgamating the Independent and Presbyterian Missions, and there is every prospect of this being accomplished. At the close of 1886 the membership of the remaining families of missions was as follows : The Methodists had 2,798 members, the Baptists 682, and the Episcopal Missions about 1,300. If these various figures show that there has been encouraging progress, they equally remind us that there is yet very much land to be possessed. If

Japan is to be won to Christ and the whole land filled with His glory, the Lord's people must pray more fervently and work more earnestly, and press forward in confident faith to the victory. And may not the hope be cherished that in a land where there are so many tokens of God's presence and power, and where the Church is growing, and the zeal of native Christians burns so brightly, the Churches will ever remain essentially one in faith and love, and eventually be united in one Native Church?

X.

THE CHURCH MISSIONARY SOCIETY'S MISSION.

(I.) *Introduction.*

"He declared particularly what things God had wrought among the Gentiles .. and when they heard it, they glorified the Lord."—*Acts* xxi. 19, 20.

T has been already remarked that some of the American Episcopal missionaries appealed to the Church Missionary Society in 1861, to take up the work they had begun. It was not, however, until several years later that the Society was in a position to commence its Japan Mission. The appeal for special prayer, addressed to Christians in Europe and America by the American missionaries in January, 1866, was received by the Society, and published in the *Church Missionary Intelligencer* of June in that year. Not only did it call forth a spirit of prayer in C.M.S circles, but within twelve months one answer came to the supplications offered, in the shape of an anonymous donation of £4,000 to the society, as a nucleus for a special Japan fund. In yet another twelve months, God who had thus provided the means gave also the man; and in the very year of the great revolution, 1868, the Rev. George Ensor, B.A., of Queen's College, Cambridge, was designated as the first missionary from Christian England to the newly opened Empire.

The first station occupied was Nagasaki, where, when Mr.

Ensor arrived in January, 1869, the American Episcopal Mission was still located. He was joined in 1871 by the Rev. H. Burnside ; but both these brethren were soon obliged, by failure of health, to retire from the field. It was in 1873, when the remarkable course of events in Japan seemed to indicate that ere long a great and effectual door would be opened, that the Society's enlarged plans for missionary operations in that country were formed ; and in that and the two following years, four new stations were occupied, viz. : Osaka, by the Rev. C. F. Warren, formerly of Hong-Kong, on the last day of 1873 ; Tokio, by the Rev. J. Piper, also formerly of Hong-Kong,—and Hakodate, by the Rev. W. Dening, transferred from Madagascar,—both in May, 1874 ; and Niigata, by the Rev. P. K. Fyson, M.A. (who had reached Tokio in 1874), in the autumn of 1875. These stations, with the exception of Niigata, which was finally relinquished in 1883, are still the centres of the Society's Japan work. Not only was Nagasaki early deprived of its first missionaries, but of the brethren just mentioned as founders of the other stations only one—the Rev. P. K. Fyson—remains in the field in connection with the Society. Mr. Piper left Tokio in December, 1880, and retired in 1882 in consequence of Mrs. Piper's health ; Mr. Warren left Osaka in March, 1885, and is compelled to remain in England for the same reason ; and Mr. Dening was separated from the Society at the beginning of 1883. But the work is still carried on vigorously by those who were associated with these brethren, or who have subsequently gone out. At Nagasaki the Venerable Archdeacon Maundrell still takes the lead in the work which he practically recommenced in 1875, and he is supported by the Rev. A. B. Hutchinson, formerly of Hong-Kong, who joined the mission in 1882, and the Rev. J. B. Brandram, M.A., who arrived at Nagasaki with his sister in April, 1884. At Osaka the Rev.

H. Evington, M.A., who joined Mr. Warren in December, 1874, is the senior missionary, and also Secretary of the Japan Mission. His colleagues are the Rev. G. H. Pole, M.A., who reached Osaka in February, 1881, and who since Christmas, 1884, has held the Principalship of the Osaka Divinity School; Miss Caspari, formerly of Sierra Leone, who went to Hakodate in 1880, and was transferred to Osaka in 1883; the Rev. G. Chapman, who arrived in December, 1884; the Rev. W. J. Edmonds, formerly of the East African Mission, who arrived a year later, and the Rev. T. Dunn, formerly of the Ceylon and North Pacific Missions, who reached Osaka in December, 1886.

At Tokio the Rev. P. K. Fyson is the Society's senior missionary, but his work has lately been of a special character, the translation of the Old Testament. The Rev. J. Williams, who was formerly in East Africa, and was transferred to Hakodate in 1876, and thence to Tokio in 1879, is the Society's active evangelistic missionary at the capital. At Hakodate the Rev. W. Andrews, who went to Nagasaki in 1878, and was transferred to Hakodate in 1882, has been the Society's only ordained missionary since the spring of 1883, but Mr. J. Batchelor who went to Japan in 1877, and was appointed catechist in 1879, and lay missionary in 1883, makes Hakodate his head-quarters, and when there, renders valuable assistance in Japanese work, though his special work is amongst the Aino aborigines of Yezo.

The details of the work are left to the missionaries at each station, who are expected to co-operate so as mutually to support each other in their several lines of work; but the Japan C.M.S. Conference, which first met, especially for conference and prayer, under the presidency of Bishop Burdon in 1878, and which since 1881 has been convened annually, now occupies an important place in the government of the mission, as all matters involving expenditure have to be referred to it before the parent committee will take them into consideration.

Until the appointment of Bishop Poole in 1883, the English missions were under the Episcopal supervision of the Bishop of Victoria, Hong Kong. Bishop Smith first, and subsequently Bishops Alford and Burdon, visited Japan officially. It was when Bishop Burdon last visited Japan in 1878 that the question of appointing a bishop to reside in the country was first raised among the missionaries. After considerable delay, the Rev. A. W. Poole, who had been a C.M.S. missionary in South India, was appointed. He was consecrated on St. Luke's Day, October 18th, 1883, and reached Japan in December, where he was warmly welcomed by the English clergy and the native Christians connected with the English Church Missions. His Episcopal career was brief; but the ten months of his residence in Japan were not lived in vain, for he won the affection and confidence, not only of his fellow-Churchmen, but of the missionaries of the various American societies, and his influence seemed likely to do much towards uniting the servants of Christ in Japan. He has been succeeded by Bishop Edward Bickersteth—son of the Bishop of Exeter, and grandson of a former secretary of the Society—who reached Japan in April, 1886, and has since visited every station and outstation of the C.M.S., from the Aino village of Horu-betsu in Yezo to Kagoshima in South Kiushiu. How important a part of the Bishop's work the oversight of the C.M.S. Mission is, will appear from the detailed account of each centre presently to be given.

Mention has already been made of the mission of the American Episcopal Church. It has never been a strong one, and was especially weak during the first twelve years of its existence. Mr. (now Bishop) Williams was practically single-handed from 1859 to 1871, as both his early colleagues had retired before the end of 1861 through failure of health; and the mission was in abeyance during his absence, extending over nearly three years. In 1869 he removed from Nagasaki to Osaka, and there and at Tokio this mission now has its two chief centres of work. In 1873, the year in which the C.M.S. resolved to extend its operations, the Society for the Propagation of the Gospel entered the field, and now has missionaries at Tokio and Kobe. With these sister Church Missions the C.M.S. missionaries have cordially co-operated in works of common interest.

The mutual friendly relations of the three missions were greatly promoted by a united conference, held at Tokio in May, 1878, under the presidency of Bishops Williams and Burdon. Previous to the conference, views had been frequently interchanged on the desirableness of having one Book of Common Prayer for the Missions of the sister Churches, and when the conference had discussed the matter in its different bearings, a resolution was passed embodying a basis of co-operation, and providing for the appointment of a Prayer Book Translation Committee. The committee nominated by the bishops were: Bishop Williams, and the Rev. J. Quinby, of the Protestant Episcopal Church of America; the Rev. A. E. Shaw, of the S.P.G.; and the Revs. C. F. Warren and J. Piper, of the C.M.S. The first portion of the joint work of this committee, embracing the Morning and Evening Prayer and Litany, the Baptismal, Confirmation, and Communion Offices and Catechism, was published in December, 1879. The Occasional Offices, Collects, and Occasional Prayers and Thanksgiving were completed and published in 1882, and the 39 Articles in 1885, and the Psalms were left to be added when published by the Bible Societies. The bulk of the translation work was done by Bishop Williams and Mr. Warren, and the latter carried the whole through the press. The adoption of one Book of Common Prayer has tended to bring the converts of the three Missions close together, and now they have formed themselves into one Japanese Church. This was done at a synod held in Osaka in February, 1887, which was attended by delegates from the different congregations. A constitution and canons were passed, together with a resolution declaring that for the present the Japanese Church adopts the Prayer Book and Articles of the Anglican Communion. God grant that with this united action in synod there may be deepening of spiritual life and a growth of brotherly love and missionary zeal, and that the Churches walking in the fear of the Lord and in the comfort of the Holy Ghost may be multiplied!

Before noticing in detail the work at the four stations at present occupied by the Society's missionaries, a brief reference must be made to that formerly carried on at Niigata. The Rev. P. K. Fyson, its founder, remained there until the summer of 1882, when he removed to Yokohama, and a year later to Tokio, to take part in the translation of the Old Testament under an arrangement with the British and Foreign Bible Society. During the whole of his residence at Niigata—more than six years—he was mainly occupied in evangelistic labours; but literary work was not neglected, and some of his earliest attempts gave promise of future usefulness in this department, of which his Old Testament translations are now a fulfilment. Preaching was persistently carried on in the town of Niigata, tours were sometimes made in the surrounding populous district, and many Chinese and Japanese Scriptures and Christian books were sold. A little school was opened in 1880, and continued until the final withdrawal in 1883, with an attendance of about 40 during most of the period.

The people in that part of the country were not at all well disposed towards either foreigners or Christianity. When Mr. Fyson opened the little school he did not visit it for several days, for fear of frightening away the children, and when he did first appear half of those present got up and ran out. Mr Fyson's own account of his work at the preaching station in the town in 1882—the seventh and last year of his residence—will best illustrate the temper of the people at this remote port. He says:—

> Almost every evening, except when the weather was very bad, I used to go with the catechist to preach there. The number of hearers varied very much; there were frequently 50 or 60, sometimes 80 and up to 100. Sometimes a very noisy set of young men came in and did their best to interrupt the meeting, to the evident annoyance of more sober-minded people who wished to hear what we had to say. The front of the house being quite open to the street, it was practically equivalent to preaching in the open air, and the people stood in their clogs on the earth floor, so that we could not turn the rowdy ones out, and their yells often completely drowned our voices. "Makoto no Kami" ("True God") would be shouted in derision, or Namu Amida Butsu—the usual Buddhist invocation—jocularly, in opposition. Abusive epithets were hurled at us in abundance. "Sorcerer," "thief," "incendiary," "murderer," and others too foul to repeat; the catechist coming in for his special share, "Traitor to your country," &c. Sometimes dirt and a few stones were thrown, or we found our table or the rain-doors smashed. I think the only person of those attending these meetings who showed any interest in Christianity was a young carpenter; he came pretty regularly, bought some books for himself, and mended our table without making any charge. However, a good many visitors from the country were discernible in the crowd, and they would no doubt carry back to their homes something of what they heard, and in this way we may hope some knowledge of Christianity would be spread over a wide surface, although there was no apparent beneficial result in the town of Niigata itself.

Miss Bird visited Niigata when she was in Japan, and a short passage from her *Unbeaten Tracks in Japan* will show the kind of influence Mr. and Mrs. Fyson were exercising during their residence in Niigata :—

> Mr. and Mrs. Fyson offer what is very important in this land of loose morals, the example of a virtuous Christian home, in which servants are treated with consideration and justice, and in which a singularly sensitive conscientiousness penetrates even the smallest details. Mrs. Fyson speaks colloquial Japanese readily, has a Bible-class, and is on very friendly terms with many of her female neighbours, who talk to her confidentially, and in whom she feels a great interest. Her real regard for the Japanese women, and the sympathetic, womanly way in which she enters not only into their difficulties, but into their different notions of morals, please me much.

The ingathering was not large, one now and then, but it has one worthy representative still working in connection with the C.M.S. This is Mr. Makioka, who, on leaving Niigata in 1883, took up his residence in Tokio, and acted first as catechist and subsequently as pastoral agent of the congregation there, and is now doing evangelistic work zealously and acceptably at Tokushima, one of the Osaka out-stations. It cannot but be regretted that want of means and men necessitated the Society's withdrawal from Niigata, just at a time when a larger ingathering might have been looked for ; but it was the unanimous opinion of the conference that concentration at fewer stations, where the missionaries could co-operate and mutually support each other in different branches of work was essential, and that Niigata ought to be given up, unless in addition to maintaining two missionaries there the Society could strengthen Osaka and Nagasaki. The Edinburgh Medical Mission has withdrawn from Niigata, as well as the C.M.S., and the missionaries of the American Board have now entered into the labours of their brethren of these two British societies, and are reaping fruit. "And herein is that saying true, one soweth, another reapeth." Mr. Fyson's present translational work, though precluding him from most of the active duties of missionary life, as well as from the joy of seeing converts gathered by his own evangelistic efforts, is nevertheless of the utmost importance to the common work of all Christian missionaries, and cannot but largely help forward the growth and development of the Churches.

XI.

THE CHURCH MISSIONARY SOCIETY'S MISSION.

(II.) *Nagasaki.*

"One soweth and another reapeth."—*John* iv. 37.

T was on the 23rd of January, 1869, eighteen days after the young Mikado gave his first State reception at Tokio to the Ministers of Foreign Powers accredited to his Court. The Rev. G. Ensor landed at Nagasaki. He took up his residence in "a neat little bungalow, the property of the American Bishop Williams, which stood at the edge of the native town, and at the extreme boundary of the foreign settlement."

At that time Christianity was a proscribed faith, and one of the first things to catch the eye of the newly arrived missionary was the ominous notice posted up—"The laws hitherto in force forbidding Christianity are to be strictly observed."

I read those words in Japanese, and I realised at once that the missionary work in Japan was thenceforward to be one of excessive difficulty. What were we to do? I couldn't gather the little ones into the Sunday-school or stand and preach in the streets. The only opportunity I had was simply to receive the visits of any inquirers who chose to come to me to my own house; and would a Japanese venture thus?

They did venture—

Ere a month had passed, day by day, hour after hour, my house would be thronged with Japanese visitors, all curious to know something about England and her science and art and progress, but, most of all, about her religion; they knew that she was a power among the nations, and believed that religion and power in a State are inseparable. More serious inquirers would wait till the darkness of night, and then steal into my house; and we used to have the doors closed and the windows barred, and as I bade them farewell when they left I scarce ever expected to see them again—for I was informed that an officer had been specially appointed to keep watch at my gate.

Some nine months after Mr. Ensor's arrival, occurred the deportation of the Romanist Christians of Urakami (see

NAGASAKI HARBOUR, FROM THE ISLET OF DESHIMA.

page 58). They were driven by hundreds past his house. "My heart bled for them," he wrote; "I had no sympathy with their doctrines, but I had sympathy with them in their sufferings; and I felt that the arm which had been lifted to suppress one section of Christendom in Japan, if the motive were political, could not afford to spare another." He goes on to relate how one night in that week, when he had "dropped into an almost despairing frame of mind," a token for good was given to him :—

I was sitting by myself in my study, and heard, in the darkness, a knock at the door. I went myself to answer it, and, standing between the palm-trees of my gate, I saw the dark figure of an armed Japanese. He paused a moment, and I beckoned to him to enter; and he came in and sat down, and I asked him what his business was. He replied, "A few days ago I had a copy of the Bible in my hands, and I wish to be a Christian." I said, "Are you a stranger in these parts? Don't you know that thousands of your people are being detained as prisoners for this?" "Yes," he said, "I know. Last night I came to your gate, and as I stood there, thinking of the terrible step I was about to take, fear overpowered me, and I returned. But there stood by me in the night one who came to me in my dreams, and said I was to go to the house of the missionary and nothing would happen to me, and I have come." And, drawing his long sword, he held it up to me in a form signifying the Japanese oath, and promised that he would ever keep true to me, and I received him.

This man was afterwards baptized by the name of Titus; "for God," says Mr. Ensor, "who comforteth those who are cast down, comforted me by the coming of Titus."*

Mr. Ensor was privileged to baptize ten or twelve Japanese, and then, after four years of most zealous labour, the failure of his health compelled him to return home. Meanwhile, however, the Rev. H. Burnside had joined him in 1871, and after his departure Mr. Burnside was able, taking advantage of the growing toleration, to work more openly. Instead of waiting for the people to come to him, he began to go to the people. On one occasion, in November, 1873, the following interesting incident occurred :—

I went into one of the large Buddhist temples in the town, and whilst there expressed a wish to enter into the place where the idol is located,

---

* Nothing is now known of this man. Some years after his baptism he was living in Osaka, and teaching in a Government school. He had then grown cold.

THE ISLAND OF DESHIMA: THE C.M.S. CHURCH, SCHOOL, AND MISSIONARY'S HOUSE.

and which, except upon special occasions, is kept closely shut up and railed off from the people. The priests, as is always the case, were very gracious and polite. They informed me, however, that nobody but priests were allowed within the sacred inclosure. "Be it so," I replied, "but I am myself a priest, the English priest of Oura,"—such is the name by which I am known throughout this whole island. Oura is the name of the foreign settlement. Upon this, judging, I presume, from my dress of the truth of my words, they instantly gave way, and told me that I might enter. This, after thanking them, and after having taken off my boots as well as my hat, I at once proceeded to do, accompanied by about twenty priests. Inside I beheld, as I expected, the idol, altar, incense, flowers, and all the other paraphernalia of heathen and idolatrous worship. My heart grew hot within me. I felt that I must speak, and so for the space of three-quarters of an hour, and in the very presence of their idol, I was enabled, by God's grace, to preach to the poor fellows of the Lord Jesus and of His great and only salvation, as also of the hollowness and fearfulness of idolatry. They confessed that very much of what I said was true, told me that I was a learned man, and some of them expressed a wish to be allowed to come and see me, in order that they might hear more about Christ. That same afternoon two of their number called and stayed conversing about the Bible for some considerable time.

At the same time Mr. Burnside opened a public service at his house in the foreign settlement, which was soon fairly attended by inquiring Japanese. He was assisted by a catechist, Mr. Midsushina, a convert from Buddhism, who had been a member of the Russo-Greek Church. Meanwhile he set about building a regular mission church. Of course such a thing was impossible in the native town —indeed he had failed even in hiring a house there for services—but he secured an excellent site on the little islet of Deshima, close to the bridge leading from the foreign settlement to the native town, within a few minutes walk of any part of it, and in full view of the harbour.* On this spot he

---

* See the pictures in the *C. M. Gleaner* of March, 1877, and Dec., 1878.

erected a neat little church; but before the day arrived for setting it apart to the service of God, he had left Nagasaki, compelled by weakened health to return to England. It was completed under the superintendence of the Rev.. H. Evington, who came from Osaka to carry on the Mission during the short interval between the departure of Mr. Burnside and the arrival of his successor, the Rev. Herbert Maundrell; and it was opened on July 11th, 1875, a few days after the latter reached Nagasaki. As this was the first C.M.S. church erected in Japan, it may not be out of place to give here Mr. Evington's account of the building :—

It is built of bamboo and plaster, and faced on the outside with boards, painted a yellowish stone colour. The building is about seventy feet long and thirty feet broad, and has a porch over the front entrance. Above the porch is a circular window with a stained-glass centre. On either side of the porch is a window going to a point at the top, with a little circular window of red glass in the point. There are four more windows of the same shape on either side, and, at what is practically the east end, though the church does not stand east and west, there is a large Gothic window, having at the top a circular window corresponding to that at the west end. On either side of this window is a small door entering the vestry on one side, and an ante-room on the other. A small Maltese cross crowns the gable at the west end. Inside, a sort of apse is formed by the cutting off of the vestry and ante-room, and this is raised from the floor two steps. The roof is supported by open beams stained a dark brown, and varnished, and the rest of the wood-work, window-frames, doors, and seats, is made to correspond; the walls are covered with white plaster. There are three rows of benches, one down the centre and one on each side; they are supplied with book-rests, and boards underneath the seat to hold the *geta* [clogs] or *zore* [sandals] which the natives always take off their feet when they enter a house. A massive stone font stands to the right of the principal entrance, and a neat Communion table, with chairs and kneeling-stools, form the furniture of the chancel.

Sunday, the 11th, was the day fixed for the opening of the church for public preaching. The notice of this was written, according to Japanese fashion, on a small board, and hung up at the door. Before commencing service we met in the catechist's house, with Mr. Stout and Mr. Wolff, two American missionaries, and two Japanese Christians, one a convert of the American Episcopal Mission at Osaka, and the other Mr. Stout's assistant, to ask God's blessing upon the work and the place, that it might prove to many to be the house of God and the gate of heaven. The service commenced at half-past three, and was conducted as follows:— I read two of the sentences preceding the exhortation, and then went on with the confession, Lord's Prayer, prayer for rulers, prayer for all conditions of men, general thanksgiving. We then sang a hymn, and I asked the catechist to read the lesson, Matt. v. This was followed by another hymn, "Jesus loves me," and, this over, I asked the catechist to preach. His text, which Mr. Maundrell had selected, was Matt. vii. 2.

The congregation was small, not numbering more than forty, who stayed throughout the service, whilst there is ample accommodation for a hundred and sixty or seventy. Still I trust that, when it is well-known that preaching is going on, there will not be a congregation wanting. May God grant that this small beginning may continue but for a short time, and that ere long there may be gathered within its walls a company of faithful men who have come, not only to hear the Word preached, but to pray to and praise Him who has bought them with His blood, and to glorify the name of the one true God.

Bishop Burdon says of this church: "Its turret, surmounted by a cross, is quite a prominent object at the head of the beautiful bay. You will remember that Deshima is the very spot where the cross was laid down to be trampled on as a test of any Natives suspected of Christianity. The raising of the cross on high at Deshima has, therefore, an additional significance that it has not elsewhere."

When Mr. Maundrell arrived, most of those who had previously received baptism had left Nagasaki, a milkman and his wife (who still remain faithful) and the acting catechist, Mr. Midsushina, being the only Christians connected with the mission. But as soon as he had mastered the language, he found a promising work growing under his hands. The first convert baptized by himself, in August, 1875, was Paul Nakamura, a native of Higo, one of the provinces of Kiushiu. Another convert, Peter Yoshidomi (=lucky riches), baptized

December 26th of the same year, belonged to another principal city of Kiushiu, Saga. It is in this way that the Gospel spreads. Nakamura brought from Kumamoto three friends of his, of the Samurai class, who entered the Nagasaki police force in order to be where they could receive Christian teaching. All three, with four others, were baptized on Easter Day, 1876; and all three, with five others, were confirmed on Whit Sunday in that year by Bishop Burdon, on his first Episcopal visitation in Japan. During the next two years there was encouraging progress, and at the close of 1878 the converts numbered forty-eight. It is interesting to notice that the little company was made up of persons of different classes, and included several entire families. Thus of the sixteen adults and five children baptized in 1878, three were Samurai, and the rest of the artizan, shopkeeping, and labouring classes. In three cases husbands and wives were baptized together, and several husbands previously baptized had the joy of seeing their wives added to the Church. The year 1878 was, too, one of preparation for future work. A two-storied school building was erected in close proximity to the Deshima church, and before the close of the year was in use for Sunday-school and Bible-class work. Most of the money needed for its erection, amounting to about $900, or £180, was raised among the European residents at Nagasaki, who were and still are, dependent on the C.M.S. missionaries for the services at the English church. Mr. Maundrell's hands were also strengthened by the arrival in December of the Rev. W. Andrews, a Cambridge graduate.

In the following year, 1879, the extension to Kagoshima and Saga took place under the circumstances and with the results to be noticed in the next chapter. In Nagasaki itself, although preaching to the heathen in the native town could not be systematically carried on, owing to the difficulty of securing a good preaching place with any continuity of tenure, there was encouraging progress. Twelve adults and five children were baptized, and the attendance of the Christians at the services, with one or two exceptions, gave general satisfaction. Two fresh efforts were inaugurated by the opening of a day-school in the building erected in 1878, and by the commencement of the Girls' Training Institution. The former took place soon after the beginning of the year. Vernacular classes were held in the morning under a native teacher, and English was taught in the afternoon by Mrs. Goodall—a lady of whom more will be said presently—and the preparandi students. From the beginning of 1880 Mr. Andrews undertook the supervision of the morning school; and Mr. Hutchinson, soon after his arrival at Nagasaki in the spring of 1882, did what he could to help it forward. But it was never very successful. During 1879 the scholars varied from twenty to twenty-five. In 1880 they fell to ten or twelve, and apparently did not increase in 1881. In 1882 there was a slight improvement owing to the diligence and zeal of Jacob Watanabe, but it was not such as to warrant the continuance of the school, and it was closed in 1883. Still during the more than four years of its existence it filled a place in offering a Christian education to those desirous of availing themselves of it, and the afternoon classes which owed so much to the earnest and persevering efforts of Mrs. Goodall, and which were attended both by the girls in her training institution, and the junior students of the college, were most useful. From the very beginning, as repeatedly urged by Mr. Maundrell, the great want was a well qualified English schoolmaster; and the school, revived in some modified form, may yet be among the most successful agencies used by the Good Shepherd in gathering and feeding the lambs of His redeemed flock.

In the year 1880 Kumamoto was occupied as an out-station, but in Nagasaki there was nothing of stirring interest. With steady plodding work on the part of the missionaries and their helpers, there was indifference on the part of the people. Out of forty-three baptized at Nagasaki and its out-stations, only nine—four adults and five children—belonged to Nagasaki. The result of the next year's work was still more disappointing. The efforts of previous years were continued, and Mr. Andrews laid himself out for evangelistic work in the villages within easy reach of Nagasaki; but out of fifty baptisms in Kiushiu in connection with the mission, only four were administered in Nagasaki, and all the four recipients were natives of Saga.

In 1882, Mr. Andrews, who had suffered from the climate of Nagasaki, was transferred to Hakodate, and the Rev. A. B. Hutchinson, formerly of Hong-kong, took his place. The year was not one of much progress, and it had its special trials. Paul Moro-oka, the catechist at Kagoshima, caused grievous disappointment, and was lost to the work. Paul Yoshidomi, who had been for some time in charge of the work at Saga, left the mission, and joined another society. On the other hand, Jacob Watanabe, a ready speaker, who had rendered good service in the Deshima school, and shown himself zealous in every good work, was appointed a catechist. The hope inspired by the promise he then gave of future usefulness is, as we shall presently see, being realised.

In previous years there had been much indifference shown by the people of Nagasaki, but in 1882 there was open opposition.

This opposition was continued during 1883 by the bitter and slanderous attacks of an anti-Christian society—a society drawing its members from those, whether Buddhists, Shintoists, Confucianists, Agnostics, Materialists, or Atheists, who reject Christianity on either religious, national, *pseudo*-philo-

I

sophic, selfish, or fleshly grounds. Added to this trial from without was the bitter sorrow caused by the withdrawal from the mission of two leading adherents at Kagoshima, and of another at Nagasaki. But others were added to the Church, and the Christians generally made considerable advances in knowledge and grace.

In February, 1884, Bishop Poole paid his first and only visit to Nagasaki. This was an event of no little importance. The Bishop manifested—as indeed he did everywhere, and at all times—the keenest interest in every department of Christian work. He examined the catechists, attended the native Church services, preached at the English service on Sunday, visited Mrs. Goodall's school, and personally examined those of her pupils who were candidates for Confirmation, went over the Sailors' Institute, and inquired into its working, visited the Japanese Hospital, and conversed and prayed with two English patients, attended the inaugural meeting of the Kiushiu District Church Council, visited the depôt of the British and Foreign Bible Society, went to see the site just purchased for a mission-room, and held a Confirmation for twenty-eight candidates.

This latter was the chief event of the visit. Mr. Hutchinson thus wrote of it :—

That Sunday will long be remembered with feelings of deepest interest. The service began at half-past eight as usual, and altogether there was a congregation of about eighty or ninety assembled, including, besides our own Christians and catechumens, a very few from other churches, and one or two heathens. The candidates, twenty-eight in number, occupied the front seats, the women having a small square of white silk folded in half and neatly tucked into their head-dress by way of a veil. The answer of the candidates was given with much fervour, and the address of the Bishop, translated sentence by sentence by Mr. Maundrell, fully and faithfully pointed out the necessity for us all of the continual indwelling and renewal of the Holy Ghost—the spiritual meaning of the apostolic rite in which we were engaged. All but three or four of the candidates had been baptized as adults, which gave additional solemnity to the service, as a renewed dedication of themselves to the Lord that bought them. . . . . One of the candidates had risen from a bed of sickness to be present, and two had come from Saga ; all felt it good to be there. . . . . In the afternoon the native congregation again assembled, and forty communicated with us, after listening most attentively to a plain and most practical address on the duties of Christians, as influenced by the Holy Spirit, and the manifesting of His indwelling by the manner in which those duties are performed.

Soon after the Bishop's visit Mr. Maundrell left for Europe with his family. This was a great, though, thank God, only temporary loss to the Mission. "It is always a strain upon a young mission," wrote Mr. Hutchinson, "when one who has been directing the work for years quits his post for a time, and the strain is greater when he into whose hands the work falls is comparatively inexperienced and unable to speak the language fluently." About the same time the Mission was strengthened by the arrival of the Rev. J. B. Brandram and Miss Brandram. Their first work was the language, but whilst pursuing their studies in it they found opportunities of usefulness, and were "cheered by real signs of successful work amongst Europeans both on shore and afloat." Twenty-five adults and twelve children were baptized during the year in connection with the Mission, of whom eight belonged to Nagasaki. One of them, a Samurai of the Goto Islands, sought the truth in vain amongst the Buddhists ; after a three years' course, finding his heart still unsatisfied, he came to Nagasaki and was "found of the Good Shepherd."

The close of the year was marked by the opening of a new mission-room in the native town. The Deshima church, and other mission buildings belonging to the C.M.S. and other Protestant missionary societies, had all been erected in the foreign settlement. This was the first instance of such a building being erected in the town of Nagasaki. So far this new departure has not resulted in any marked improvement in the outlook; for notwithstanding the excellent position of the building, the attendance on the regular preaching days has been small.

There were ten baptisms in Nagasaki in 1885, and several have been received since. When Bishop Bickersteth made his first visitation tour in Kiushiu in the autumn of 1886, and held Confirmations at seven different places, fourteen of the

C.M.S. JAPANESE STUDENTS' RESIDENCE, NAGASAKI.

sixty-four candidates were Confirmed at Nagasaki.* This is sufficient to show that progress is being made, even if it is slower than we could wish.

Mr. Maundrell, who returned to Nagasaki in the spring of 1886, and who has since been appointed Archdeacon by the Bishop, laments the continued indifference of the people, notwithstanding the absence of the determined and active opposition of former years.

---

* The Confirmation at Nagasaki was held on January 1st, 1887.

Mr. Hutchinson writes :—" Nagasaki remains dry ground. Pray for the dew to fall and quicken it to life."* " Can these bones live? O Lord God, Thou knowest." "It shall come to pass in the last days, saith God, I will pour out of My Spirit upon all flesh."

Two special branches of the work must be separately mentioned before the out-station work is described. In 1877, Mr. Maundrell established a little college for training candidates for missionary work among their own countrymen, in the first place as evangelists, and then, if it please God to call them, as ordained ministers of the Church. Mr. Maundrell thus wrote :—

> The building for which the committee made me a grant has been finished, and it was opened on St. Andrew's Day.
> The young men admitted as students are Stephen Koba, of Kumamoto, and Paul Yoshidomi, and Paul Moro-oka, of Saga. Another young man, John Ko, is equally desirous of becoming a teacher, but his (as yet heathen) wife and parents do not sympathise with him in this desire, so for the present he is a non-resident student. Admiral Ryder, before he resigned his command of the China Fleet, paid a visit to Nagasaki, and came up to see the college just as it was being finished. He was so pleased with it, and felt so strongly the necessity of each student having a room to himself, that he afterwards sent me 50 dols. "towards a new wing when required." Some of his officers made this sum up to 100 dols.

During 1878 the same four students pursued their studies, and at the beginning of 1879 another, John Inutsuka, was admitted. During 1880, all the five were doing active work. Stephen Koba was at Kagoshima and Paul Yoshidomi at Saga. John Inutsuka was temporarily sent to Kumamoto, and John Ko and Paul Moro-oka did good service in Nagasaki whilst continuing their studies in the college.

In training native agents Mr. Maundrell's admirable plan

---

* Annual Letter, January 19th, 1887.

was to combine study with work, and by moving his men from time to time to give them in turn the advantage of being under his own immediate influence at the central station, and of further training in the college. Thus in 1881, while the

CATECHISTS AT NAGASAKI.

other four were at the out-stations—increased to three by the occupation of Kumamoto in 1880,—Stephen Koba, who had been located at Kagoshima nearly two years, and had done good service there, was brought back to Nagasaki, where, in addition to helping considerably in the preaching at the

Deshima church, he was reading Divinity—chiefly the Thirty-nine Articles and the Holy Scriptures—and Church History.

From this time, too, the name of Jacob Watanabe must be associated with the college. Although he was only baptized in the previous year, his attainments, age, and experience soon placed them in a position of equal rank with the members of the senior class. Mr. Maundrell speaks of him as a married student who attended the classes at the college in the morning, and assisted at Deshima day-school in the afternoon, combining active work in the present with preparation for the future.

Simultaneously with the training of the student-catechists the junior class was continued with varying numbers—some leaving and others joining from time to time. In 1880 and the following year there were eight junior students, in 1882 six, and in 1883 eight, of whom, however, two were placed with Mr. Maundrell by the Rev. A. Shaw of the S.P.G. Tokio Mission.

Throughout the entire course the study of the Holy Scriptures was steadily pursued, and Pinnock's *Analysis of the Old Testament*—of which Mr. Maundrell published a translation—and Dr. Smith's *Scripture History* were used as text-books. Among the subjects taken up from time to time were the Prayer Book and Thirty-nine Articles, Paley's *Natural Theology*, *Pearson on the Creed*, and Robertson's *Sketches of Church History*; besides which there was a general course embracing Ancient History, Mathematics, Greek and English. In the last named subject the senior students early attained a good degree of proficiency, and at the close of 1878 Mr. Maundrell wrote of them :—" Thanks to Mrs. Goodall, they are now able to make good use of English Commentaries and historical works bearing on the Old and New Testaments, which are helping them to a more intelligent knowledge of the

Bible and of the Christian religion than they could otherwise obtain. Their knowledge of English will also enable them to proceed at once to theological works and Church History." The training of native agents was only a branch of Mr. Maundrell's work, and the constant pressure of other missionary duties made it impossible for him to give undivided attention to it. The classes were at times "greatly interrupted, the students' time not made the most of, and their progress impeded." Yet in spite of this, the effort commenced in faith and carried on with prayer and painstaking perseverence, has not been without encouraging, and, it may be hoped, lasting results. There have been failures, as might have been expected. Some of the junior students manifested unfitness for spiritual work, others failed in health and had to discontinue their studies, but six have been transferred to the Osaka Divinity School, which is now the central training institution for the C.M.S. Japan Mission.

Of the four original students, two have caused grievous disappointment, yet the other two—Stephen Koba and John Ko—together with John Inutsuka and Jacob Watanabe, have proved themselves zealous workers, as the following pages show. This branch of Mr. Maundrell's work has been noticed and much commended by naval officers and others. The following letter from Admiral Coote, when on the China Station in 1880, speaks for itself:—

H.M.S. " Vigilant," May 27th, 1880.

DEAR MR. MAUNDRELL,—Having visited your little college, it has been much on my mind that an effort should be made to render it more efficient; and finding that there is every probability of getting more Japanese young men for training as teachers, and eventually for ordination, I have much pleasure in placing at your disposal $500 towards increasing the present small collegiate building, with the hope that the Committee of the C.M.S. will see the necessity of sending, at an early date, a thoroughly efficient helper in the educational department.

You are at liberty to communicate my views to the Secretary of the C.M.S.
Wishing you much success in your Master's service.

I am, yours truly,

R. COOTE.

Mr. J. C. Hall, H.B. Majesty's Consul at Nagasaki, who had met two of the catechists trained by Mr. Maundrell at Kagoshima and Kumamoto, referred to them in the following terms:—" I feel that Mr. Maundrell has gone the right way to work with the right sort of men." When Bishop Poole visited Nagasaki in February, 1884, he "spent some hours in examining the catechists individually, and particularly as to their attainments"; and he was afterwards heard to say how much he was pleased with all of them.

The Girls' Training Institution also demands a brief notice. Its history is a record of quiet and unobtrusive, but solid and excellent work. It may be well to mention that Mrs. Goodall is the widow of an Indian chaplain, who, instead of electing to spend the remainder of her life in a quiet English home, volunteered to become Mr. Maundrell's associate at Nagasaki as an honorary missionary, and reached Japan a few months after he did. Her chief work has been the training of a few Christian girls in the little institution which owes its existence mainly to her efforts. A house was purchased, and Mrs. Goodall commenced her work by taking two girls, who were with her during most of 1879, and a third was added at the close of the year. In 1880 there were eight under training, and from that time to the close of 1884 this was the usual number. In the spring of 1885 there were ten in residence, and although applications have been received from others desirous of entering, it has been impossible to entertain them, as the present house will not accommodate more.

In gathering this little number the object has been to

educate them in the duties of domestic life, to train them in habits of truthfulness, and to form and develop their Christian character. They receive instruction both in Japanese and English; what may be called the three R's are emphasized, the Holy Scriptures taught, and Christian truth inculcated and music and singing taken up as accomplishments, with a view to future usefulness in the services of the Church. So far the girls have been almost entirely supported whilst under training, partly by local contributions, and partly by donations of money and work from the supporters of the "Missionary Leaves Association," and other friends in England.

The case of Mary, the third girl received by Mrs. Goodall, shows the value of the Christian training given in this unpretending little institution. At the time she was taken she was engaged to be married to Paul Moro-oka, but after his sad defection, although he obtained a good Government appointment, she declined to fulfil her engagement. This gave great offence to her parents and friends, who threatened to disown her unless she married him. At her mother's request she returned home to Saga, and was kept in anxious suspense some two years, during which every effort was made to induce her to consent to be married either to Paul or to a heathen. But her purpose was firm, and she steadily refused to be yoked with an unbeliever. In a letter written to Mrs. Goodall during this period of trial she said :—" It helps me much to think that you are praying for me daily. Do not be too troubled about me. I believe our heavenly Father will guide me and keep me safe." She was both kept and guided. Mr. Paul Nakamura—*not* the convert baptized in 1875—for several years teacher of Chinese to the college students, and himself a member of the theological class, and later an acting catechist, had expressed a desire to marry her previous to her return to Saga. Her parents refused consent for a time, but ultimately it was given, and Mary's marriage to a Christian husband was celebrated in the Deshima church, on June 25th, 1885, amidst tokens of sincere Christian rejoicing.

Other work amongst the females has not been neglected. A Bible-class for women—both Christians and inquirers—has been held at Mrs. Goodall's house every Wednesday for two or three years past. Mrs. Goodall attends, but the teaching is done by Mr. Nakamura. From fifteen to twenty have attended, and have been greatly benefited and helped by the instruction they have received. The lady members of the Mission have also sought to reach and win their Japanese sisters to Christ, and by precept and example to lead them on in the path of holiness and truth. Their efforts are for the most part quiet and unobtrusive, but they are none the less effectual. The following reference to one such effort will suffice as an illustration, and it will be read with the deeper interest now that Mrs. Maundrell has been removed from the sphere she occupied.

"The present governor and his late wife have done much during the past year to bridge over the gulf that separates foreigners and natives. His wife, Mrs. Kusaka, had begun to read the New Testament with Mrs. Maundrell, and we had hope that she would be the means of access to many upper class ladies, when she was suddenly removed by death."

Both in Nagasaki and in the Kiushiu out-stations there is a wide field for work amongst both girls and women, which can only be done by ladies without the house duties and cares connected with married life. The Church of England Zenana Missionary Society has been able, in response to the pressing invitation of the C.M.S. Japan Conference, to extend its operations to Japan, and Mrs. Goodall has been received as an honorary missionary of that society. May God speedily give more lady workers to gather the whitening harvest!

XII.

THE CHURCH MISSIONARY SOCIETY'S MISSION.

(III.) *Kiushiu Out-stations.*

"Speak unto the children of Israel, that they go forward."—*Exodus* xiv. 15.

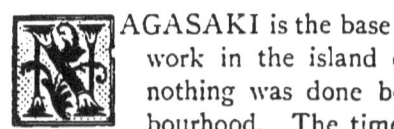AGASAKI is the base of operations for the Society's work in the island of Kiushiu. For ten years nothing was done beyond its immediate neighbourhood. The time for extension had not yet come. At length it arrived, and the workmen whom the Lord had been preparing were ready to go forward. Kagoshima and Saga were occupied as out-stations in 1879, and Kumamoto in 1880. These towns, although worked as out-stations from Nagasaki, are themselves important missionary centres. In speaking of them Mr. Maundrell says: "The towns themselves are equal in size to Nagasaki, and being centres of large districts, which are far more extensively cultivated than the hills around Nagasaki can possibly be, their suburban population is greater." The work at these out-stations, and in the districts reached from them, will now occupy our attention.

1. *KAGOSHIMA.*

Kagoshima is the capital of the Satsuma province. It was here that Xavier landed in 1549, and that the last struggle in the Satsuma Rebellion of 1877 took place. The town itself does not present an imposing appearance, but its surroundings are pretty. It stands on the western shore of the Gulf of Kagoshima, about twenty miles from its mouth, and is backed by well-wooded hills three or four hundred feet high. In the gulf opposite the town is the volcanic island called Sakura-jima (Cherry-tree Island), with its lofty peak, to the north of which is "a magnificent harbour some twelve miles in diameter, surrounded by lofty hills." The town is divided into two portions, which are connected by "a good road, lined with shops, and much frequented"—the one being the principal centre of trade, and the other chiefly occupied by Samurai families. "The streets are much wider than those of Nagasaki, and better kept, and there are some tidal canals running through the town."

The Gospel seems to have been carried to Kagoshima by some of the Nagasaki converts, who were there on business. In March, 1879, Mr. Maundrell, on hearing from them that "not a few were anxious for Christian teaching," sent down Stephen Koba, one of the students who had been under training two years, who at once hired a room to preach in, held services every evening, and instructed those who had asked for baptism. Three weeks later Mr. Maundrell received a message, begging him to come to Kagoshima at once. It is significant of the progress made by the Japanese since the opening of the country, only twenty years before, that this message came by *telegraph;* that Mr. Maundrell responded by proceeding to Kagoshima in the Japanese steamer *Yoshi-no-Maru*—and that during his stay he visited a spinning-mill, belonging to Shimadzu (the famous Satsuma Daimio, see p. 85), fitted up with machinery purchased at Manchester and Oldham.

In the outward aspect of things at Kagoshima there was much indeed to sadden, for during the recent rebellion its "inhabitants had suffered severely. Not only were hundreds and thousands deprived of their husbands, fathers, or brothers, or other relatives on whom they depended, but the greater portion of their houses were burnt"—the fifth time within a few years that the town was in a great measure destroyed by fire.

But the work presented many features of encouragement. There were numerous hearers, and some candidates for baptism, whom Stephen had carefully instructed. One of these, a medical man, was admitted to the visible Church by baptism on April 26th, "the first convert of our Church at Kagoshima."

The preaching every evening, commenced by Mr. Koba, was continued during Mr. Maundrell's visit, and such notes as the following—"This evening about thirty persons were present"; "A crowded room again this evening"; "Preached to a full room"—show that the attendance was good. No less encouraging was the earnestness of the inquirers. Referring to what took place on Sunday evening, April 27th, Mr. Maundrell wrote: "Eleven persons adjourned, after the preaching, to the 'upper chamber,' and in a few minutes it was delightful to see them naturally divide into parties to be instructed in the Creed, the Lord's Prayer, and Ten Commandments. While Stephen Koba and Yoshidomi were instructing others, I had an aged man, a young man, and two young women—all of one family—and in a short time the aged man was taking my place as teacher. He understood more than the rest what I had been saying about the sufferings of the Saviour, and in pure Kagoshima idioms he explained it to them. . . . All seemed to be interested in the truth, and athirst for it. It is the first time that I have witnessed in Japan anything approaching to the earnest desire for Christianity which one so frequently witnessed in Madagascar."

Mr. Maundrell baptized five more adults and one child on May 1st, and six adults and six children on May 5th, so that on his return to Nagasaki he left a little Church consisting of fourteen adults and seven children, and in addition there were several others who had given in their names as desirous of becoming Christians. Further visits were paid in July and November, and Mr. Maundrell was cheered by evident signs of progress. Stephen Koba had endeavoured to extend his influence by opening a day-school for children and an evening school for young men. There was at the time full scope for private enterprise in this direction, as the Government had done much less for education at Kagoshima than at many other places, and no difficulty was experienced "in commencing a small Christian school in the heart of the city on the mission property." These new efforts were not without results. Writing of his visit in November, Mr. Maundrell says: "The night school has borne fruit. Among the twelve baptisms that I had this time at Kagoshima were five young men who have been reading the Gospels with Stephen Koba at this school." These twelve baptisms made, with those administered at the two previous visits, a total of thirty-seven —twenty-five of the recipients being adults and twelve children. Such was the most promising commencement at the first occupied of the Kiushiu out-stations. But even then all was not sunshine, for in his Annual Letter Mr. Maundrell thus refers to the Kagoshima work: "The attendance at the Sunday services is not so good as at Nagasaki, neither is the Sunday observed by some of the native Christians so strictly as it ought to be."

Two incidents of the November visit may here be mentioned. The first illustrates the opportunities the travelling missionary often has of speaking to persons of position and influence, and also the attitude of many of the better educated in

Japan towards Christianity. It is thus referred to by Mr. Maundrell :—

There were two passengers from Nagasaki in the saloon besides myself. We were thrown together a good deal, and I was anxious to find out more about them, for they evidently knew me better than I knew them. I was amused at their reticence on the subject of Christianity. One told me that he had been in Worcester Cathedral, and that he had studied six months in America under a Unitarian, hinting that both in England and America there were many Unitarians! This led to a long talk on the Divinity of our Lord, and my friend seemed somewhat sorry that he had so far revealed that he knew anything of the foreign religion. . . . They were the Government directors of the new dock and iron foundry at Nagasaki. When this dock was opened, every foreign resident in Nagasaki received an invitation to be present at the ceremony, except the missionaries; these were purposely uninvited because the director of the dock, Mr. Watanabe, is opposed to Christian teaching —the very gentleman that I have mentioned above as my fellow passenger!"

The other incident illustrates the interest often manifested by naval officers and others in missionary work. It is thus referred to by Mr. Maundrell :—

In addition to the joy of the work, and of further intercourse with Stephen Koba, whose cheerful disposition makes him an agreeable companion, there was, for Kagoshima, the rare occurrence of a British man-of-war in harbour, the captain and officers of which, through their frequent attendance with their crew at the English church at Nagasaki, are so well known to me, and not a few of whom take a deep and sympathising interest in our work. It was a real pleasure to see Captain Aldrich and Dr. Hart take a lively interest in the little day-school, to accompany them, together with Stephen Koba San and Paul Moro-oka San, to the late Daimio's cotton mill, and then, on their return, to see them enjoy a cup of tea on the second floor of the Society's preaching-house, in this extreme out-of-the-way part of Japan—I may almost say, of the world.

Mr. Maundrell's next visit to Kagoshima was in April, 1880. He found Stephen Koba "working very diligently and carefully both in the day-school and among the adults." At the morning service on the Sunday spent there, there were no less than thirty-five children present. The outlook was, therefore, still cheering, but during the year only three adults and five children were added to the Church by baptism.

In January, 1881, Stephen Koba returned to Nagasaki for a year's further study, and Paul Moro-oka took his place at Kagoshima. Paul worked zealously and acceptably, and considerable progress was made during the year. Out of fifty baptisms in Kiu-shiu in connection with the Mission, forty-two were at Kagoshima, which was therefore bidding fair to become our strongest post in Southern Japan. Writing at the close of the year, Mr. Maundrell says :—

> The work is full of promise. There are now nearly 100 persons, including children, who have attached themselves to our Church. At my last visit, only a short time ago, I had the pleasure of giving the Holy Communion to nineteen persons, besides the catechist, and of admitting to the Church by baptism two gentlemen Samurai, father and son, with their respective families, who have shown unmistakable evidence of their sincerity. Like Cornelius, before becoming Christians they had "given alms," and done what they could for the good of others. They built a school 36 ft. long by 15 ft., which must have cost them between two and three hundred yen,* for the sake of their poorer countrymen.

But the remarkable prosperity of the first three years did not continue. The year 1882 was one of great trial. Paul Moro-oka, who had commenced so well, proved unsatisfactory. He became "embarrassed in pecuniary difficulties," and there were also "rumours of immorality against him, which he rightly judged would, if proved, lead to his dismissal." He therefore voluntarily withdrew from the Mission. It was a

---

* About £40 or £50.

sad disappointment, and a severe blow to the work. Mr. Maundrell thus refers to it :—

It is a grievous fall for him, poor man, and such a disappointment is never without its baneful influence on others. At the same time it is partly by such illustrations of failure, as well as by good example and precept, that an infant Church learns what is required in its teachers, and so its status is gradually raised, and its idea of what the members of the Christian Church should be more accurately realised. Who can measure the good teaching the Church has reaped from the fall of St. Peter and the error of Simon Magus? So now in the missionary field, it is in the weakness and sinfulness of some, as well as by His grace given to others, that the Lord instructs and edifies His Church.

Stephen Koba now returned to his old post, and although he "worked with his usual care and steadfastness," there were not the same visible signs of success. Buddhism, which had long been excluded from the province by the Satsuma clan, was becoming a power, and the activity of the missionaries of the Shin sect seems to have seriously affected the work. Some of the Christians were "shaken in their faith, and became less regular in their attendance at the Sunday services ; the number of inquirers was smaller, and there were fewer baptisms." In May, 1883, there were ninety Church members—fifty adults and forty children—and six candidates for baptism ; but the work showed no signs of recovering from the check it had received in the previous year.

Mr. Hutchinson, who was left in charge of the Kiushiu work on Mr. Maundrell's departure for England on furlough in March, 1884, was unable to visit Kagoshima during the year. The accounts from Stephen Koba were very disheartening, and in his report at the close of the year Mr. Hutchinson wrote :—

Twenty of those baptized formerly at Kagoshima are not to be found now; whilst twenty-eight (children included) have given up all external profession of Christianity. These last are our trials. The flesh has overcome some; the world ensnared others.

But in the midst of much to sadden, when Mr. Hutchinson visited Kagoshima in May, 1885, tokens of encouragement were not wanting. On one of the days he spent there he baptized a family, husband and wife and three children—and the infant son of the catechist; and on another day a Samurai, sixty-nine years of age, whose "answers were clear and decided," and to whom "the 'blessed hope of everlasting life' in Christ Jesus seemed very precious." Work had also been commenced at Kajiki, a village at the head of the gulf, fifteen miles north of Kagoshima. Mr. Hutchinson thus refers to it:—

Koba San has been preaching here twice a month for some time past. One Christian, a tax-collector, resides here, but was away on duty when we arrived. . . . In the evening about seventy people listened attentively to our preaching for some two hours, and then some fifteen or eighteen of the principal men remained, asking questions and looking at Scripture pictures till nearly midnight.

But whatever may be the future of the work at this out-station and the places visited from it, the present outlook is not at all cheering. "Both Kagoshima and Saga," writes Mr. Maundrell, in his Annual Letter for 1886, "are low in numbers, low in knowledge, and low in means." The removals and defections leave but a "little flock" in either case. At Kagoshima, when Bishop Bickersteth visited it in 1886, only ten persons of all those baptized from the first were presented for Confirmation. But if thus far the work has disappointed the hopes and expectations inspired at its promising commencement, let it only stimulate us to pray more earnestly for the few who remain faithful, that they may "shine as lights in the world, holding forth the word of life."

2. *SAGA AND CHIKUZEN.*

Saga lies to the north-east of Nagasaki, a few miles from the coast at the head of the Shimabara gulf. "It is not the capital of a *Ken* (prefecture) like Kagoshima; but having formerly been the residence of a Daimio it is an important centre." Mr. Maundrell first visited Saga in November, 1879. He gives the following account of his journey thither, and of the place and its surroundings :—

Our route lay round Cape Nomo to the south of Nagasaki, eastward of the Shimabara gulf, and then up this gulf, passing close to the foot of the Shimabara mountain (which, to my regret, we did at midnight), to the mouth of the Ogawa river, at the extreme north of the gulf. We ascended this river some distance to a village called Wakatsu, where Paul Yoshidomi was waiting for us, and with him we soon took jinrikishas to proceed to Saga. The country here is exceedingly flat— one vast rice-field—presenting a strong contrast to the hilly land of Nagasaki. It is one of the largest rice-fields in Kiushiu. The town of Saga is situated in the middle of it, about five or six miles from Wakatsu. It was a delightful ride. Harvest was in full progress. A large portion of the rice was still standing; some was cut and lying on the ground, some cut and standing in sheaves; some had been carried, and the ground already prepared for the next crop of wheat or beans. So quickly in succession does one crop follow another in Japan that the land has no time to get weedy. The country full of ripe corn, the busy harvesters, the level roads, and the beautiful autumn day, all contributed to make our ride most pleasant.

The circumstances which led to this visit are thus given in a letter written immediately afterwards :—

Four of the preparandi students are natives of Saga, viz., Paul Yoshidomi, Paul Moro-oka, John Ko, and John Inutsuka. It was a place, therefore, that I have always looked upon with interest and hope, and that I had long wished to visit, hoping that at the least, among the relatives and friends of the students, some would be found ready to listen to the Gospel message. This hope had been considerably strengthened of late by the fact that a teacher in one of the Government schools at Saga came to Nagasaki a few weeks ago for the express purpose of receiving baptism, having been taught the Truth by the students during last summer's vacation. He represented that there were not a few at Saga who were wishing to be instructed, and asked me to come there as soon as possible, and, in the meanwhile, to allow Paul Yoshidomi to precede me, to open a preaching-place. I left Nagasaki on Sunday morning, the 2nd inst., on board a small Japanese steamer called *Kiu-kawa-maru*, taking John Inutsuka San with me.

During his stay Mr. Maundrell was hospitably entertained by John Ko's father, who was formerly a retainer of the Daimio of Saga. He visited the large Government school of 600 pupils, in which the gentleman already mentioned as having come to Nagasaki for baptism was a teacher. The head-master and teachers appeared to be very friendly. Of the encouraging outlook Mr. Maundrell thus wrote:—

> I stayed at Saga a week, and had preaching every evening, at which from 150 to 200 persons were present. Happily my host's house was most elastic. The sides of my rooms were only screens, and, these being removed, two or three additional rooms were available. Old people and young alike came to hear the new doctrine. The parents and friends of the students were present regularly.. I could not but see that the time has come for trying to begin a permanent work in Saga, for which the way has certainly been prepared.

Before he left Saga he baptized John Inutsuka's brother, a girls' school teacher, and his wife, and a medical student and his sister, five altogether. Paul Yoshidomi, who had received two years training at Nagasaki, continued as catechist in charge. His marriage to a Christian young woman, trained in a mission school, enhanced the hope of his future usefulness, a hope which, as we shall presently see, was not realised in connection with the C.M.S. Mission.

In returning to Nagasaki by land Mr. Maundrell passed through a village where he found a young man of his acquaintance in charge of a school of 200 children, who had often attended the mission services at Nagasaki, and who, as a native of Saga, was much interested in hearing what had happened there. When Mr. Maundrell next visited Saga, in April, 1880, this young man, Jacob Watanabe, now one of the most zealous and efficient catechists in the Kiushiu Mission, was one of six persons who received baptism.

In Saga not only was there no parallel to the rapid growth which characterised the work at Kagoshima in its early days, but there were no baptisms after those just referred to until 1882, though four natives of Saga were baptized at Nagasaki in 1881. In 1882 the work was much tried by the defection of Paul Yoshidomi, who joined another mission, and took over with him some of the Christians who were related to him. John Inutsuka was sent to take his place, and in October Mr. Maundrell visited Saga in company with Mr. Hutchinson. The pen of the latter tells us that on the Sunday spent there "about twenty-five were present at morning service and eight partook of the Holy Communion," and that an attentive congregation of between sixty and seventy assembled for prayers and preaching in the evening. During the visit two adults— "a widow lady, 65 years of age, and a quiet, earnest, young farmer from a neighbouring village," and three children were baptized; and another, Mr. Oba, was publicly received as a member of our Church. Mr. Maundrell thus speaks of Mr. Oba's case:—

He was one of the first inquirers that I saw on my arrival in Japan in 1875, when he was frequently coming to talk with Mr. Evington, who had come to look after the mission for a short time. During my second visit to Saga three years ago, I baptized his wife and children, but he himself was away from home at the time in Government service at Fukuoka, and living with a second wife. Soon afterwards a missionary of the American Board of Missions, while travelling in Kiushiu, met with him, and not knowing all the circumstances of the case, baptized him. He has now employment at Saga, has put away his second wife, and is likely to prove a considerable strength to the work in the town.

Mr. Hutchinson's account of an evening's lecturing may be quoted, as illustrating one branch of evangelistic work often, as in this case, shared by converts, catechists, and missionaries :—

In the evening the room was crowded, over a hundred being present for the *yen-zetsu*, or lecturing. The catechist commenced, after hymn and prayers, with an earnest address on " Doubt and inquiry necessary to faith." Oba San followed on the " Fear of God needed to keep men straight." I was then privileged to sketch the " Entrance and progress of the Gospel in China," Mr. Maundrell interpreting. One illustration by Oba San was much enjoyed. It is not enough to hold a gun firmly and aim straight; you must take care, first of all, that you put the powder in *before* the bullet, otherwise all the effort is in vain. Faith in God is the essential preliminary to a right life.

The subsequent history of the Saga Mission has never been of a very encouraging character. In 1884 the little band of Christians was much discouraged and depressed by the efforts made by their opponents to suppress Christianity in the town, and not a single convert was baptized at either of Mr. Hutchinson's two visits. In 1885 there was some encouragement, and during his second visit in July Mr. Hutchinson baptized three adults and two infants. The conversion of one of them, a man forty-three years of age, Otsuka by name, is thus referred to by Mr. Hutchinson :—

About six years ago Mr. Maundrell, in crossing from Tokitsu to the place from which I am writing, was in imminent danger, owing to a storm bursting over the Omura gulf. His fellow-passengers were in a state of great alarm; Mr. Maundrell offered up prayer in a clear voice, the cry was heard, and all landed here safely. One of the passengers went to his home near Saga, and told how a *Kiyoshi* (teacher) had prayed to the true God, the God of the Christians, and how plainly their deliverance was the answer. His adopted son, Otsuka, was deeply moved by this, and he became an inquirer, convinced and converted, and it has now been my privilege to admit him to the Church by baptism. The father, alas! remains undecided; impressed, but not converted.

The Christians at Saga are still a small and feeble flock. Of those baptized since 1879 some have transferred their allegiance to another mission, others have migrated, and "the two most intelligent members of the Church, who ought to have been a help and strength, have proved rather the reverse." Thus it was that when Bishop Bickersteth visited Saga in 1886, and held a Confirmation there, only four candidates were presented. That there is a small remnant of true believers in Saga we cannot doubt. Let us pray that they may be clothed with power from on high to witness for their Lord, that the weak things of the world may by the power of His Spirit confound the mighty, and the little one become a thousand.

But the town of Saga has now become the centre of a more extended work in the province of Chikuzen, in which, at the important town of Fukuoka, and at other places there are several little groups of Christians. Towards the end of 1882 the leading men of several villages in Chikugo—the province adjoining Chikuzen at its south-eastern extremity— invited our Nagasaki missionaries to visit them. After Mr. Maundrell had promised to go a rumour was circulated that a sum of money would be given to every person embracing Christianity. Jacob Watanabe was sent to expose the falsity of this rumour, and to declare "the true nature of our Mission in Japan and of the Gospel of Christ." "He returned with a list of nearly two hundred families, who, apart from all pecuniary considerations, had resolved to become catechumens." In the following spring he was sent again, in company with two colporteurs of the British and Foreign Bible Society. The three were alike impressed with the importance of the opening, and brought back a further request for a visit from Mr. Maundrell.

After Easter, 1883, Mr. Maundrell, accompanied by Jacob Watanabe and John Inutsuka, the Saga catechist, set out for the district. Passing through many villages and the town of

Kurume—a place as large as Saga—they at length reached Hongo, where Sunday was spent in instructing the villagers, of whom eight families had given in their names. A part of Monday was similarly spent at Takata, another village, outside which a Buddhist temple, the property of six families, was offered for Christian purposes. In the evening at another place, Hisamatsu, two hundred persons assembled to hear the Gospel, some of them coming long distances. On Tuesday the mountain range between Chikugo and Chikuzen was crossed, and the latter province was entered. At Nishigo on two consecutive days large preaching services were held. Some Buddhist priests made efforts to oppose, but to no purpose. Here seven families had "given in their names as resolved to become believers in Jesus." The next morning twenty-five families belonging to another village sent in their names. Altogether nearly eight hundred families, some few in Chikugo and Buzen, but for the most part belonging to the Chikuzen province, declared themselves ready to become Christians. The ignorance of these professed inquirers was great, and the motives of many of them questionable, but the open door was a call to prayer and effort. The movement was not in the main a genuine one, but, as in so many similar cases, among the many there were a few sincere seekers after truth, and of these some further particulars must be given.

The early efforts just noticed were followed up, and in due time fruit began to appear. In June, 1884, John Inutsuka visited Chikuzen, and met with much to encourage him. At *Onodani*, a village of eighty houses, many attended the preaching on the day of his arrival, and the day following there was much conversation about Christianity, which resulted in seventeen heads of families enrolling themselves as candidates for baptism. Mr. Hutchinson visited them in the following November, and encouraged them to persevere in their search for truth ; and on the occasion of his next visit in July, 1881, he had the joy of receiving into the Church three families, consisting of seven adults and three children. Mr. Hutchinson gives the following interesting account of these first-fruits of Onodani :—

We received a hearty welcome from Kuwano San the elder and the members of his family. Ere long his younger brother, Yasuyemon, who had been our host on the occasion of my former visit, came in, accompanied by his wife, and a little later, Oba San. We soon plunged into serious matters, and whilst the wives were busied in culinary preparations for their guests and servants, I had a long and most interesting conversation with the husbands on the grounds of their faith. I found that for more than six months they had quite given up all idolatry, to the intense vexation of their neighbours, who had, to punish them, cast them out of the village association for mutual help. In fact, they had become social outcasts for Christ's sake. Every Sunday they meet for prayer and praise and the reading of God's Word. I found they had made good use of the New Testament I left with them in November last, and they had also purchased others, besides prayer and hymn books for themselves. Their faith is simple, grasping the salient points of our own sinfulness, of righteousness through Jesus Christ, forgiveness of sins through faith in His precious blood, and of daily need of divine grace to help us to follow in the way of God's commands to our life's end. Their knowledge was defective of course ; the wonder was that with irregular and but brief periods of instruction they had learned so much, and that to the saving of their souls. Last November they were heathens faintly recognising that the light of a new day had dawned upon them. Now, after suffering persecution and scorn for their Saviour's sake, they were ready openly to confess their faith in Him, and cut themselves adrift from all the old delusions and idolatry. I wish you could see the real earnestness of these dear brethren in Christ. Salvation is to them a very serious matter. Weariness and fatigue were forgotten in the presence of such lively proofs of the gracious working of the Holy Spirit. Then the three little children, the eldest only seven years of age, joined in singing the translation of " Great God, and wilt Thou condescend," the sweet child-voices helped occasionally and memory prompted by the fathers' voices.

To return to John Inutsuka's visit in 1884. From Onodani he went on to Kuchi-no-hara, where he arrived about 2 P.M. on Sunday, June 29th. He was both surprised and delighted to find " three families assembled in the house of an energetic inquirer, engaged in Divine worship, with Hymn Books, Prayer Books, and New Testaments spread out before them." It was their custom thus to meet together on the Lord's Day, to read and talk over the hymns and portions of Scripture, and to join in common prayer. John appeared amongst them as one "sent from God," and by his exhortation and prayer they were greatly comforted under persecution.

Shortly afterwards Mr. Tanaka, one of the catechumens, came to Nagasaki and brought the good news that a police-officer had appeared in the village, "and inquired why the family of the bath-keeper were living in the cowshed, and ordered the restitution of the bath-house. He also asked of the headman the meaning of the high fences along the path leading to Tanaka's house, and ordered their removal. Thus it was shown that the authorities are sincere in securing freedom to the individual to worship according to conscience. Of course they cannot go further, and make neighbours trade with Christians against their will."

Tanaka had really come to Nagasaki to ask for baptism. Mr. Hutchinson thus speaks of his preparedness for this holy Sacrament :—

" I made a careful examination into Tanaka San's case. He was with me for about two hours on two successive days. I was indeed pleased with his answers. Remember, he has only on three or four occasions before this heard preaching during the last ten months. But he has read the New Testament through prayerfully *twice* in that time. This, and the Morning and Evening Prayers in the Prayer-book and the Catechism, have been his study and comfort. We really feel that he has been taught of God. Sin, the Atonement, the mediation of Christ, the unity in Trinity, the resurrection, and eternal life, are to him realities. It did us good to hear his voice in the Confession and Lord's Prayer on Thursday evening at our service. He has suffered much for Christ already, and yet withal is so humble in his ways. I felt here was indeed an exceptional case, and gladly granted him his request.

One unexpected but gratifying result of this visit and baptism is thus referred to by Mr. Hutchinson :—

> His coming and his object led one of whom we have long been hopeful to make also the grand decision. Really a fruit of Mr. Andrews' loving labours, Sadakichi San has been kept back by a mistaken view as to some sensible sign being required of the incoming of the Holy Spirit to the heart of the believer. Bishop Poole's address to the confirmees on this point much impressed him, and at last he too has declared for Christ openly. He has been for four years past the manager of our Sailors' Institute—a man of tried integrity. These two I had the great privilege of baptizing on Sunday evening.

In the following November Mr. Hutchinson visited Kuchi-no-hara and baptized other catechumens, so that at the close of the year there were nineteen Christians in this village, "the fruit of seed sown by Mr. Maundrell and Watanabe San, and watered by John Inutsuka San, and two of our students in the long vacation."

When Mr. Hutchinson spent a night at Kuchi-no-hara, in July, 1885, he found the believers "full of joy," "all walking earnestly and rejoicingly in the ways of the Lord." In returning home on this occasion he visited Hakata, a seaport thirty-three miles from Kuchi-no-hara, and baptized the mother of one of the Nagasaki pupils. An interesting incident connected with this baptism was the presence of Takanabe, one of the Kuchi-no-hara Christians, who had walked to Hakata to bring the headman of a neighbouring village—an earnest inquirer. Of these two Mr. Hutchinson wrote :—

> Our inquirer was up with us again the next morning, earnestly asking questions; and with him the noble brother who had voluntarily taken the

thirty-four miles the previous day to help on a soul towards the light of the Gospel. Which of us does not feel reproved by such evidences of love and faith?

The work has now extended to Fukuoka, where, during his visitation tour in Kiushiu, Bishop Bickersteth confirmed two persons. With such evidence of spiritual life in the Chikuzen Christians as the preceding narrative affords, may we not confidently hope that He who has began a good work in them will perform it until the day of Christ. The Saga catechist, with several groups of Christians in Chikuzen to feed and guide, and multitudes of heathen in his district to whom the Gospel must be preached, specially needs the prayers of the Lord's people. In the circumstances of his work we seem to hear his voice saying to us, "Brethren, pray for us, that the word of the Lord may have free course and be glorified, even as it is with you."

3. *KUMAMOTO.*

Kumamoto, which is due east of Nagasaki, is some eight or nine miles from the east coast of the Shimabara Gulf. It is the capital of the province of Higo, the garrison town for the southern portion of the Empire, and, from a native point of view, second to no town in Kiushiu. Its importance, therefore, as a missionary centre cannot well be overrated.

Mr. Maundrell paid his first visit to Kumamoto in 1876, in company with Bishop Bardon. His second visit, to commence active missionary operations, was nearly four years later. During the Christmas vacation of 1879 two of the Nagasaki students, Messrs. Mekata and O-Hara, visited Kumamoto and did some quiet evangelistic work there. The result was an earnest request from a few natives of the town for a resident catechist; in response to which Mr. Mekata was sent to commence systematic work. On his arrival he secured a small room where he had regular preaching, and when Mr. Maundrell visited Kumamoto in April, 1880, he was delighted to find how well he had been getting on. There were no baptisms during this visit, but inquirers were instructed, and there was preaching every evening. One interesting incident —the preaching at Yatsushiro, a town of 15,000 inhabitants, about 30 miles from Kumamoto—is thus referred to by Mr. Maundrell :—

Mekata San had made two or three friends at Yatsushiro. One especially, ———, a local officer, though not a Christian, is deeply interested in the welfare of his countrymen, both materially and religiously, and he thinks rightly that their welfare could be best advanced by the belief and practice of Christianity. This man, immediately on my arrival, tried to find a room where I might preach. But, as he expected a large audience, he could find no private building that would be suitable. He accordingly made an agreement with a Buddhist priest, by which a part of a temple was placed at my disposal. It was soon reported throughout the town that a foreign Kiyoshi (teacher) was going to preach at this temple in the evening. It was not the *vads*, in which the image of Buddha stands, that became for the time being our lecture-room, but a spacious side chamber in which the Buddhist priests themselves often preach to their people. On reaching this place I found three or four hundred persons already assembled, and others pressing in. At the further end of this chamber the priest had very kindly and considerately provided a table, on which stood two large candles and a chair. Presently he himself came and made my acquaintance, bringing for me some tea and cake. After this he retired to a smaller room close by, both visible and within hearing. It was a novel situation—a Christian missionary admitted to a Buddhist temple as a teacher of religion, with a congregation of about 500 people, all curious to hear "what this new doctrine is." After Mekata San had explained that the religion of Jesus was one inculcating order, reverence of and submission to those in authority, and mutual love, I preached for about an hour myself. Many of those present were of the leading men of the town, Government officials, and school-teachers. No doubt they were more curious to hear than eager to learn; but the circumstance fully shows how great a change is coming over their minds, and how rapidly the hearts of the people, if not the country, are being thrown open to the proclamation of the Gospel.

The C.M.S. Mission.—(III.) Kiushiu Out-stations. 159

Already there were signs of the springing of the seed, and when Mr. Maundrell again visited Kumamoto in July he had the great joy of baptizing twelve adults and four children. These first-fruits included a family consisting of three adults and two children, another member of which had been in Mrs. Goodall's school more than three years, a Government Inspector of village schools, a nurseryman who had heard the gospel at Yokohama and Tokio, when he was there on business, a widow sempstress and her daughter—the former of whom was an old friend of Mr. Midzu-shina, the first catechist employed at Nagasaki, and a native doctor and his two children.

Later in the year Mr. Mekata's health failed and he retired from the work. Mr. John Inutsuka, another student, took his place, and at the close of the year the work looked promising, as in addition to attending the Christian services and preaching for the heathen, " not a few came to the preaching place to talk with the catechist."

During the year 1881, the work was carried on in the midst of opposition. Again and again was the preaching place stoned, and once Mr. Inutsuka had to escape for safety at the back of the house. But the Christians continued to meet for worship on Sundays, and preaching to the heathen was carried on regularly. Mr. Nakamura, one of the converts who had formerly been an inspector of Government schools, rendered real service to the mission. He started a tentative school for young men in the hope of overcoming heathen prejudices, and at the close of the year there were eleven under instruction. Four baptisms during the year brought up the number of Christians to twenty-eight, of whom seven were children, and in addition there were three inquirers and one candidate for baptism.

During 1882, John Ko, a married catechist, was in charge.

He worked steadily and under much more favourable circumstances. Referring to the change, Mr. Maundrell says :—

There is a very numerous and influential body of advanced Liberals amongst the upper classes who are strongly agitating for representative institutions. Though not Christians themselves, they are not hostile, but regard Christianity with favour, believing that it will serve their object. Consequently there has been little or no demonstration of hostility against the preaching-place this year similar to what I had to report last year. During my last visit I noticed a great difference in this respect. It is quite remarkable to see how the tables are turned. Last year it was our lecture-room which was decried and stoned : this year the persons who then stoned us and tried to suppress the preaching—the Conservative and anti-foreign party—have themselves been stoned, and their meetings attempted to be suppressed, because they are regarded as obstructionists !

One specially hopeful sign was the large sale of Holy Scriptures—during the year more were "sold at Kumamoto than in all other parts of Kiushiu." The school commenced in the previous year was continued, and ten or twelve young men from fifteen to twenty years of age lived with John Ko as boarders at their own expense, and were thus constantly brought under direct Christian influence. Mr. Hutchinson, who accompanied Mr. Maundrell on a visit to Kumamoto in October, 1882, thus speaks of John Ko's household and the school :—

One realised, at evening and morning family worship, the happiness of being in a Christian household. Ko San's wife and two little children, with their servant and the schoolmaster, and eight youths who form the school and sleep on the premises, made quite a daily congregation; their singing was very good. Three of the lads earnestly asked for baptism during our stay, but it was felt best to encourage them to persevere, and promise baptism on our next visit. Every day they receive a certain amount of direct scriptural instruction from the catechist, and this with the full consent of their parents.

In the same communication he mentions a Saturday evening prayer meeting which was attended by eighteen adults, and thus describes the Sunday morning service :—

> On Sunday morning twenty-three were present at service, of whom seven besides ourselves partook of Holy Communion, which I was privileged to administer, Mr. Maundrell taking the morning prayer and preaching; after which he baptized the infant child of the catechist. In these services, I should say that whilst a chair is provided each side of the table for us as Europeans, the natives all sit round on the mats, just as they do at the temples. In prayer they incline forwards till the head nearly touches the ground. Those who use Prayer Books lay them on the ground before them.

During 1883, the work seems to have gone on steadily.

In 1884, Mr. Hutchinson again visited Kumamoto, and baptized ten persons—the fruit of John Ko's earnest and faithful work. The school was continued with an average attendance of ten young men; but two left to enter the local medical school, and two were withdrawn by their parents through fear of their becoming Christians.

Mr. Hutchinson's next visit in May, 1885, was a still more cheering one. He thus describes the new premises which had just been rented for the mission :—

> Really they are two houses thrown into one; the left hand having a European front, its ground floor being used as the preaching-place, and the upstairs room forming the school; the lower portion of the right forms the catechist's home, and the upper floor the place of meeting for the Church members.

Mr. Hutchinson was much cheered by the attendance at the evangelistic services held for preaching to the heathen. Referring to one held on the day of his arrival, he says :—

> In the evening we had preaching to the heathen, Koba and Ko San speaking for more than two hours. About seventy listened attentively. A stone was thrown through the window, but that was the only interruption, and was not repeated.

L

Another feature of encouragement was the interest shown by the Christians in these services. Referring to a service held the following evening, Mr. Hutchinson says:—

The crowd was greater than before. I noticed that singing is a very prominent element in the work at Kumamoto. The Christians come to the evening preaching, and help with the opening hymn, which at once attracts a crowd; and prayer is always offered *in presence of the heathen* for a blessing on the Word spoken, both before and after preaching.

But the crowning joy of the visit was the admission of six persons to the fellowship of Christ's flock by baptism. They are thus referred to by Mr. Hutchinson:—

There was the same evidence of careful preparation on the part of the catechist I noted last year, and there was much to cheer us in the fact that now not only did Mrs. Ushishima come forward again, but her husband also, and their son aged 15. Last year he threatened his wife with death if she received baptism; now he came confessing his sin and his faith in the crucified and only Saviour. Another point of interest is that the eldest son is a student at the Osaka College, at his own charges; and the wife's brother is the energetic student, Fujitomo San. Besides these were a medical student, Ida Asakichi, aged 21; Uyemura Kahei, 20, a barber; Uchi Koga Saiyi, 26, a fishmonger,—young men not ashamed to be known as Christians. These, with Dr. Sata's infant, I decided to baptize on Sunday afternoon, being exceedingly pleased with the testimony they gave as to the grounds of their faith.

The subsequent progress of the work has been most encouraging, and it was, under God, greatly helped by the visits of Mr. and Miss Brandram in 1886. When Mr. Brandram was there in March he found that the Christians connected with the three missions represented in Kumamoto "were arranging for a series of united preaching." Four meetings were held on two successive days, and audiences of four or five hundred listened attentively for more than two hours on each occasion. The success of this united effort marks a new era in Christian work in Kagoshima.

At the time of this visit Mr. Brandram baptized five adults and one infant. The case of one woman is especially interesting. Mr. Brandram thus refers to it :—

One was a woman sixty-four years of age, who had for some time past been a most zealous Buddhist, going daily for five years to a temple several miles distant. Her grandson, a medical student, died the year before last. During his illness one of our Christians, a young doctor, visited him, and spoke to him of Christ. The word thus spoken was brought within reach of the grandmother, and after his death she came to our catechist inquiring about Christ. She told me the day and hour when she first heard. She is wonderfully earnest, and people, seeing her happy face, have asked her the reason for her joy. She is most regular in attending the services. Another grandson of hers, a schoolboy aged fourteen, was baptized at the same time.

Mr. Brandram's second visit, this time accompanied by his sister, extended over three months. There were numerous openings for work. Miss Brandram "taught knitting and English to some ladies and children. Her classes were usually closed with Bible-reading and prayer. Amongst those in whom she was especially interested were the four children of an officer belonging to one of the regiments stationed there."

Of his own work he thus speaks :—

On Sunday mornings Inutsuka and I preached alternately; in the afternoon I took a Bible-class; in the evening I preached to the heathen. On Monday evening we had preaching in our house ; on Wednesday, at the catechist's ; on Friday, a prayer-meeting in one of the Christian's houses. I had numbers of visitors: and before I left two young men came, New Testament in hand, with difficult passages marked for me to explain.

It was towards the end of this interesting and helpful visit that the Bishop, accompanied by Archdeacon Maundrell, visited Kumamoto and held a Confirmation. There were twenty-four candidates. Mr. Brandram "had the pleasure of examining them—it was a real pleasure. Most of them were plainly showing by their lives that they wished to be Christ's faithful soldiers and servants unto their lives' end." During the same visit thirteen more were baptized.

The Church at Kumamoto is the "most active and flourishing Church" connected with the C.M.S. Kiushiu Mission. With its steady growth, it has manifested a spirit of manly self-reliance, and its desire to become a self-supporting Church seems to be very near realisation. Referring to this subject in his Annual Letter for 1886, Mr. Hutchinson says:—

> The Kumamoto Christians are making great efforts to become self-supporting. They are intent on erecting their church, the fund for which is nearly completed, and the site has already been purchased. That and the residence for a pastor or catechist settled, there is nothing to hinder them from energetically pushing on their pastorate fund. Mr. Brandram, who has spent nearly three months at Kumamoto, tells of one innkeeper who sets aside a fraction from the account of each guest for the church, and of an earnest sister who devotes half the profit on every article she knits and sells towards the church fund.

Another hopeful and encouraging feature of the Kumamoto work is the gradual extension of its influence in the surrounding neighbourhood. When Mr. Hutchinson visited Kumamoto in May, 1885, he was privileged to gather in some of the first fruits of these outlying places. He thus speaks of a visit to a candidate for baptism and his family at a place eight miles from Kumamoto:—

> An attack of illness prevented his coming to meet me. He had come in with his family on the previous Sunday in vain—Itsuno Shokiyo, aged 54, a farmer; his wife, Omoju, aged 44; their daughter, Tsunayo, aged 22; and her daughter, Matsumi, aged 3; constituted this interesting family. I was much struck with a remark made by Itsuno San. "I thought," said he, "that God had sent me this illness to keep me from coming in to be baptized because of my sins, which have made me unworthy to join His family. 'Yes,' I said to myself, ' God knows I am not good enough to be a Christian.'" Of course it was my privilege to point him to the Saviour's own words, "Come unto

Me, all ye," &c., and He "cleanseth us from all sin ; " and to show that not our loving Father but Satan it is who tries by all means to keep us back from Christ.

In journeying from Kumamoto to Saga he visited Yamaga, twenty miles from Kumamoto, and Oshima twenty-three miles further on, at both of which places he found catechumens waiting for baptism. Two were baptized at Yamaga, Mrs. Nakamura, the wife of the governor of the prison, and Sakamoto Sentaro, a cooper by trade—of whom Mr. Hutchinson thus speaks :—

This latter is very earnest, and possesses a good memory. He frequently preaches in the bath-house, and often gets pelted with the shingle at the bottom of the bath. He is quiet in appearance, and very earnest in his manner. May God bless him to his countrymen in Yamaga! Mrs. Nakamura is a lady of exceptional mental ability, combined with great humility. She rejoices in the comfort and peace which are the fruits of the indwelling Spirit. Her husband and his brother, also an official, came to see me, but whilst keenly alive to the affairs of this world, seemed to care nothing for the things which belong to the life eternal.

Oshima, the next place visited, is described as " one of many villages that line the road by the shore of the Shimabara gulf. At many of these salt is manufactured on an extensive scale, in a very primitive manner : firstly, by evaporation from the sun's rays ; and lastly, in small furnaces, heated with wood fires. The inhabitants of these fishing villages seem very poor, contented with the bare necessaries of existence. Shrines and temples are rare, another evidence of poverty."

Of the entrance of the Gospel to Oshima and the baptisms then he adds :—

At Oshima, the host of the *yadoya*, or inn, awaited us. He first heard the Gospel from one of the converts at Kumamoto, whom I baptized last year, who had come to Oshima on law business. He visited Kumamoto, and invited Ko San to come and preach, which he has done several times; as a result, Kuroda San, aged 30; his wife, 24; and his uncle, a fine old Shizoku, 72, presented themselves for baptism. Kuroda San's sister, aged 30, had also for a time received instruction and given her name as a candidate; but it seems the Buddhist priest residing near had got hold of her, and effectually frightened her by tales about Christianity being a very bad religion; though why she could not say, except that it would rob those who entered it of all their money.

Mr. Brandram visited both Yamaga and Oshima in the spring of 1886, and administered the Lord's Supper to two or three Christians at each place, and when Bishop Bickersteth and Archdeacon Maundrell visited the district in the autumn, two were confirmed at Yamaga and eight at Oshima.

Both in Kumamoto and the places visited from it, the fields are ready for the reaper. "There are open doors on all sides. The Christians are awake and at work." "Just now Kumamoto calls for our earnest prayers and help." A resident European missionary would, with God's blessing, do much for the consolidation and extension of the work. It is for the Church at home to join in earnest prayer, and to supply the means to enable the Society to give the vigorous Church at Kumamoto the help that it needs.

XIII.

THE CHURCH MISSIONARY SOCIETY'S MISSION.

(IV.) *Osaka*.

"Precept must be upon precept, precept upon precept; line upon line, line upon line; here a little, and there a little."—*Isa.* xxviii. 10.

HE Rev. C. F. Warren, the first C.M.S. missionary to Central Japan, reached Kobe early in December, 1873, and on the last day of the year removed with his family to Osaka. He was warmly welcomed by the American Episcopal and American Board missionaries who were already located there, and shortly after his arrival was cheered by witnessing some of the first Christian baptisms in that city. During the first year of his residence he visited Kobe fortnightly to conduct services for the English community at that port, a duty of which the Rev. H. Evington relieved him soon after his arrival in December, 1874. But the acquisition of the language was his chief work, and in twelve months he had, by dint of hard study and constant intercourse with the people, so far mastered it as to be able to attempt preaching in his own house. The first of a series of Sunday afternoon services was held on January 3rd, 1875, and a few friendly natives whose acquaintance had been previously made, or who were specially invited, came together and listened to a simple statement of Gospel truth. These services were carried on for three months with

an average attendance of about a dozen, and prepared the way for a more public effort.

More than two years had elapsed since the withdrawal of the edicts against Christianity, but it was still impossible to procure buildings in the city of Osaka for Christian purposes, except within the narrow limits of the district where foreigners were allowed to reside, and it was determined to commence a tentative work in a small building on the Foreign Concession where there was no fear of interference from the native authorities. Accordingly a small chapel or mission-room, 24 feet by 15, with a recess at one end, 6 feet by 3 feet 6 inches, for a small Communion-table, was erected at the back of Mr. Warren's house. It cost $300, about £60, all of which with the exception of £5 was subscribed in Osaka and Kobe.

The opening service—if such it may be called—held on May 30th, 1875, was very encouraging. Sixty or seventy persons filled the little building, and many more stood at the door and windows. As there was not a single native Christian or inquirer connected with the mission, the proceedings were of an informal and evangelistic character, and Mr. Warren gave an address on the purpose of the mission, of which the following is an outline :—

OUTLINE OF THE FIRST SERMON PREACHED IN THE C.M.S. CHAPEL AT OSAKA.

This is a place of worship. Why is it so called? Because here we shall meet to worship the one living and true God. In Japan many gods are worshipped, but not this one true God. Christians do not worship many gods like the Japanese, because they believe in the one and only God, the Creator and Preserver of all things. In ancient times, indeed, we in England worshipped other gods; but through God's mercy the true way was made known in our land, and we, having the knowledge of the one true God, worship Him alone. This is the first article of our Creed,

"I believe in God the Father," &c., as our Lord Jesus Christ taught (Mark xii. 28, &c.). We believe that He is the only object of worship, as Jesus said to Satan (Matt. iv. 10). We follow the moral teachings of the sages; we reverence parents and those in authority; but we pay Divine honours to the one true God alone.

But why come here to worship? Is this the only place where God can be approached and worshipped? God is omnipresent—can be worshipped everywhere, as Jesus said (John iv. 20, 21). Now, where two or three meet, Jesus is in the midst of them (Matt. xviii. 19, 20). We can pray alone everywhere—in secret, where none but God can hear (Matt. vi. 5, 6). When we meet with our families, we can meet in our houses; but when we come from different families, it is meet that we should have a place for united worship. Hence, whilst places of worship are not the only places where God can be sought, they are necessary.

But where is the representation of our God, or the symbol of His presence, such as the Japanese have? We need neither. God has no form (John i. 18). God has forbidden any representation or symbol (2nd Com.). God is a Spirit. Must be worshipped in spirit and truth (John iv. 24). How shall we worship this true God? What offerings shall we offer? Not food and drink, for God needs none of these things ; but with a penitent, believing, obedient heart we shall praise and worship Him. Our prayers will not be vain repetitions, like the vain repetitions of the heathen (the *Namu Amida butsu* of the Buddhists being instanced) (Matt. vi. 7); but we shall confess our sins, and seek pardon and grace to be holy and good.

Here, too, we shall read and preach God's Word. His message of love to man—to all men—written for our learning. From this we shall teach the way of truth : that God is one eternal, almighty, omniscient, omnipresent, merciful and good, Maker and Preserver of all things. We shall teach that man, created pure and holy, has sinned—ought to be punished; that God, to save man from punishment, sent His dear Son Jesus Christ; that Jesus Christ came, lived, and died to atone for man's sin; that all who believe in Him shall be saved—have sins forgiven and eternal happiness (John iii. 16).

If it be asked why we came to Japan with this new way, we reply—(1) because Jesus commanded His disciples and us (Mark xvi. 15, also Matt. xxviii. 18, &c.); (2) because God is the Creator of all, and Jesus came to save all men (1 John ii. 2); (3) because there is no other Saviour from sin and its consequences (Acts iv. 11).

Believe on the Lord Jesus Christ. Come and hear the good news from time to time.

The little chapel at once became the centre of systematic efforts to disseminate the knowledge of Christ. On Wednesdays and Fridays there was public preaching to small congregations, sometimes less than a dozen, but generally between twenty and thirty being present. Larger congregations assembled on Sunday afternoons; and almost daily inquirers were received and passers-by conversed with. Sometimes one or two, and frequently twenty, thirty and even fifty entered the chapel or stood at the door, and were spoken to individually or collectively in a single day. Copies of single Gospels in Japanese, which were the only portions of the New Testament then published, were frequently lent to those who appeared to be interested in Christianity, and many more, as well as copies of the Old and New Testament, and other Christian books in Chinese were sold to visitors.

Whilst these efforts were being made to scatter the good seed far and wide, line upon line teaching was provided for those who professed to have some interest in Christian truth, by commencing services of a devotional character with Bible-reading. This is illustrated by the following account of a Sunday's work from Mr. Warren's journal :—

FIRST SERVICE FOR INQUIRERS.

Sunday, June 13th, 1875.—This morning carried out my intention of commencing a service and Bible-reading for inquirers. In addition to my teacher, there are several who have expressed a desire to know the way of God more perfectly, and I felt that it would be well to make such a beginning at once. My purpose (D.V.) is to have the morning service somewhat shortened, with a hymn and Bible-reading on Sunday mornings, and a Bible-reading with prayer and singing on Thursday evenings. When we commenced this morning, there were two Japanese present; but another young man, who had promised to be with us, came in later. I trust that the Lord was with the two or three thus meeting in His name. Having sung a hymn at the close of the morning prayer, the chapel door was thrown open, and before we had procceded far quite a number came in, and paid great attention to the Word spoken. At 3 P.M., opened the chapel for preaching. There were about twenty inside and quite as many more at the door and windows. I preached on the Resurrection of Jesus, the subject having been suggested by an article which appeared in a native newspaper, written to prove that the Resurrection of our Lord was not an historical fact. In speaking on the subject, I quoted largely from the Gospels, and was followed most eagerly by those who were supplied with books. The whole party, with the exception of two, who left just as I was concluding, remained and listened most attentively to the end. I am thankful to observe some of the same faces again and again at these preaching services. God grant that the interest they feel may grow, and ripen into faith in the one name given under heaven amongst men, whereby we must be saved. One young man who was present—he is a student in the Imperial College here—expressed his determination to come to the Bible-readings, so that he might hear the matter from the beginning to the end.

During the year ending June 30th, 1876, there were held in the chapel 228 public services, beside which there were 209 attendances for conversation with inquirers and visitors, and thousands heard something about the true God, and the gift of eternal life in Christ Jesus, and carried away small tracts containing elementary statements of Christian truth.

By the beginning of 1876 there was a little class of avowed candidates for baptism, and on June 25th, eighteen months after the first service held in his own house, and thirteen after the opening of the chapel, Mr. Warren had the joy of admitting six persons into the Church by baptism. One of them, his own teacher, was baptized with some hesitation, as although his faith was apparently sincere, it was a faith rather of the head than of the heart, and he afterwards had to be excluded from the Church. Of the rest, Mr. and Mrs. Aratani were fruits of the chapel work, and the other three were led into light in the way detailed in Mr. Warren's interesting account of them:—

Mrs. Kumei, an old lady of fifty years of age, was, I believe, the first of the party known to me, and the first Japanese to whom I administered

THE MISSIONARIES AT OSAKA AND THE FIRST SIX CONVERTS, 1876.

baptism. She first visited our chapel in the summer of 1875, and after attending a few services, quite settled down as a member of our congregation. It will interest you to know how she was first introduced to

Christian truth and teaching, as it shows how wonderfully God overrules all things for the accomplishment of His gracious purposes in leading the blind to Himself by a way that they know not. Japan, as you well know, has during the last few years opened her gates to the commerce, science, and civilisation of the West. This has necessitated the employment of many foreigners by the Government, both imperial and local. Too frequently, I grieve to say, they do not help but hinder the missionary in his work; for their impure lives, their indifference to all religion, and in some cases their avowed infidel principles, too often prejudice the natives against, and repel them from, Christianity. But there are noble exceptions—Christian men and women, lights lit up of Christ, who let their light shine before men, and by holding forth the Word of Life as they have opportunity, endeavour to lead souls to Him Who is "a light to lighten the Gentiles," the "true light which lighteth every man who cometh into the world." Two of these witnesses for Christ, a lady and gentleman from America, engaged in school-work at the garrison town of Kumamoto, in Kiushiu, whilst pursuing their ordinary calling, have made efforts to teach the truth as it is in Jesus. Here we have the instruments God would make use of to plant the first seeds of Christian truth in Mrs. K.'s heart. But she was not a native of, nor was she resident at, Kumamoto, and had therefore, in the providence of God, to be brought thither. This came about as follows:—After the death of her husband, which happened many years ago, she had her son—I believe her only son—educated for the medical profession under Dutch physicians. Ultimately he became a surgeon in the army, and in the ordinary course of duty was sent to the garrison of Kumamoto. Thither his mother accompanied him, and was there introduced to the lady and gentleman already mentioned, and by intercourse with them learned to care for the things of God. A short tract, *Easy Introduction to Christianity*, by Dr. Hepburn, written in an easy style, and a translation of the *Peep of Day*, were amongst the earliest books placed in her hands. Here she learnt her first lessons in the kingdom of God. Both the mother and son appear to have been impressed, and to have had a desire to learn of Christ and to become Christians. Last year Mrs. K. came on to Osaka, it being the intention of her son to follow her as soon as possible, and to join her in seeking admission to the Church of Christ. On reaching Osaka she found her way to our chapel, as I have already noted. After a time she was put under a regular course of instruction, with a view to baptism. The old lady has given many proofs of her earnestness and sincerity. She has seldom been absent from any of our Christian services, and has often attended the preaching services held for the benefit of those who know nothing about Christianity. She has learned to value the Lord's Day, and has not been ashamed to confess her regard for it before her heathen neighbours. She has made efforts, too, to lead others to the truth. For presentation to some she has purchased portions of the Holy Scriptures and Christian books. She has invited many to come and hear the Word, and has not unfrequently brought her friends with her.

Mr. and Mrs. Nakanishi, aged 49 and 35 respectively, I have not known so long as the rest of the party, but after a careful consideration of all the circumstances of the case, I felt that their baptism ought not to be delayed. Mr. N.'s case is one, too, of some interest, as showing how the changes going on in this country are not without their influence even in the conversion of souls. You are aware that the opening of Japan has necessitated the sending to Europe and America of a number of persons for education and other purposes. One gentleman, now at the head of an important department of the administration, who was formerly in America, in writing to his friends, gave his impressions of Christianity, and stated that he was convinced that sooner or later it must become the religion of Japan. Whether that gentleman has pursued his studies in Christian truth further, and is not only not far from, but actually within, the borders of the kingdom of God, I know not; but certain it is that his statements were not without their influence on the mind of Mr. N. He at that time was an officer in the same department, and by the statements just referred to, had his mind directed to Christianity. Although a Buddhist of the most influential and popular sect in the country, he determined, more than a year ago, to cleanse his house from idols, and accordingly did so, leaving only the ancestral tablets before which to worship. These, as further light dawned upon his mind, he ultimately removed. Finally, he found a Christian tract in his house, not knowing by what means it had been brought there. After reading this most carefully he determined to seek instruction, that he might the better know what he ought to do. In this interesting state of mind he came to me. I found that he had not only put away what he knew could not profit and help him, but was praying to the one living and true God, so far as his light and knowledge enabled him to do so. I found him a most intelligent and earnest inquirer, and as time went on he showed himself desirous of leading his friends to the truth.

His wife, who was baptized at the same time, is a nice little woman.

They have two daughters, aged about fourteen and eight respectively. It was interesting to notice the spontaneous desire of the parents for the baptism of their children as soon as they themselves were numbered amongst the followers of Christ. The young people were baptized on August 20th.

These six converts were all confirmed by Bishop Burdon on July 23rd in the same year, during his first visitation, and on August 20th—the day when Mr. Nakanishi's two daughters were baptized—they received the Holy Communion at the first Japanese Communion Service ever held in connection with the C.M.S. Osaka Mission.

A touching remark respecting their first converts occurs in Mr. Evington's journal. "One soon learns," he says, "that there is nothing to fear from repeating over and over again the same thing to those who are anxious to learn. They like to hear 'the old old story' '*slowly*' and '*often*,' that they may '*take it in*.'"

Mr. Warren was now no longer working single-handed. Mr. Evington, who since his arrival in December, 1874, had relieved him of the English work at Kobe, was now similarly relieved by the timely arrival of two S.P.G. missionaries, who settled at Kobe in August, 1876. He had made good progress in the language, and commenced to assist Mr. Warren early in 1876, especially in the work of receiving visitors and inquirers in the chapel; and now the weekly Bible-class, which had for some time been held before the Sunday afternoon service, was divided, and Mr. Evington regularly took the junior portion. Thus these true yokefellows, with one heart and united effort, devoted themselves to the task entrusted to them, and waited for fresh openings for aggressive evangelistic work.

The attitude of the local authorities was still uncertain, and it was doubtful whether the public preaching of Christianity would be allowed in the heart of the city; but as there was apparently no objection to a missionary or native Christian meeting a few persons in a private house, the newly-baptized Church members placed their houses at the disposal of the missionaries, and made efforts to gather little companies of people to hear the Gospel. Mr. Aratani was the first to move in the matter. He offered Mr. Warren the use of his cottage, and then, once a fortnight for nearly a year, little companies of eight, ten, or a dozen met to hear and talk over the Word of God with Mr. Warren or Mr. Evington. In February, 1877, Mr. Nakanishi similarly opened his house for evangelistic work, and meetings, often quite public, were regularly held there until September, when he removed to the neighbourhood of the Foreign Concession. Mrs. Kumei also arranged for a fortnightly meeting at her house from October, 1877, until she left Osaka in the June following; she also secured the loan of a room in another house, where meetings were held either weekly or fortnightly from February to August, 1878. Meetings were also held at the houses of two professed inquirers; but, sad to say, one of them subsequently joined the Roman Catholic Church, and some years later died, it is to be feared, without any Christian faith whatever; whilst the other, an ex-Buddhist priest, eventually returned to his old profession, and quite recently was in charge of a temple a few miles from Osaka.

These meetings, which were one of the chief features of the Osaka work all through 1877 and a good part of 1878, showed that the native Christians were not ashamed of their Lord, and that they desired to do all in their power to hold forth the Word of Life to their fellow-countrymen. They worked heartily and zealously with the missionaries, bore all the expense of lighting and warming their rooms, and generally provided tea and cakes for refreshment; and as the efforts gradually became more public, lanterns were in most cases suspended at their doors when meetings were going on, bearing the notice, " Preaching of the doctrine of the true God. Come in and listen."

The following account of the first meeting at Mrs. Kumei's house, from Mr. Warren's journal, will show the character of many of these meetings :—

October 12th, 1877.—In the evening went to Mrs. K.'s for a meeting for the first time. She has recently taken quite a large house in anticipation of her son's return from the seat of war—he being a surgeon in the army—and has asked me to hold a meeting there once a fortnight. Gladly have I consented, and to-night our first meeting was held. There were fifteen of Mrs. K.'s neighbours present, and five of our native Christians and inquirers. I spoke for about an hour on the one living and true God, and of His love to man. Our good friend Aratani, who was present, followed me in an admirable address just suited to the occasion.

This meeting, whatever may be its results, shows that at least one of our Christians is letting her light shine—not a solitary instance, I hope. Mrs. K. does not, I feel sure, hide her candle under a bushel. She must speak to many, as she frequently purchases portions of the Scriptures and other books for those who have been led to desire them through her conversations with them. The meeting to-night is the result of her personal efforts. Her house does not stand on a thoroughfare, but behind. All, therefore, who were present were invited by her. May God own and bless her efforts !

Whilst most of these meetings were of an evangelistic character, some of them were devotional. Mr. Warren thus describes one held at Mr. Nakanishi's house on November 3rd, 1877 :—

In the evening, went to Mr. N.'s house by appointment, There most of the Christians and inquirers met for united prayer. I have suggested to our people that they should thus meet once a week, and unite in singing, reading, mutual exhortation, and prayer. I purpose (D.V.) attending only occasionally—perhaps once a month—the evening before our monthly Communion service. I want our Christians to feel that they

M

are to stand alone, and not to lean upon us for everything. May God enable them to lean upon Him! The meeting was pleasant and profitable. I gave out a hymn and offered prayer, and, after reading a few verses and saying a few words, I threw the meeting open. N. N. offered prayer. A. proposed that we should sing "Jesus loves me, this I know," a translation of which was in the book we were singing from, and then prayed. Aratani followed with a few appropriate remarks, and concluded with prayer. After another hymn I pronounced the benediction. Mr. Evington was present, but took no part, as we felt it would be better to leave it as much as possible to our native brethren. I thank God that this step has been taken, indicating, as it does, further progress in the development of our work. The Lord add His blessing!

Attempts were also made to carry the Gospel into some of the villages in the Osaka plain. Short journeys were made on foot, extending over two or more days, and groups were addressed at the way-side tea-houses, and when possible companies of people were gathered for preaching in the inns where the nights were spent. The following extract from Mr. Evington's journal will suffice to show the character of this work:—

November 20th, 1877.—We got away about ten o'clock this morning, going across the fields from Osaka westward, intending, at the time, to take the line of villages below the railway, on our way to Nishi-no-Miya, and to return by the coast. Passing through Yebiye, I spoke to an old woman, who was spreading out her rice to dry, and collected about twelve or fifteen people, besides several children, to whom I spoke of the True God, the Giver of all mercies. We then crossed the Juso-gawa, into a large village called Nejima (about 1,000 houses). When we came to the first resting-place, I found the old woman's finger bleeding, and offered to bind it up with court-plaster. The operation was sufficient to attract a crowd, and, during the address which I gave, some sixty or seventy people, if not more, including children, came together. We then walked through the town, and went into a *chaya** to have some lunch, and quite a crowd collected round the door; and when I had finished my rice, I addressed fifty or more in the street. From this

---

* Tea-house.

place we passed on to Owada, and in the middle of the village there I must have had more than 150 grown-up people and children round me. At all these places I spoke chiefly of God as the great Creator of all things, and the only One who could give pardon of sin and true happiness. Both I and my teacher spoke on the same subject at Tsukuda to fifteen or twenty people. In the evening we stayed at Ama-ga-saki, and the hotel people brought in their neighbours to the number of thirty. May the Lord bless the word spoken to-day! We must have addressed over 300 of different ages, and may we not look for the Lord's promise to make the seed bring forth fruit in His own good time?

An unusual number of inquiring visitors were received by the missionaries in the chapel, and at their homes, during 1877. Daily, and at all hours of the day for several months, they were much occupied in this way. It was the year of the Satsuma rebellion, and among the inquirers were many convalescent soldiers from the over-crowded temporary military hospitals. One case deserves special mention. The man, Fujita by name, came for conversation, and purchased a copy of St. Luke's Gospel in Japanese. He subsequently visited the missionaries for instruction, and finally declared his determination to become a servant and soldier of Jesus Christ. He manifested much zeal for the good of his comrades, and took small tracts, for which he was willing to pay, to distribute among them. In this way many were induced to come to the Mission House for conversation, and to purchase New Testament portions. Fujita San was subsequently removed to Tokio, and later sent back to his native province. All along he persevered in his search after truth, and he was eventually baptized by a native pastor in Shikoku, connected with the American Board Mission. He has proved a faithful and zealous Christian, and as lately as 1885 was employed in the store of the National Bible Society of Scotland, at Yokohama.

It was in this year too that a special effort was made to

reach and instruct the women. Mr. Warren thus wrote of it in his Annual Letter:—

In July I commenced a weekly class for women. The average attendance has been from eight to ten. Lessons on fundamental truths, chiefly based on the Apostles' Creed, have formed the course of instruction. Mrs. Warren always joins us. Some of the meetings have been very interesting. One one occasion I asked each of them to bring a text that had particularly struck them. One gave, "God so loved the world," &c. Others gave, "Behold I bring you glad tidings of great joy," &c.; "Except a man be born again," &c. "Blessed are ye when men shall revile," &c.; "Whosoever eateth my flesh, and drinketh my blood, hath eternal life." These texts were paraphrased by the women who brought them. The remarks of the woman who mentioned the last text struck me most. They were somewhat as follows: "Jesus Christ is the Son of God. He became flesh, and in the flesh suffered, shed His blood, and died for sinners and all who believe that He came down and died, making His incarnation and death their only hope of salvation, the food of their souls, will have everlasting life."

The class steadily grew, and during 1878 the average attendance was about a dozen. Mrs. Warren commenced a class for needlework, and the class for women followed. Among its members there were several illustrations of the beneficial effects of Christianity in addition to its direct spiritual help. When some of them became Christians they could scarcely spell out a word; some time afterwards they could read the New Testament with comparative ease, and could turn to well-chosen passages in illustration of the subject under consideration.

Whilst these and other efforts were being made to win souls, and to build up the little flock of believers, the tiny room or chapel which had been erected in 1875 proved too small for the expanding work, and was replaced by a larger building about 45 feet long and 22 wide—the portion fitted up for Divine service being 36 feet by 22, the remainder forming a class room. It was opened on August 23rd, 1877, just two years and three months after the opening of the building it replaced. The need of a larger building was in itself a mark of progress, but the opening service indicated what a real

HOLY TRINITY CHURCH, OSAKA, AS ERECTED 1877.

advance had been made since June, 1875. *Then* there was not a single convert or catechumen, and those who attended the opening service (or rather preaching) were for the most part there out of curiosity. *Now* there was a congregation of eighty persons, a fair number of whom were either Christians, catechumens, or hearers of the Word ; a native Christian read the Lesson, and the singing and responding were such as " would put to shame scores of well-attended churches in our own favoured land." *Then* there could be no communion service. *Now* six converted Japanese united with the missionaries in commemorating the Lord's death. *Then* Mr. Warren could only deliver an elementary statement of Christian truth, and explain the object of his coming to Japan. *Now*, addressing the Christian converts, he could take for his text, " Ye are the light of the world," and remind them that it was their duty to reflect the light of truth, purity, and love as lights lit up of Christ.

The year 1877 was thus one of expanding influence and growing opportunities, but the infant daughter of Mr. Nakanishi was the only one received into Christ's flock by baptism. Yet, the year closed with many signs of the springing of the seed, and during 1878 seventeen adults and three children were added to the Church. Fully half of these were relations and friends of Christians, no uncertain proof that they had been witnesses to Christ in their homes and among their friends.

The second visit of Bishop Burdon, in 1878, strengthened and encouraged the now growing flock. He preached at the usual morning service on Trinity Sunday, Mr. Warren, interpreting, and in the evening he dedicated the little church— thenceforth called Holy Trinity Church. On the following Thursday, June 20th, he held a Confirmation, when seventeen Japanese and one European were presented. They went up as much as possible in family groups, husband and wife, parent and child, kneeling side by side to receive the imposition of hands. At the Communion with which the service closed, twenty-four native Christians—three of them belonging to the American Episcopal Mission—knelt with nine Europeans at the Lord's Table. The number of communicants was now increased to twenty-two, as against six at the first Communion less than two years before. There was, too, progress in other respects. Messrs. Nakanishi and Aratani, two of the first six converts, and Mr. Kimura, who received some of his first lessons in Christian truth from Mr. Warren during his stay at Kioto in 1875, rendered valuable assistance at the various services and meetings, and began to receive regular instruction with a view to increased efficiency in such work.

At Easter a Church Committee had been formed, and later in the year resolutions were passed providing for the establishment of prayer meetings, and for visiting the sick and other absentees from public worship, as well as for the collection and disbursement of Church funds. In this way it was sought to promote brotherly sympathy among the Church members, and united action in all things affecting the welfare of the Church, and to lay the foundation of a strong, vigorous, aggressive, and self-supporting Christianity.

It was in this year, too, on Feb. 16th, that the first C.M.S. preaching-room was opened, in which fifty-one preaching services were held during the year with an average attendance of fifteen, exclusive of Christians, and at the book-store connected with the preaching-room nearly $50 worth of Bibles, tracts, &c., in Chinese and Japanese were sold.

During the following year, 1879, aggressive work was somewhat interrupted by a cholera epidemic, which necessitated the discontinuance of meetings for a time. In October a second room was opened in the city, the Christians taking the financial responsibility, though Mr. Warren and Mr. Evington guaranteed $2 a month towards the expenses for a year. This arrangement was modified in 1883, when the Christians undertook larger responsibilities in connection with the Church of the Saviour. Another forward movement was the opening of a boarding and day-school for girls by Miss Oxlad, of the Society for Promoting Female Education in the East, particulars of which are given on a subsequent page.

Early in 1880 Mr. Warren left Osaka on a flying visit to this country. He returned to Osaka in the autumn, and resumed his work before Christmas. During Mr. Warren's absence, Mr. Evington and the native Christians shared the work in and around Osaka. Eight adults and one child were baptized. Three of these were the first fruits of Mr. Evington's preaching-room work, and one was from a village in the Osaka plain which Mr. Evington had frequently visited when itinerating.

In February, 1881, Mr. Evington returned to England for a brief furlough, and Mr. Warren was left single-handed. Shortly after Mr. Evington's departure the Rev. G. H. Pole arrived. He was well known to the Osaka missionaries, having been formerly engaged as a civil engineer under the Japanese Government. He returned to England in 1876, and went to Cambridge to study with a view to taking Holy Orders. Whilst at Cambridge he offered himself to the C.M.S. for work in Japan, and after spending a year at Tunbridge Wells as curate to Canon Hoare, he went to Japan as a C.M.S. missionary.

The year was one of marked progress. In Osaka fifteen adults and eight children, and at Tokushima, the first out-station of the Osaka centre, which was opened this year, three adults, were baptized. One of those baptized in Osaka was Dr. Kumei, the son of one of the first six converts. He had been an army surgeon, and was at the time of his baptism residing in Osaka, practising as an ordinary physician. The hope that he would become one of the most substantial and influential members of the Church in Osaka was not realised, as he subsequently removed to his native province, and there died in 1886. But the year's increase included two whose names will, it is hoped, be long known in connection with Christian work in Osaka and its out-stations. Mr. Yamashita was baptized on Easter Day, and received the name of Paul. He was a custom-house officer, and was sometimes on duty on the foreign concession. In passing the door of the church he stopped to listen to the word which was eventually to bring light, joy, and strength to his soul. He was at that time a sorrowful man—worse than a widower, for his wife had to be put away for unfaithfulness—and he drank in the truth. His New Testament, well-worn and marked from reading and searching, showed how earnestly he sought to know the way of the Lord. In 1882 he joined the theological class just then started by Mr. Warren, and since 1883 he has been engaged in evangelistic work at Tokushima, Fukuyama, and in Iwami.

Mr. Terasawa was baptized on Trinity Sunday. He was in Osaka waiting for official employment, and spent as much of his leisure as possible in studying Christianity. After he received an official appointment he spent alternate days in teaching Mr. Pole. In the following year he joined the theological class, and was one of the first students admitted to the Osaka Divinity School. From November, 1884, whilst continuing his studies for the ministry, he performed the duties of pastoral catechist in connection with Holy Trinity Church, for which he received Bishop Poole's licence, and on March 6th, 1887, was admitted to Holy Orders by Bishop Bickersteth.

Another sign of progress was the removal and enlargement

of Holy Trinity Church. This building, like its predecessor, was moved bodily across the road to its new site. The enlargement was effected by throwing the class-room into the body of the church and adding a chancel. A school-room was added, and matted in native fashion for prayer meetings, Sunday-school, &c. The church in its enlarged form was re-opened on Christmas Day, 1881, and Mr. Evington, who had just before returned to Osaka with Mrs. Evington, occupied the pulpit. He was struck by the signs of advance which he saw, and especially by the increased numbers of communicants, for on that day thirty-four knelt at the Lord's Table.

With the beginning of 1882, a station committee was formed for directing the growing work at the station, and a daily prayer meeting was also commenced. Thus, whilst the desire was to do everything with order and system, it was not forgotten that the secret of all harmony and success is in the presence and power of the Holy Ghost.

The year was not without its trials. One of the native helpers was entirely laid aside, and Mr. Warren's health was much impaired for more than six months. Still the work went on, and a second out-station was opened, in the province of Iwami, under circumstances of great interest. It was not a year of remarkable ingathering, for the total number of baptisms was only fourteen, and of these nine were at the out-stations—the net gain in Osaka being only three—and the missionaries were saddened by the coldness of two who neglected the means of grace, and were removed from the communicants' roll. Thus is the evil ever mingled with the good in the Church, and the wheat and tares grow side by side.

A regular theological class was commenced in June, and placed in Mr. Warren's charge; and Messrs. Terasawa and Yamashita entered as the first students, and were accommodated in spare rooms in Mr. Warren's house, who was then living quite alone, as Mrs. Warren and the rest of his family had returned to England.

The year 1883, though one of abounding mercies, was not without its trials. The illness of Mr. Kimura, who was for some time a catechist, continued, and his name had to be struck off the list of workers. Mr. Aratani, who had been working for more than two years at Tokushima, returned to Osaka in August, and shortly afterwards retired from the work. It was a grievous disappointment that one who by his early zeal had given such promise of usefulness, drew back, and this disappointment has been aggravated by his subsequent unchristian conduct. But it was, perhaps, well that both these trials came when they did, for they led the Osaka missionaries to rely less on paid agents, and more on voluntary helpers, and to push the theological students to the front.

Among the mercies of the year, mention must first be made of the showers of revival blessing which fell on the Lord's people in Osaka, as in other places in Japan. From the beginning of the year the first droppings had been felt in the neighbourhood of the capital, but the copious shower was given later. The unity of the Protestant missionaries had been conspicuous at the General Conference held in Osaka, and the unity of the native Christians was equally shown at a general meeting of Christians and Christian workers held in Tokio. Was not the shower of blessing which followed a token of God's presence in the midst of His united people ? In Osaka the movement began with a few brethren who daily met to pray for the outpouring of the Holy Spirit. The spirit of prayer gradually extended, and soon pervaded the whole of the Churches in Osaka, and united prayer meetings were held every evening in one or other of the church buildings. There was no excitement, but intense fervour and definiteness, both in prayer and exhortation. Whilst these meetings were being held, news of the blessing experienced at Tokio was sent by the delegates from Osaka. One short telegram simply said "The Holy Ghost has descended. Pray for us." When the delegates returned they were like new men. They had evidently received fresh light, grace, and power from on high. Speaking of this time of refreshing, Mr. Warren wrote :—

During the whole of my ministerial experience of nearly twenty years, whether in China, England, or Japan, I never before witnessed such manifest tokens of the presence and power of the Spirit of God. It was a blessed time of refreshing, and, thank God, the results have not been transient.

From that time Christians connected with the different missions in Osaka were drawn together in closer union. The deep sense of a common need had drawn them together to pray for the outpouring of the Holy Spirit, and now, when His fuller indwelling was realised, their hearts were aglow with mutual love; and when the daily prayer meetings ceased, it was unanimously agreed to hold a united weekly meeting for prayer and exhortation. This was the more remarkable in that whilst the week of prayer in January had been annually observed with profit, no attempt to hold united prayer meetings periodically throughout the year had been successful.

Nor was the union only one for prayer, for the strength of the different Churches was united in special evangelistic efforts in public halls and theatres. This unity was never more conspicuously manifested than at the meeting held at Osaka to commemorate the 400th anniversary of the birth of Martin Luther. It was entirely organised by the native Christian workers—was presided over by a native, and the only foreign missionary who spoke on the occasion was the Rev. C. F. Warren of our C.M.S. Mission.

But remarkable as the year was, there were only nineteen persons baptized in connection with the C.M.S. Osaka centre, and of these only eight adults and three children were living in Osaka. But the spiritual life of the Church was deepened. There was a manifest growth in brotherly love, in power to witness for Christ, and in zeal for His glory; and the year closed with the conviction and believing expectation, that God who had revived and strengthened His dear children, would ere long through them bring blessing to others.

One of the principal events of the year—the opening of the Church of the Saviour in the city of Osaka as a new centre of Christian worship and work—has yet to be noticed. It has already been stated that Mr. Evington commenced evangelistic work in a hired house in February, 1879. In less than two years this house had to be vacated. Another house was taken, but in a less eligible position, and early in 1882 yet another move became necessary. As considerable difficulty had been experienced in renting buildings in the city, the native Christians agreed to ask the C.M.S. to grant them $1,000 as a loan, to purchase and fit up a suitable building for Church and mission work, and they engaged to refund the money by instalments. The request was granted, and the Church of the Saviour—a dwelling-house internally fitted up as a mission church—was opened on Sunday, October 14th, with a service and the Holy Communion. All the C.M.S. Osaka Christians attended, and the three resident missionaries divided the service—the Rev. C. F. Warren preaching the sermon. Two of the first six converts—Mr. and Mrs. Nakanishi—and seven other communicants and several children now severed their connection with Holy Trinity Church and formed the nucleus of a new congregation. This was a real step forward, and placed new responsibilities on the Christians. The now separate congregations are still one in sympathy and effort; they have a united monthly meeting for conference, mutual exhortation and prayer; and their division into two bands was the occasion of forming the first Church Council for the Osaka district, delegates being sent from both congregations to confer on all matters where joint action and responsibility are concerned, and to administer all common funds.

The year 1884 opened with promise. Bishop Poole's arrival, and his first visit to Osaka in January, encouraged the Christians. On Sunday, January 13th, he preached at the morning service in Holy Trinity Church. In March he confirmed nineteen at the same church, and a few weeks later twelve at the Church of the Saviour. The work at both the churches in Osaka, and at the out-stations, showed a very decided advance, and altogether sixty-two souls—forty-two in Osaka and twenty at the out-stations—were added to the Church by baptism. Of the Osaka baptisms thirteen were at the Church of the Saviour, the congregation connected with which thus doubling itself during the first fifteen months of its existence.

Whilst the spiritual work of the mission was thus prospering an important addition was made to its machinery by the erection of Holy Trinity Divinity School, which, although located at Osaka, is the central college for the C.M.S. Japan Mission. Particulars of this institution, as well as of the day-school for boys, opened about the same time, will be found on subsequent pages.

But another movement, dating from the autumn of 1884, has yet to be noticed. At the beginning of the year there was no regularly-appointed catechist at Osaka. Mr. Yamashita was acting in that capacity at one of the out-stations, though nominally still a member of the theological class; Mr.

Nakanishi, whose salary was paid from a local fund, was working regularly in connection with the Church of the Saviour; and Mr. Terasawa, another of the students, rendered valuable assistance at Holy Trinity Church.

During the year the Home Committee intimated that instead of appropriating money for the direct support of catechists at Osaka, they would make a grant to the pastorate fund of the Osaka Church Council. This necessitated a forward movement, and threw more financial responsibility upon the Christians, which their action proved they were not unwilling to assume. It was ultimately decided to appoint two lay pastoral agents—Mr. Terasawa to Holy Trinity, and Mr. Nakanishi to the Church of the Saviour—and to engage Mr. Yamashita as an evangelist. In addition to paying all current church expenses as before, the Holy Trinity congregation undertook to provide the whole of their pastoral agent's salary, and the younger and smaller congregation at the Church of the Saviour made itself responsible for half the amount needed for the same purpose, whilst the Church council, representing both congregations, guaranteed 40 per cent. of the evangelist's salary and expenses. Bishop Poole cordially approved of the arrangements made, and licensed the agents employed by the council.

At the close of 1884, the Rev. G. Chapman arrived at Osaka to join the mission. But in March, 1885, Mr. Warren, the senior missionary, was compelled to return to England, and his connection with the work in which he had taken so large a share, terminated. In addition to the general work of the station, Mr. Warren acted as Secretary of the Japan Mission from the close of 1880. He also took an active part in the translation of the Book of Common Prayer, and gave considerable time to other literary work.

On Mr. Warren's departure, as Mr. Pole was very fully

occupied with his college duties, and could only assist at Sunday services, and as Mr. Chapman was only a student missionary, almost the whole of the general work of the station and its out-stations devolved on Mr. Evington and his native helpers. But in spite of the numerical weakness of the staff available for aggressive work there were many encouraging signs of progress during the year, although there were fewer baptisms by fifteen than in 1884. Fukuyama, first visited the previous year, was occupied as an out-station, and its first-fruits gathered. Work was commenced at Matsuye in Idzumo—the province north of Iwami, in Western Japan, and at Matsubara, a village some ten miles to the east of Osaka, under the hills that skirt the plain; and in both these places there have since been baptisms.

The year 1886 witnessed a larger ingathering than any previous one. Altogether ninety-eight adults and forty-six children were baptized at Osaka and its out-stations, of whom sixty-two adults and twenty-one children were baptized in Osaka. This remarkable increase is the more gratifying because it is the result, under the Divine blessing, of the efforts of the native brethren Nakanishi and Terasawa, and the more earnest members of their congregations.

Holy Trinity Church labours under the disadvantage of being on the Foreign Concession, which in the altered circumstances of the country is less suitable as a missionary centre than in former years, when it was difficult to secure buildings in the city. But in spite of this the congregation continues to grow, and is still the larger of the two connected with the Society in Osaka. At the close of 1886 its membership was nearly 150, including forty children, and the communicants were seventy-six. The congregations on Sundays are larger than ever, and they include an average of nearly forty from the Boys', Girls', and Divinity Schools. On

Christmas Day there were 132 present, and more than fifty received the Lord's Supper.*

At the Church of the Saviour the number of baptisms was exceptionally large in 1886—forty-seven of the adult and fifteen of the infant baptisms having been administered there out of a total of ninety-eight and forty-six respectively for the Osaka centre. The average attendance at the Sunday morning service was more than fifty, and at the afternoon service forty. At the close of the year the total baptized membership was eighty-one, and the communicants were fifty-six.

Both congregations are alive to the importance of self-support and self-extension. The year 1885, with its disastrous floods, a cholera epidemic, and the great depression of trade, was a trying one. The contributions of the Christians were seriously reduced, and sometimes Mr. Terasawa received from his congregation 6 Yen instead of 10 Yen a month. There was a great improvement in 1886, and the Holy Trinity congregation, in addition to raising sufficient for their pastoral agent's salary, and current Church expenses, made a small contribution to evangelistic work. The total amount of the contributions of this congregation in 1886 was Yen 201·23, only some 16 cents more than the year before, but allowing for the decrease of contributions from foreigners, students, and others, and the discontinuance of a monthly offering of 2 Yen from the catechist, the actual increase from the congregation was 50 Yen. Ever since the arrangement was made in the autumn of 1884, the congregation of the Church of the Saviour have paid the moiety of their pastoral agent's salary and the whole of their church expenses, in addition to contributions towards the Evangelistic Fund of the Church

---

* Whilst these pages are passing through the press, we hear that Holy Trinity Church has been taken down to be re-erected in the city.

Council. The total amount of their offerings in 1886 was Yen 111·18. In his report for 1886 Mr. Nakanishi thus speaks of the prospect of the second church becoming self-supporting :—

> The number of believers has greatly increased, still the greater portion of the people are poor, many have removed to a distance, and the number of separate families is small, so that we are not yet able to stand alone; nevertheless by degrees, through the mercy and love of God, I trust that within the next year we shall be able to free the hands of the mother society, whence we have received so much help, and to walk alone.

The congregation of Holy Trinity Church look upon the room rented by the Society in the city as their evangelistic outpost, and they also make the work at Matsubara, ten miles from Osaka, their special care. This latter place has been visited by Miss Caspari, as well as by the catechist, students and others, and in 1886 two adults and one child were baptized there.

The Church of the Saviour, being in the heart of the city, is well situated for preaching to the heathen, and this is regularly carried on every Sunday and Friday evening, and on other stated days of the month. The congregations vary from twenty to fifty. The pastor and members of this congregation also conduct evangelistic meetings for their non-Christian fellow-countrymen at Moriguchi, a village five miles from Osaka in the direction of Kioto. Thus whilst the two congregations are being built up in their holy faith, they are striving to be "lights in the world, holding forth the Word of Life."

These two congregations are now ministered to by native clergymen : Messrs. Terasawa and Nakanishi, who, together with Mr. Terada for the Hakodate station, were admitted to deacon's orders by Bishop Bickersteth on March 6th, 1887.

The ordination took place in Holy Trinity Church, which was matted in native fashion for the occasion. Mr. Evington preached the ordination sermon from 2 Tim. iv. 5 and 1 Thess. v. 13. Mr. Pole read the Litany, the Rev. W. J. Edmonds (formerly connected with East Africa, who reached Osaka in December, 1885) the Epistle, and Mr. Nakanishi the Gospel. The total congregation was 320, of whom 276 were in the body of the church, and about forty in the schoolroom beyond the chancel, the windows between being thrown open. Sixteen foreigners, including the Bishop and clergy, and one hundred Japanese received the Holy Communion.

Less than eleven years before, Mr. Warren baptized the first six converts at Osaka, and now one of them, Mr. Nakanishi, has been ordained as pastor of the congregation of the Church of the Saviour, which he has been mainly instrumental in gathering since October, 1883; whilst Mr. Terasawa, who received many of his early lessons in Christian truth from Mr. Nakanishi, has become the ordained pastor of Holy Trinity Church. What hath *God* wrought! " I planted, Apollos watered ; but God gave the increase. So then neither is he that planteth anything, neither he that watereth ; but God that giveth the increase."

But one or two branches of work in Osaka must be specially mentioned before the out-stations are dealt with. The establishment of a boarding and day-school for girls has been already mentioned as one of the forward movements of 1879. It was opened in June, and at the end of the year there were three boarders and eleven day-scholars connected with it. Miss Oxlad's house was small and inconvenient for a boarding-school. The little chapel, built in 1875, had been removed bodily to a site behind Miss Oxlad's house, and was available for a school-room; but even when a small room had been added to it, and additional accommodation was provided for boarders, there was but little room for expansion. Yet there was steady growth, and in 1883 nineteen boarders and sixteen day-scholars were under instruction for a longer or shorter period; and at the beginning of 1884, fourteen boarders and ten day-scholars returned to resume their studies. But the building was already overcrowded, and all further development absolutely stopped. Matters grew worse in 1885, when less eligible premises had to be taken, and so they continued until the beginning of 1886, when, through the kindness of a lady visiting Japan, it became possible to rent a better house. From that time the school, which had been merely existing for two years, began to grow again, and there are now some fifty girls connected with it, about half of whom are boarders. Since Miss Oxlad's return to England in October, 1884, Miss Boulton, who joined her in December, 1883, has been in charge, and she is now assisted by Miss Hamilton, who reached Osaka in the spring of 1886. A new school building, as recommended by the C.M.S. Japan Conference, is to be erected at a cost of £1,500,* and will be called "The Bishop Poole Girls' School," in memory of the short but helpful episcopate of the first English Bishop in Japan. Although the building will be the property of the C.M.S., and the school will be carried on as heretofore under the supervision of the Society's missionaries, the Society for Promoting Female Education in the East will still be responsible for the teaching staff and the current expenses.

The mental, moral, and religious training afforded by this school is now bearing fruit. Three of the former pupils are now engaged in Christian work—a substantial proof that one object aimed at in establishing the school is being attained. Already one of the first pupils, a bright and promising girl,

---

* Of this amount £900 has been contributed, and the building will be erected as soon as the remainder is forthcoming.

has been taken to be with Christ, whom she early learnt to love and follow. She was the daughter of Mr. Nakanishi, and one of the first two children baptized in Osaka. Not only did

REMOVING THE FIRST OSAKA MISSION CHAPEL ACROSS THE STREET.

she give proof of conversion to God, especially from 1883, but her death and its attendant circumstances in a missionary hospital in 1885, so influenced one of the female patients in the same ward, that she and her husband have since become Christians, and are now members of Mr. Nakanishi's congregation.

Not only has the work of the ladies just referred to been useful to the girls and women, but it prepared the way for the establishment of a school for boys. For some time Christian boys had been allowed to attend the girls' school, and when this was no longer possible after the summer vacation of 1884, it became necessary to decide whether the children of Christians should be left to the purely secular influences of a Government school, or have some provision made for their education on Christian principles. The latter course was adopted, and a school was opened in the room at the rear of Holy Trinity Church on September 4th, with eleven boys, and at the end of the year there were twenty-six. To accommodate this school, and to make room for a few boarders, a building was purchased, re-erected, and adapted for the purpose, the entire cost being met by funds raised locally and private help from home. Mr. Pole has taken the oversight of it from its commencement, and opens it every morning with prayers. The Japanese studies are in the hands of duly qualified native teachers, and the students of the divinity school give the Scripture lessons week by week in turn. English has been taught several hours each week, and in this work Miss Carpari—who was formerly in Sierra Leone, but was transferred to Japan in 1880, and joined the Osaka station in 1883—has rendered valuable assistance. Mrs Edmonds also assisted during the first half-year of 1886; and now the Rev. T. Dunn, who reached Osaka in December, 1886, and Miss Dunn, have taken over the responsibility of the English classes. The school has steadily grown, and at the close of 1886 there were forty-two boys on the roll, of whom fifteen were boarders. They are for the most part the children of Christians, all pay their own fees, and there are no "charity" scholars on the list at all.

The Osaka Divinity School is one of the several training institutions in China and Japan which owe their existence to the munificence of the late William Charles Jones, by whom the China and Japan Native Church and Mission Fund, which bears his name, was established. As soon as the location of the proposed institution was decided on, the committee of this fund made a grant of £2,000 for the building. A site was secured at the end of 1883, and building operations were at once commenced. The corner-stone was laid by Bishop Poole shortly afterwards. It bears the simple inscription—in Japanese on one side, and in English on the other—" To the glory of God this corner-stone was laid, March 3rd, 1884," a testimony to the fact, as the Bishop remarked on the occasion, that the college was erected not for the glory of the Church of England, or of the Church Missionary Society, or of the munificent donor of the fund from which the building grant was made, but for the glory of God alone. In a few months the building was ready for occupation, and on September 29th it was formally opened. Bishop Poole, who was just leaving for California, presided at the opening ceremony, and subsequently made the following entry in the *Visitors' Book* :—

On September 29th, 1884, St. Michael and All Angels' Day, I presided at the opening ceremony of the Holy Trinity Divinity College. There was a large attendance of Japanese Christians, and their hearty singing, and the readiness with which they joined in the responses, as well as their attention to the speeches, was very striking. At the conclusion of the meeting Mr. Warren conducted me through the building, and it is pleasant to record that it is substantial, well-fitted, and admirably arranged for its purpose. It reflects great credit on the hon. architect, the Rev. G. H. Pole. The term, I understand, will begin with six or seven students. If their training is as substantial and thorough as the building, they will be a great power for good in the native Church.

The Rev. H. Evington, who had been in charge of the theological class since the previous January, at once entered upon his duties as Principal *pro tem*. Ultimately the Committee appointed Mr. Pole to the principalship, and he took charge of the college at Christmas. At the close of 1884 there were seven students, Nagasaki and Hakodate each contributing two, and Osaka three. There are now some fifteen students under training, and two of the seniors—Mr. Terasawa, of Osaka, and Mr. Terada, of Hakodate—together with Mr. Nakanishi, who attended the divinity lectures, have been ordained. Mr. Pole has spent an immense amount of time and labour in the preparation of his lectures. They have all been carefully written out both in Japanese and Roman characters, so as to be available for those who may sooner or later share or take up his work, and to form the basis of textbooks on Bible History, the Creeds and Articles, the Prayer Book, Christian Evidences, Church History, &c.

Whilst every effort has thus been made to render the training thorough and solid, the students have been kept in constant touch with practical mission work. Even during term-time they teach in the boys' school, and give evangelistic addresses as their help is needed and can be utilised without interfering with their studies; and during the vacations they are frequently sent out two and two to evangelise in districts where there are openings for work. This will account for the frequent allusions to their presence and work at the outstations.

From the year 1877, when Mr. Warren commenced a special class for women, work amongst the females has been systematically carried on. The wives of the missionaries, the ladies connected with the Female Education Society, and, since the beginning of 1885, Miss Caspari, have taken part in it. Miss Caspari took over the responsibility of carrying on Mr. Warren's class, and in addition to this and other gatherings for women in the city, she has frequently visited Matsubara and other places doing similar work. The door is now open for making enlarged efforts in this direction, and the call for more lady workers is loud and urgent. Who will respond, saying, " Here am I, send me "?

XIV.

THE CHURCH MISSIONARY SOCIETY'S MISSION.

(V.) *Osaka Out-stations.*

"So that ye were ensamples to all that believe. . . . For from you sounded out the word of the Lord."—1 *Thess.* i. 7, 8.

1. *TOKUSHIMA IN SHIKOKU.*

HE important town of Tokushima, formerly the seat of a Daimio, and now the capital of the Tokushima *Ken*, with a population of about seven thousand, was the first C.M.S out-station occupied from Osaka. It is in the island of Shikoku, near its north-eastern coast, and is distant from Osaka sixty or seventy miles, in a south-westerly direction, whence it is reached by steamer under favourable circumstances in six or seven hours. It stands on one of the four streams of the delta of the Yoshino river, two of which form the "Island of Virtue" (Tokushima) from which the town takes its name. Immediately behind the town on its eastern side there are mountains, and near its western suburb there is a solitary hill, rising like an island from the alluvial plain, which once formed the fortified stronghold of the feudal lord of Awa. The massive granite walls raised for its defence, the foundation stones of the residences within the fortified enclosure, and the artificial rock-work and miniature bridges which formerly adorned some of the gardens, may still be seen. "Castle hill" is

well-wooded, and is now a public park; and from its summit may be seen the town and its suburbs, and the numerous villages with which the plain is thickly studded, forming together a grand field for missionary work.

In September, 1880, Mr. Evington spent a few days at Tokushima for change and rest. He was visited by a number of the local officials, and by some of the members of the Greek Church, of whom there were about thirty in the town, and to these and others he had numerous opportunities of speaking the Word. Early in the next year (1881) one of the Greek Christians came to Osaka, and in the name of several others requested that some one might be sent to teach them. Mr. Evington was just leaving for England, and it was determined to send Mr. Aratani, one of the first six Osaka converts, to commence work if there appeared to be an opening. He had the benefit of the counsel and advice of Mr. Thomson, the agent of the National Bible Society of Scotland, who went to visit Tokushima at the same time. There appeared to be an open door, and a house was secured and work commenced. In March and June Mr. Warren went over, and on the latter occasion spent six days there, and was much cheered by the evident signs of interest in the Gospel and progress in the study of it. On three evenings quiet services were held, each of which was attended by a dozen professed inquirers, and on two other evenings there were open meetings for public preaching, one of which was attended by fifty persons. Among the most pleasant reminiscences of this brief visit were the seasons spent in the homes of the people. Evidences were afforded of a careful study of the Word of God, and the greatest interest was shown in turning over the pages of the New Testament; and there was an evident unwillingness to allow the conversation to proceed until texts which had been quoted or referred to had been found verified.

Among those who showed interest in the Gospel were Mr. Kodama, a photographer, and his father and mother, of whom Mr. Warren thus wrote :—

Mr. Kodama is an earnest and intelligent inquirer. He is married, and his father and mother and one of his sisters live in the same house. The father, Mr. Fukui, has not advanced so far as his son, but light seems to be breaking in upon his mind, whilst Mrs. Fukui seems to be quite at one with her son, and considerably in advance of her husband. I paid more than one visit to this family, and was privileged to direct their attention to many things in the written Word. All that passed on these occasions showed a deep thoughtfulness and earnest spirit of inquiry on the part of Mr. Kodama, and a gradual advance towards the truth on the part of his parents.*

But before the first-fruits were baptized there was trial. The Greek Christians, who had been mainly instrumental in moving the Osaka missionaries to attempt work at Tokushima, caused disappointment. For personal reasons, as it appeared, they were unwilling after a time to receive instruction from Mr. Aratani, the acting catechist, and on the arrival of a Baptist missionary from Tokio, they joined themselves to him, and were shortly afterwards re-baptized. The rite was administered publicly in the river. This led to determined opposition to Christian work on the part of the Buddhist priesthood and their followers, and disturbances were created at the preaching rooms of the Baptist and Greek missions. The room in which the work of the C.M.S. had been carried on had to be vacated, and for a time the enemy appeared to triumph. But the inquirers remained steadfast, and in October three of them were baptized. Mr. Kodama was one, but his father and mother held back, as they were apparently afraid that further attacks would be made on the Christians. The

---

* Some years before the son had become the foster-child of a Mr. Kodama, and, according to Japanese custom, had taken his name, and hence the difference of name between parents and son.

fear of man thus hindered them, and their want of decision was a cause of their son's stumbling; for, during the next year, he and another of the converts—both of them photographers—were engaging in business on the Lord's Day. Faithful and loving admonition on the part of Mr. Evington—who returned to Osaka in December, 1881, and took charge of the Tokushima work—recalled both to their duty and privilege; and Mr. Kodama had the joy of seeing his father and mother baptized in August. It was serious illness, which terminated fatally a fortnight after his baptism, that led Mr. Fukui to repent of procrastination and indecision. He confessed his sin, but was told that this would not suffice unless he brought forth fruit worthy of repentance. Among other things it was suggested that he should close his shop on the Lord's Day, which he promised to do, and the Sunday after his baptism it was duly closed, and a notice affixed to the door stating that it was a rest-day. When he died, a few days later, the family had to bear the reproach of being Christians in connection with his burial. Of this Mr. Evington thus wrote :—

A grave had been already purchased in the grounds of a Buddhist temple, but the priest refused permission to bury, closing the gates and offering to return the money. A Shinto priest was then applied to, but it was not till after a night and a day had been spent in running hither and thither, and a promise not to specially mark the grave, that a grave was obtained. The service was performed in the house, and the priest simply acted as registrar. . . . A paragraph relating their troubles was inserted in the local paper, doubtless with a view to ridicule.

There was another baptism before the close of 1882, and several more in the early part of 1883, but the work was marred by a want of unity and hearty friendliness among the few native Christians; and especially by a gross act of indiscretion on the part of the catechist in charge, which was made the occasion for two of the first three converts to join the Greek Church, though laxity in regard to the observance of the Lord's Day, which is allowed by the Greek Church, was probably one of the chief reasons for the transfer of allegiance.

Mr. Aratani returned to Osaka, and his official connection with the mission was soon afterwards closed. To supply his place Mr. Terasawa, one of the theological students, spent his summer vacation at Tokushima, and in September, Mr. Yamashita, another member of the theological class, took up the work. These changes were beneficial, and at the close of the year the outlook was more encouraging than it had ever been before. The attendance of heathen at the preaching services was larger; there were several interesting inquirers; whilst the Christians manifested "greater earnestness, more love and unanimity amongst themselves," and were more regular in their attendance at the means of grace, one man walking quite seven miles to church on the Sunday, and returning in the evening.

From the beginning of 1884 Mr. Evington took charge of the Osaka Theological Class, and the practical oversight of the out-stations devolved on Mr. Warren. He visited Tokushima in January, and spent a very happy week in intercourse with the native Christians and inquirers, and on Sunday, January 27th, he had the joy of baptizing four adults, and three children of parents previously baptized. Two of the adults were Mr. Mori, a local Government official, and his friend Mr. Miyaki, an elementary school teacher. The day after their baptism they showed their colours by inviting their friends and neighbours to a meeting, which was held in Mr. Mori's house, to hear addresses from Mr. Warren and two of the native brethren. Mr. Mori is now a student in the Osaka Theological College, and gives promise of future usefulness.

In the following May Mr. Warren spent another week at Tokushima, and, in addition to other interesting work, prepared some of the Christians for Confirmation. Thursday, May 13th, was a red-letter day in the history of the little Church. Bishop Poole arrived early in the morning. After breakfast he received a number of the Christians, and in the afternoon met the Church committee, which had been formed earlier in the year. From the first the duty of self-support had been inculcated ; but a year before the Bishop's visit the Church expenses were not fully met by the contributions of the native Christians. A little temporary help was sent from Osaka, and when this ceased at the beginning of 1884 the catechist in charge contributed a small sum monthly ; but from March the Christians decided to contribute the necessary sum—$2 50c. a month—without any such assistance. The Bishop was much pleased with the progress thus shown, and urged and encouraged the Church committee to go forward in their work.

The Bishop had much pleasant intercourse with the Christians in their homes, and at the inn where he stayed ; but the principal event of the visit was the Confirmation, which in true apostolic fashion took place in "an upper room" on the evening of May 13th. Owing to the removal of three adult Christians to Osaka, where they were subsequently confirmed, and the absence from home of two others, seven, instead of twelve, were presented to the Bishop.

During a part of the summer vacation, Mr. Yamashita was assisted in his evangelistic work by one of the theological students. Mr. Warren paid another visit in August, and baptized four more adults, making for the year a total of eight adults and three children. Owing, however, to changes and removals, there was not that apparent growth in the congregation which is so desirable in the infancy of a mission.

Still the year had been one of decided progress, and but for a dark cloud which appeared just at its close—the reported immorality of two of the Christians—the outlook would have been most cheering. When Mr. Evington visited Tokushima in January and March, 1885, the shadow of this cloud was making itself felt, and the little band of Christians was further weakened by the removal of another—one of the most consistent of the number—to Tokio. Since the commencement of the mission there had been altogether eighteen adults baptized. Of these two, as already noticed, had joined the Greek Church, one had died, and eight had removed to Osaka and elsewhere, and of the remaining seven only four regularly attended the services. Mr. Yamashita and others continued their evangelistic efforts during 1885, and since March, 1886, Mr. Makioka, formerly of Niigata and Tokio, has been working zealously. But during 1886 there were no baptisms, though at its close there were three catechumens under instruction. Tokushima has proved a difficult field. The people, as Mr. Makioka remarks, are "shallow and wanting in moral strength," and "their customs are very loose, and lewdness and impurity are rampant."

The American Baptists have closed their work at Tokushima, and several of their converts and one or two from other places have in some measure repaired the loss by removals. At the close of 1886 there were, including these, twelve baptized Christians and eight communicants.

But if the progress in Tokushima has been tardy, a very encouraging commencement has been made at Tomioka, some fourteen miles distant. Both Mr. Yamashita and the students who helped him in their vacations, and Mr. Evington, visited this place in 1885. A doctor with whom Mr. Evington came in contact, and who professed to be interested, told him of his wife's father who had "read the New Testament through seven times, and rejoiced to find himself beginning to understand the meaning." The case of this man, who is living at Kotajuna-mura, a village between two and three miles from Tomioka, is thus given by Mr. Makioka:—

This man is forty-nine years of age and very peculiar. Seven or eight years ago he was a policeman, and afterwards became "kocho" (head of the village.—H. E.). Whilst kocho he bought a copy of the New Testament in Chinese, with diacritical marks to assist in the reading, and by degrees perceived that he ought to worship Christ. From this time he gave up his whole time to the study of the Scriptures, and, finally (dreadful to relate), placing bread and wine upon a shelf after assembling his family, brake the bread and said, "This is Christ's flesh," then taking the wine, he said, "This is Christ's blood." He then caused his family to eat and drink. He punished his wife because she did not believe in the true God, and told her that such as she were unfit to live, rather she ought to have a mill-stone tied to her neck and be drowned. For five years he gave up his work and made the reading of Scripture and prayer his duty; latterly, however, he has perceived his mistakes, and grieved over them, and has received baptism.

How marvellously was this man led from darkness into light! And how beautifully in his case was the promise realised, " If any man willeth to do His will he shall know of the teaching." Not only has he received Christ himself, " but he has led his wife and family, a neighbour and his family, and his married daughter with her husband and family, to the truth," so that the year 1886 closed with seventeen baptized Christians—five men, five women, and seven children— and one catechumen in Tomioka and its neighbourhood.

2. *IWAMI.*

Iwami is one of the provinces at the western extremity of the main island, and to reach its coast district from Osaka a journey of several days is necessary. The usual route is by steamer down the Inland Sea to Hiro-shima (Broad-island), on the coast of Aki, a voyage of from twenty-four to thirty hours, and thence by road across Aki and Iwami, both mountainous provinces, a walking journey of two or three days. Another route is sometimes taken from Hiro-shima, a day's *jinrikisha* ride to Miyoshi, and thence by boat for some fifty miles down the river to the coast. There are some rapids in the river, though not of such a character as to cause much excitement, and the mountain scenery through which the river flows the entire distance is most charming. Hamada, the chief town of Iwami, may be reached by steamer direct from Osaka in the summer months, but the dates of sailing and delay *en route* are uncertain, and it is generally more expeditious to travel by one of the routes just mentioned.

The Osaka missionaries were led to commence work in Iwami under deeply interesting circumstances. Mrs. Kubota, a widow, one of the Osaka Christians, who ever since her conversion in 1878 has been a humble but earnest worker for Christ, became a shampooer, and she chose this occupation because, whilst it enabled her to earn something towards the maintenance of herself and her two daughters, it gave her opportunities of placing the Gospel before strangers who might employ her in the Osaka inns.

In the spring of 1882 she in this way made the acquaintance of a young medical man and his wife, who were spending several weeks in Osaka. From what she told them they became interested in Christianity, and at her invitation subsequently attended the Sunday services at Holy Trinity Church. By this means their interest was deepened, and they purchased the New Testament and other Christian books, and began to study them. When the time came for them to return to their village home in Iwami, they expressed their determination to renounce idolatry, and serve the living and true God. Communication was kept up with them by letter, and soon they wrote to say that others to whom they had spoken, and shown the Christian books, were equally with themselves desirous of receiving instruction in Christian truth.

During the summer vacation, Messrs. Terasawa and Yamashita, two of the Osaka theological students, spent several weeks in Iwami, and as it seemed desirable to follow up the work that had been commenced, one, Mr. Terasawa, remained until December. Mr. Evington then paid his first visit, of which he gives the following account in his Annual Letter for 1882 :—

I found eight or ten people taking a greater or less interest in the way of salvation, six of them looking forward to baptism. My visit extended over ten days, during which time I preached, &c., in Gotsu, Watadzu, and Kawanobori,* as well as visiting for conversation at their own homes those whom the acting catechist had put forward as ready for baptism. These were the doctor, his wife, and grandmother, and a man named Noda, with his wife. I was very pleased with the earnestness of Dr. Santo and his wife, who do not seem to hide their light under a bushel, and instead of being moved by the opposition that was raised their faith became strengthened. I baptized them, with their grandmother, an old lady of about seventy, on December 17th. Noda's case is an interesting one. He was originally a Buddhist priest of the Jodo sect, but had resigned his office and married some ten years ago; since then he has been engaged in trade. When Terasawa and Yamashita first arrived in Watadzu he came forward to oppose them; . . . seeking to argue and cavil. However, before he had become an inquirer, not more than three days after their arrival, when they were obliged to leave their hotel because of the landlord's fears, he offered them shelter under his own roof. Since he has become an earnest inquirer we have had testimony from all around to the change in his character. His rough, boisterous manner towards both his wife and others has wonderfully toned down, and he is willing to listen and be taught. He, with his two children, were baptized on the same day with Dr. Santo. His wife, I felt, had not sufficient knowledge and personal interest to justify her baptism at present, although she partly expected it; she feels the power that it has had over her husband.

* Gotsu is on the left, and Watadzu on the right bank of the river Go, not far from its mouth, and Kawanobori some distance higher up the river.

At the time this interesting opening occurred it was impossible to locate an evangelist in the district, and the Christians were instructed to meet on the Lord's Day, and at other times, for united prayer and mutual exhortation and instruction, and do what they could to win their neighbours to Christ.

The faith of one of this little band—Mr. Noda—was soon severely tested. Mr. Evington thus refers to it :—

He was summoned by his relatives to his home, and his mother, who is now an old woman, expressed her grief upon hearing that he had become a Christian. She begged him to recant, saying that if he would she would give him a certain amount of land ; his brother also offered him a house as an additional inducement. The old lady further added, that if he would continue his connection with Christianity, though she was aged, and the parting would be an immense grief to her, she should nevertheless cease to have any communication with him. After a moment or two's hesitation, he told them that he had been brought out of darkness into light, and that even if he lost the property and his relatives he could not go back to darkness.

Nor was this all, for on his return home he was turned out of his house by the landlord, and another house he was desirous of renting was refused to him, solely because he was a Christian. These trials not only failed to move Noda San, but they were the occasion of an expression of practical sympathy on the part of the Osaka Christians for their persecuted brother, to whom they sent a sum of money to help him in his difficulty.

Mr. Evington visited the district twice in 1883—in May and November—and Mr. Tsuda and Mr. Yamashita, two of the students, spent their summer vacation of two months there, in teaching the Christians and preaching in the neighbouring villages. On the occasion of Mr. Evington's November visit he baptized the innkeeper at Watadzu, and his wife and child. This man had been interested in the Gospel some months, and had allowed the use of his upper room for the regular meetings of the Christians without charge, and now having given proof of his decision for Christ by removing every vestige of idolatry from his house, he was received as a member of the little flock.

There was another most promising catechumen, well acquainted with the Scriptures, but as his father was opposed to his becoming a Christian, and refused to allow him to rest from his ordinary occupation on the Lord's Day, his baptism was deferred. This young man—Mr. Sakata—was, however, baptized during Mr. Pole's visit to Iwami at Easter, 1884, when Mr. Noda also had the joy of seeing his wife received.

Mr. Evington's November visit was, however, chiefly characterised by some interesting work at Hamada, the important town already mentioned, which is about fifteen miles from Watadzu. In the evening of the day of his arrival he preached to forty persons assembled in two adjoining rooms—thrown into one by the removal of the paper sliding screens by which they were separated—in the inn where he was staying. Of the next day's preaching, Sunday, November 25th, Mr. Evington thus wrote :—

In the evening, for want of a preaching-place, I was obliged to stand and preach in the open air. Kowari, the servant of a society which had its offices in the back of my hotel, rendered us considerable service, by securing permission to use a piece of open ground, and then fixing up table and lanterns for pulpit and light. Quite 100 people stood and listened, in spite of the cold, and, with the exception of a few cries of " Yes, yes," " No, no," and their Japanese equivalents, no disturbance whatever was made.

On three other evenings similar audiences were addressed. On the first occasion the place of preaching was the inn—the people, numbering about 100, being accommodated in two or three small adjoining rooms, or standing outside. On the second and third evenings, as the landlord of the inn refused to open his house in the same way again, other arrangements had to be made. Mr. Evington thus speaks of them :—

We were going outside to preach in the open air again, in spite of the cold, when an old man said we should have either his son's house or his own. We were soon afterwards conducted to the house, taking our audience with us. When the preaching commenced, the three rooms of the house, thrown into one, were filled with 100 people. I took for my text Rom. vi. 23, and was listened to with attention. The day following we repeated the experience of this evening. Both Noda and I addressed a full house.

Several incidents of the visit afforded evidence of the spread of Christian truth in remote parts of the country, among those who are outside the Christian Church. One young man, a lawyer, " spoke loudly in favour of Christianity." Another who had "received Christian instruction" at Nagasaki, and knew Mr. Maundrell, though having some difficulties about the Trinity, said " that he read his Bible and prayed." Several others were " in possession of the Scriptures, and partly convinced of the need of Christianity for Japan," whilst many had taken in, at any rate intellectually, " the idea of the unity of God the Creator, and also the substitution of Jesus Christ for the sinner." Sad it is to add, that in the midst of so many apparently feeling after truth, a baptized Christian was met who was hiding his light, and who was subsequently reported to be " quietly opposing the truth."

The work thus initiated was followed up by Mr. Pole, Mr Terasawa, and Mr. Warren. Mr. Pole paid a second visit in November, and in addition to interesting preaching services in Mr. Kowari's house, he had the joy and privilege of administering baptism to Kowari and four others. If the unfaithfulness of one baptized Christian was calculated to discourage the inquirers, the earnest and patient efforts of another, who was detained in Hamada for some time on business, did much to help them forward. This was Mr. Hori, a member of the

Presbyterian Church, who did everything in his power to assist the C.M.S. missionaries during their visits, and to lead on the catechumens in the way of truth.

In May, 1885, Mr. Evington baptized three more adults and one child; and during his visit a Church Committee was formed, and it was agreed that each family should make a monthly contribution, to defray any expenses connected with Christian worship or evangelistic services.

Bishop Bickersteth visited Hamada in October, 1886, and confirmed five persons, and on the day following they met at 5 A.M. for Holy Communion, before the Bishop and Mr. Evington left for Misumi.

The Iwami province is comparatively thinly populated, and as it has not been possible so far to keep a catechist steadily at work there, the growth of the work has been comparatively slow. Evangelistic efforts have, however, been made from time to time not only in Watadzu and Hamada and the neighbouring villages, but also at Masuda, twenty-five miles south-west of Hamada, which was first visited by Mr. Pole in November, 1884, and Misumi, midway between the two places, which was first visited by Mr. Warren in the summer of the same year, and several other places. But the harvest is yet future.

3. *MATSUYE, IN IDZUMO.*

The chief feature of interest in the work in the far west of the main island in 1885, was its extension to Matsuye in Idzumo—the province adjoining Iwami on the north-east. Mr. Evington thus describes the position of Matsuye :—

Matsuye is situated on an inland sea about twenty-seven miles in length, and in most places from twelve to fifteen miles wide. It is entered from the Japan Sea by a long but narrow channel. At Matsuye, which is built about the centre of this sea, it becomes so narrow that it can be crossed by a bridge, and the town lies on either shore.

It is the seat of Government for the Shimane *Ken*, which includes the provinces of Idzumo, Hoki, and Iwami, and is the largest town in the prefecture, having a population of about 30,000 or 40,000, and being better built and to all appearances more prosperous than Hamada, the chief town of Iwami. Among its principal buildings are several Government offices, the building occupied by the normal and middle-schools, and a public lecture-hall, called the Ko-do-kuwan. The remains of the former 'daimio's castle are very picturesque, chiefly "on account of the trees, which have grown to a great size within its massive stone walls." There are "good shops of every kind," well stocked "with native and foreign articles."

It was from Iwami that the Word of the Lord sounded out into Idzumo, and reached Matsuye. In the autumn of 1884, when Mr. Pole was in Iwami, "quite a little company, who expressed a desire to know something of Christianity, offered to meet him half-way, if he would go to them." This was not then possible, and the proposed meeting did not take place. In January, 1885, one of the Iwami Christians—Mr. Noda, a Bible colporteur—met these people, and found that most of them were influenced by mixed motives, being desirous of pecuniary help to buy some land. Further communications were received subsequently both by letter and telegram, and eventually in the spring of 1885 two native Christians— Mr. Arato, a theological student, and Mr. Hara, a colporteur —visited Matsuye. On their arrival they arranged with those who were interested in their visit to have a week's preaching in the Ko-do-kuwan—the public hall already mentioned. Mr. Evington joined them the day after the first meeting was held, and on the remaining six nights of the week they preached to crowded audiences. On each of the first two nights 600 were crowded into the room of sixty mats, equal to a room 30 feet by 16. On one wet night the *geta* (clogs) or shoes showed that at least 700 were present, and "on several nights it was necessary to close the doors, and many were unable to get in at all." These meetings, which were times of broad-cast seed-sowing, were followed by quieter and more private gatherings, for the few who appeared to be really interested. Out of at least eleven who assisted in making arrangements, only three were found among the special inquirers. Eventually seven altogether promised to meet on the Lord's Day for prayer and reading the Scriptures. They were visited and instructed by one of the theological students during the summer vacation of 1885, and in the spring of 1886, on the occasion of Mr. Evington's second visit, six adults and four children were baptized. In November Bishop Bickersteth visited Matsuye, and held a Confirmation for the adult Christians. The town is an important educational centre, and the Bishop gave two addresses to some of the students, "seventy of whom attended and listened with interest." "The number of inquirers steadily increases," and there is a prospect of a large in-gathering of souls.

4. FUKUYAMA.

Fukuyama is a town in the province of Bingo, a few miles distant from O-no-michi, a port on the Inland Sea. The Rev. G. H. Pole was the first of the Osaka missionaries to visit this town. On his way to Iwami, in November, 1884, he spent a night at the house of his teacher's father, who was residing there, and had an opportunity of addressing some twenty persons who assembled to hear him. In returning from Iwani he paid a similar visit, and from 200 to 300 attended the preaching. An interest was created, which was deepened and extended by the visit of Mr. Evington and three of the theological students in the following spring. All four in turn addressed a large meeting of 400 persons. Two of the students left on the day following for Iwami and Matsuye respectively, but the third, Mr. Kodama, and Mr. Evington remained. They preached to another large audience in the evening. On Sunday, April 12th, quiet services were held in the room which Mr. Evington occupied at the inn where he was staying. In the evening there was a further meeting for the inquirers at the house of a Dr. Kamegawa. It took the form of a prayer meeting, and Mr. Evington and his native associate again exhorted those present. On this occasion nine asked for baptism. Mr. Evington left for Matsuye two days later, but Mr. Kodama remained, and during the fortnight he continued his efforts three more catechumens were added to the number. The Rev. G. Chapman, who was staying at Fukuyama for some time during the progress of this interesting work—though only as a student-missionary, for he had only reached Japan in December, 1884—no doubt did much by his presence and teaching to help and encourage the catechumens. Mr. Kodama subsequently spent his summer vacation there, and in September Mr. Nakanishi and Mr. Chapman went down (Mr. Evington being unable to go owing to some difficulty about his passport), and after examination, Mr. Chapman baptized ten adults. Two others would have been included in the number, but one was removed by death shortly before, and the other had gone to a distant town in Government service, where, however, he attached himself to a body of Presbyterian Christians.

Mr. Kodama, whose name will ever be associated with the foundation of the Fukuyama Church, and who gave promise of being most useful in building it up, was taken by the Master to a higher sphere in the spring of 1886. He was one of the first three baptized at Tokushima in October, 1881, and in the spring of 1884 he removed, with his family, to

Osaka to join the theological class. His wife died in the summer of 1885, and he followed her a few months later, leaving his widowed mother and two children behind. A passage from a simple English letter which he wrote to the Rev. C. F. Warren in October, 1885, may well follow our brief notice of this promising young worker.

> In April I went to Fukuyama with Mr. Evington, and remained there three weeks and preached. Many persons came there; and every day many of them came to my hotel to hear the Gospel. Some Sunday about twelve of them told me they wished to be baptized, and I preached to them about baptism. After that they always met in the name of Jesus Christ, and they are greatly comforted. In the summer vacation I went there again and remained two months. All brothers are faithful to the Lord. 20th September ten brothers were baptized by Mr. Chapman, and they are therefore the beginning of the Fukuyama Church.

The work has since spread to the village of Yera, six miles distant from Fukuyama, and the small town of Fuchiu, apparently a little further off, as Yera-mura is spoken of as the half-way house where the Christians of the three places sometimes hold united meetings. "Rooms for Christian worship have been secured in all three places," and the Christians "are not backward in giving of their substance to the Lord."

"The movement towards Christianity," in Fuchiu, "has been specially encouraging." Mr. Chapman, who spent the autumn of 1886 at Fukuyama, says of the Fuchiu work:—

> The Christians are all of the better class and are all very earnest, especially an influential merchant. He has opened a school for the teaching of English, and would almost give all his possessions to get some resident English teacher, which at present seems impossible. There have been six baptisms here, and two have been admitted as catechumens.

Among the Christians at the village of Yera is one man

baptized in January, 1886. "He is a farmer of no special education." Before his baptism he used to drag his heavy cart over the bad roads to Fukuyama on Saturday, spend Sunday with the Christians, and return home on Monday morning. He is now the peacemaker—"the great settler of disputes for the village." Referring to this, Mr. Evington says :—

It was related of him in my presence, a few days ago, that instead of doing as the ordinary middlemen do, going to the house of each and speaking ill of the others, he gets the disputants together and sits between them, then laying open the New Testament, explains to them their duty of being reconciled to one another, with the general result that a true understanding is come to, and the cause of trouble removed.

Bishop Bickersteth visited Fukuyama in October, 1886, and confirmed "ten persons of all ages in the back room of the Japanese inn, and afterwards gave them their first Communion," and in a few days later another was confirmed at Fuchiu.

At Fukuyama there were six catechumens at the end of 1886, and two more asked for baptism early in 1887. Mr. Chapman says :—" The outlook is promising, as many outsiders are now interested in our religion and wish to know more about it." God grant that these " Churches " may have rest and be edified, and walking in the fear of the Lord, and in the comfort of the Holy Ghost may be multiplied. " Brethren, pray for us, that the word of the Lord may run and be glorified, even as it is with you."

XV.

THE CHURCH MISSIONARY SOCIETY'S MISSION.

(VI.) *Tokio.*

"Ye shall be gathered one by one."—*Isa.* xxvii. 2.

THE first C.M.S. Missionary to Tokio was the Rev. J. Piper, who with Mrs. Piper, reached Yokohama in April, 1874, and shortly afterwards removed to the capital. A little later they were joined by the Rev. P. K. Fyson and Mrs. Fyson. We do not think of missionaries in civilised Japan having to undergo much personal privation, as in Africa and North-West America, but the experience of our first missionaries to Tokio shows that discomforts were not unknown even there. Mrs. Piper thus describes their first dwelling :—

There is a corner or bit of land near the sea, outside the city proper, which has been allotted to foreign residents; this is the only place where they are free to buy, build, or rent houses. The place is called Tsukiji. My husband found one place, and only one, where we might live in Tsukiji. Several of our friends who have seen the house since we left say, " How *did* you live in such a place?" and indeed I often wonder how we did pass two hot summers in such a close, low dwelling. The house was half a house, if I may use such a contradiction of terms. There were eight rooms all under one roof, all the rooms exactly alike—twelve feet square, no kitchens, no outhouse, nothing but walls and floors. Four of these rooms were occupied by a Scotch missionary, and Mr. Piper secured the other four rooms for our first residence in Japan.

Of course we must have a kitchen of some sort. My husband engaged a carpenter to make us one, which when completed looked more like a large packing-case at the side of the house than a kitchen; no windows and no chimney, for the place was too small to hold a foreign cooking-stove. We used nothing during the year and a half we lived in that house but Japanese charcoal and native fireplace, for there no chimneys are made; the smoke goes where it can, or where the wind drives it to.

We spent many happy days in that funny little house, and often now we recall the first evening spent there, the joy we felt at having a home of our own; and after five years in Japan we think of our first home with great satisfaction.

BAY OF YEDO (TOKIO).

During the eighteen months that Mr. and Mrs. Piper occupied this humble cottage residence their chief work was the study of the language. But time was found for numerous other occupations. Visitors were received and acquaintances formed, and in 1875, a Bible-class for natives was commenced. Besides, Mr. Piper as secretary of the Japan Mission, had much business of a general character to attend to. He also took a leading part in forming local committees of the British and Foreign Bible and Religious Tract Societies, of which he continued one of the most active members during the whole of his residence in Japan; and he and Mr. Fyson, in the absence of an English chaplain at Yokohama, carried on the English services there for more than a year, and also conducted services for the officers and men belonging to the British Navy who were employed as instructors in the Naval Training School at Tokio. In the autumn of 1875 Mr. Fyson was transferred to Niigata; and from that time until May, 1879—nearly four years—Mr. Piper was the only C.M.S. missionary at the capital.

Whilst the residence of foreigners is by the Treaty of 1858 limited to the settlements at the open ports, Government permission has often been obtained for them to reside elsewhere. In this way many foreigners, either directly employed by the Government as professors, teachers, or in some other capacity, or engaged by companies or individuals for educational, manufacturing, or commercial purposes, reside beyond the limits of the settlements, and in other places than the open ports. Missionaries desirous of getting into the country and extending their influence have sometimes made engagements to teach in schools or families in order to obtain this privilege. It was in this way that Mr. Piper was able to rent and occupy a more suitable house some distance from the foreign settlement, to which he moved towards the close of 1875. Preparation was now made to commence active and aggressive work. A portion of the premises, which had formerly been used as a shop, was fitted up as a mission-room, and became the centre of the Society's Tokio work for more than two years. The year 1876 was one of hopeful beginnings. On the Feast of the Epiphany, the first public service was held in the newly occupied premises; on Whit Sunday, June 4th, a young man who had attended the Bible-class commenced by Mr. Piper in the previous year was baptized; on October 1st there were four more baptisms, and on the same day the first Confirmation was held by Bishop Burdon; on October 15th the Holy Communion was administered for the first time to the Christians; and on Christmas Day the first informal Church Committee was formed. Mr. Piper having thus early invited the converts to consult with him on the affairs of the Church and the work of the mission.

During 1876, preaching and other services and Bible-classes were regularly held, and good congregations assembled from time to time to hear the Word of God. These efforts were continued in the following year, although the congregations were not so large, owing in part to the diversion of traffic by the closing of a bridge for some months for repairs, but chiefly in consequence of the Satsuma rebellion having unsettled men's minds. There were, nevertheless, good audiences nearly every time Mr. Piper preached.

The work was extended by renting a second room for evangelistic services, and then Mr. Piper preached regularly during the latter part of 1877. He also made several excursions into the suburbs, "distributing tracts, and telling of Jesus." These public efforts were frequently followed by private intercourse with individuals, some of whom appeared to be near the Kingdom of God, but afterwards discontinued their visits, and were lost sight of.

During 1877, five adults and three children were baptized, one of whom was Mr. Fuyeki, a builder and contractor, who continued faithful until he fell asleep in 1885.

In reviewing the work of the year Mr. Piper thus speaks of the "little flock":—

There are two features in our little flock which especially encourage me to hope for and believe in its permanency and growth. (1) They begin to associate with and visit each other because of their common faith. (2) The majority of our married Christians, both husband and wife, have embraced the truth—thus they help each other. As an instance of this mutual help I may mention that only last Sunday a young man who was baptized last year, told me that if he forgets to say "grace before meat," his wife looks at him and says, " You have forgotten."

Towards the close of 1877 the Government, for some reasons, seemed to be desirous of reducing, as far as possible, the number of foreigners residing outside the foreign settlements

MISSION CHURCH AT TOKIO.

and the permission granted to several missionaries to live in different parts of Tokio was withdrawn. Mr. Piper was affected by this action, and was compelled to seek a residence on the Tsukiji Settlement. He was fortunately able to secure suitable premises, which from the spring of 1878 became the centre of the Society's Tokio work. A neat little church was erected on the corner of the mission lot, the entire cost of which, exclusive of old material which was available

P

for the building, was $1,200—say £240—all of which was contributed by friends on the spot or in England. The labours of our Tokio brethren amongst the English residents both there and at Yokohama have been already referred to. Some of those who appreciated their ministrations manifested great interest in the erection of the church. To their generous and loving gifts Mr. Piper thus refers :—

> In justice to some who have sent me sums without asking, it may be said that one gentleman handed me a cheque for $100 (£20), and a like sum was put into my hands by a British seaman, for some time in the service of the Japanese Government, and who was really brought to Jesus through the means of a Bible-class carried on by Mrs. Piper, and an English service which Mr. Fyson and I used to hold whilst we were studying the language. This seaman, who is now in England, and writes to Mrs. Piper, wished to show his gratitude to Almighty God, and felt that he could not do it in a better way than helping His cause in the land where his own soul had been savingly converted. $25 (£5) were sent to me some time ago by an English nurse in Yokohama, through the chaplain at that port, in remembrance (as she said) of my services during the time there was no chaplain there.

The new church was dedicated on May 5th, 1878, by Bishop Burdon. Mr. Piper thus wrote respecting it :—

> The church will seat 150 persons comfortably, and many more might find room on special occasions.
> We held the first service in it on Sunday, April 7th, when four persons were baptized, and the Holy Communion was adminstered. It was a day of great joy to Mrs. Piper and myself, and to all our Christians, now 18 (*i.e.*, baptized) in number.
> On May 2nd Bishop Burdon came up from Hong-Kong to be present at our C.M.S. Conference, and on Sunday (May 5th) we had a Dedication Service in English. I commenced our ordinary Japanese service at 9 A.M., an hour earlier than usual ; and at its close we had the Holy Communion. At eleven o'clock the English service commenced. It was well attended by the English and American residents, among whom were Sir Harry and Lady Parkes, and the American Minister and his wife. The Bishop preached an appropriate sermon, after which a collection was made

amounting to $100 (£20), and thirty-five persons stayed for the Holy Communion.

In the afternoon of the following Sunday (May 12th) we had a special service in Japanese, inviting all the members of the American Episcopal Church and S.P.G. to join with us. There were at least 120 Christians present, and about 100 others, mostly heathen. The church was crowded, and the whole service, which lasted three hours, was a joyous sight, and will not be easily forgotten by those who were present.

In addition to the services and meetings in the new church, evangelistic services were held in the room which Mr. Piper had secured in the city before the close of 1877. Three times a week the Word was preached to good congregations, and much precious seed was sown by the distribution of small tracts at the close of the services. In making full use of both these means of disseminating Christian truth Mr. Piper showed much commendable zeal. He was contented to be "a sower," knowing that if he himself did not reap, fruit to God's glory would be found in due time.

In 1878 there were fewer baptisms than in the previous year, but the case of Mr. Tsurumoto was a particularly interesting one. Mr. Piper thus wrote of him :—

He was a policeman in this city, with a very slight knowledge of English. He was led to think and inquire about Christianity by a few sentences in (I think) Peter Parley's book. He came to see me first at the close of 1876, and, as usual with inquirers, I proposed that we should read a Gospel together. He expressed his willingness to do so, and we commenced reading that of St. Matthew in the Japanese language, as his knowledge of English was very limited indeed. He came very regularly, as his duties would permit him. We read as far as the twelfth chapter in the course of a few months, during which time he manifested a thoughtful and anxious interest. In March, 1877, soon after the Satsuma rebellion broke out, he suddenly disappeared. Of course I felt anxious to know what had become of him. I had become very much drawn towards him, and looked upon him as one "not far from the kingdom of God." About two months passed away without our hearing a word from or of him, when, to my thankful surprise, a short letter came from him, written amidst the scenes of the civil war. He therein told me that he had been suddenly ordered to the south, and had no time to come and tell me. He further said he had not forgotten the truths he had learned with me—indeed, they had comforted him amidst the dreadful scenes through which he was passing.

Three months more passed over, and further tidings came from him. Again, at the end of that time, I received a few lines from him, informing me that he would like to come and see us, but was unable because he was suffering from a bullet-wound received in the war, and had been brought back to Tokio, and was in a hospital some two miles from our house. One of our Christians and I took an early opportunity of finding him out at the hospital where he was lying. We found him cheerful, and with the Gospel by his bedside, not afraid of speaking of Christianity in the presence of his fellow-sufferers. We visited him several times, and he seemed to be gradually improving, when, to our sorrow, at our next visit, we saw him in a separate room in a state of madness! His wife and child were there, but he did not know her or us. The dreadful sights at the seat of war had so told upon him, and the wound was so severe, that madness ensued. The next time we went to see him he was still raving, and even worse than before.

We came away feeling certain that he would soon die, and our hearts were very sad. You can imagine the feelings of gratitude and utter astonishment which came over us one morning at breakfast, when the servant came and announced the presence of this very man, restored, and "in his right mind"! He had come as soon as he could to thank us for all our kindness, and to ask that he might soon be baptized. His lameness, and the strange, somewhat wild, look on his face, excited in our hearts mingled feelings of sorrow and praise to God. After a short time I baptized him in our new church on Sunday, May 26th, rejoicing with all our Christians that this our brother, whom we had two or three times given up as "dead," "was alive again,", and the more than once seemingly "lost" "found." It was meet that we should be "merry" in the highest sense. In our estimation his case is a deeply interesting episode connected with the great Satsuma rebellion.

Tsurumoto became an intelligent and earnest Christian, and his conduct did much to commend the Gospel to his heathen relatives. When he first became interested in Christianity his wife and most of his relatives were devoted idolators, and nothing seemed less likely than that they—especially his wife and father—would become Christians. But, by God's mercy, it was otherwise. His wife was the first to be won, and she was baptized in December, 1879. It was mainly through his influence, combined with the teaching at a Bible Class held by Mrs. Piper at his father's house that Tsurumoto's father, aunt, elder brother, and sister, were led to Christ. They were baptized in 1880, some two years after Tsurumoto's conversion.

Although he never fully recovered from the wound he received in the war of the Satsuma rebellion, Tsurumoto was always a zealous worker for Christ in connection with the mission. He frequently assisted at the preaching services in the Mission-room, and did excellent work as teacher of the mixed school, presently to be noticed. After a faithful and consistent course of more than four years he entered into rest on the 12th September, 1882. Mr. Williams, who was then in charge of the Tokio work, thus wrote of his funeral :—

> The day after his death, the Christians of our own and other missions assembled to pay the last mark of respect to all that remained of their departed brother. Bishop Williams, of the American Episcopal Mission, was present; and it was very touching to see assembled the school children for whose good poor Tsurumoto had so patiently laboured. After the first part of the service was ended many of those present followed the corpse to the cemetery in the suburbs; and there, in the grounds of the Buddhist temple, we committed the body of our brother to the earth with Christian rites, in "sure and certain hope of the resurrection to eternal life." He was in many respects a most estimable man, and his death has been a great loss to us.

Mrs. Piper's zealous labours not only helped individual souls towards the kingdom of God, as in the case of the members of Mr. Tsurumoto's family, but they led to the establishment of the Sunday and day schools which are still carried on. Towards the close of 1878 she commenced a little Sunday-school in the city preaching room. In the following February Mr. Piper, with the assistance of one or two of the native Christians, commenced another in the church. In March the two were amalgamated, and the united school was carried on under Mrs. Piper's superintendence. From that time, whether carried on under Mr. and Mrs. Piper and their successors, or, as in 1884, by Mr. Makioka, the pastoral catechist in charge, the great and fundamental truths summarised in the Creed, Lord's Prayer, and Ten Commandments were systematically taught, and many important passages of Holy Scripture were committed to memory by the children. The attendance has varied from twenty to fifty.

How the mixed day-school, which has proved one of the most successful vernacular educational efforts in connection with the C.M.S. Japan Mission, was commenced, will appear from the following extract from one of Mr. Piper's letters :—

From a small sewing class which my wife formed in 1878, the idea of a day-school arose, and in September last (1879)—after circulating notices in our neighbourhood—we used the vestry behind the church as a school, till we could ascertain whether we should be justified in going to the expense of building one. The plan more than answered our expectations, and consequently we have built a small school adjoining the church which will seat fifty or sixty scholars. It was built and furnished with funds which we had received from friends in England. The native Christians spontaneously gave yen 15—somewhat more than £2. The new building was opened on December 1st, and now there are thirty-one scholars on the books. The teaching is all in the vernacular. The man who was wounded in the Satsuma rebellion, and of whom I spoke at some length in my last year's Report is the teacher. In addition to the ordinary subjects which are taught in Japanese schools, Mrs. Williams and Mrs. Piper give instruction in knitting and sewing ; and religious teaching, with singing and prayer, form a part of every day's work.

In 1880 the attendance improved to between thirty and forty, and later it rose to nearly fifty, and in 1886 to between fifty and sixty. The value of such schools is shown by two interesting incidents, mentioned in Mr. Fyson's Annual Letter for 1885. The son of Mr. Tsurumoto, the late master of the school, is the first boy referred to. Mr. Fyson says:—

A boy about six years old, son of the former master of the school, is now living with his grandfather at the other side of the city and attends a day-school there. Last year the teacher of his class was one day explaining to the pupils that the person called "God" in the text-book, and described as the Ruler of all things, was the sun-god whom all Japanese have been accustomed to worship. This boy said, No: it meant the True God; that his father and uncle had taught him so. The teacher maintained that it was the sun-god, and the boy stuck to his point that it was the One True God; but he was of course silenced by the teacher, and went home. The next day the teacher called at the grandfather's house and half-apologised for the way he had treated the boy, and added that he did not know but what the boy might be right; and after this he adopted the boy's explanation, and taught his class that "God" meant the One True God.

The other incident is that of a young lad, a former pupil of the school, now an apprentice in a bookseller's shop. His fellow-apprentices, observing that he held his head down for a short time before beginning his meals, asked what he did that for, and also wanted to know the reason why he did not pay reverence to the Kamidana (god-shelf) as they and the rest of the household did every morning. The lad replied that he always said grace to God before his meals, and that he believed in the One True God, the Creator; he had learned that at school, and that it was foolish to worship a Kamidana. They jeered at him for forsaking the gods of his country and worshipping the foreigners' God; but they have so far come round to his way of thinking, that they have given up paying reverence to the Kamidana, and the master of the house himself is half-ashamed of doing so. The lad's grief is that his master will make him work on Sundays as well, but he means to be baptized when he gets a bit older. There are no doubt more cases like these that we never hear of.

In May, 1879, the Rev. J. Williams was transferred from Hakodate to Tokio. Additional strength was now thrown into the work. Mr. Williams, whilst continuing his studies in the language, shared the preaching at the city preaching room with Mr. Piper, and Mrs. Piper and Mrs. Williams worked together in the day and Sunday-schools. During the year seven adults and five children were baptized.

On December 26th, 1879, a terrible fire broke out about a mile from the mission premises. It spread with alarming rapidity, and destroyed thousands of houses in its onward march until the mission property was threatened. The buildings belonging to some other missions in the vicinity were burnt to the ground; but the houses, church, and schoolroom of the C.M.S. Mission were all spared. Allusion is made to this calamity because it was the occasion of an exhibition of the practical benevolence of Christianity. Two years before, when a great fire took place, the missionaries undertook relief work; but on this occasion the relief was on a more extensive scale, and in the four months which followed the fatal day on which thousands were deprived of all that they possessed, Mr. Piper received from European residents in Tokio and Yokohama, and distributed amongst the sufferers, about £1,600. Mr. Matsuda, who was then Governor of Tokio, thanked Mr. Piper for his conspicuous services in a highly complimentary letter; and Mr. Piper wrote :—

> The beneficence of foreigners shown through the missionaries has produced a profound impression on the minds of many Japanese in favour of Christianity. May it result in some souls being eternally saved "so as by fire."

The year 1880 was not characterised by any large accession to the little flock at Tokio, for only five adults received baptism. One of these was the fruit of seed sown in Osaka; the other four were the members of Mr. Tsurumoto's family already referred to. But the slowness of the Church's growth did not interfere with the discharge of the missionary's first duty to "preach the Gospel to every creature"; and the Tokio brethren continued their efforts in church, and school, and mission-room with unflagging zeal—thankful for "the great privilege of unfolding 'the old, old story,' and urging large numbers to cast away idolatry and indifference, and turn to the living God."

Towards the close of 1880 the Tokio station lost its first missionary workers by the return to England of Mr. and Mrs. Piper, through the failure of the latter's health. In taking leave of them a few words must be said about Mr. Piper's literary work. As a member of the Tokio Committee of the Religious Tract Society he did much to promote the creation of Christian literature in Japanese. Amongst his small tracts for general distribution may be mentioned one on "The True God," and another on "The Resurrection," which have been circulated by tens of thousands. He also prepared a "Life of Christ in the Words of the Evangelists," after the plan of a little book compiled and arranged by a lady in America, of which an edition of 10,000 was printed. Before the appointment of the Prayer Book Translation Committee in 1878, Mr. Piper joined with Bishop Williams and other Episcopal missionaries in Tokio in preparing a translation of the Morning and Evening Prayer and Litany, which were the first portions of the Prayer Book ever published in Japanese. After the General Conference of Episcopal Missionaries in 1878 he was appointed a member of the Prayer Book Committee, and shared in the work of preparing and revising those portions of the Prayer Book which were printed in 1879, and brought into general use on Christmas Day in that year. In the translation and circulation of the Holy Scriptures he took an active interest. As a member of the Revising Committee he offered a number of valuable suggestions on some of the Books of the New Testament.

He joined with several other missionaries in preparing and publishing the first three, and later the first eleven chapters of Genesis ; and his translations of Jonah, Haggai, and Malachi were the first complete books of the Old Testament ever published in Japanese. But his chief Biblical work was the Japanese Reference New Testament, which contains 12,000 references taken from the "Revised English Bible"— a book of immense value to the Church of Christ in Japan.

Mr. and Mrs. Piper left Tokio just at a time when their presence seemed so necessary to develop and strengthen the work they had commenced. But the work is the Lord's, and it is with unerring wisdom that He orders the movements of His servants. Mr. and Mrs. Williams now assumed responsible charge of the work which they had for some time shared with their former colleagues. In 1881 Mr. Williams baptized two somewhat remarkable women—Mrs. Ozaki, the sister of Mr. Ito, who was the first convert baptized by Mr. Dening at Sapporo several years before—and Mrs. Hada, the wife of Dr. Hada, now one of the most influential members of the Church of Christ in Tokio.

Mrs. Ozaki was at Sapporo in June, 1880, and met Mr. Dening there. She was then expecting shortly to leave for Rome to join her husband. She did not leave Japan, but returned to Tokio, where she made the acquaintance of Mr. and Mrs. Williams, and from November she attended the services and meetings to get instruction in the truths of Christianity. On the last Sunday in May, 1881, she was baptized, and Mr. Williams wrote of her as follows :—

> She is the most intelligent Japanese woman I have met, and, like her brother, possesses great force of character, so that I hope she will become a really useful member of the Church of Christ. She and Mrs. Williams seemed to take to each other from the first, and my wife says that she feels that she has quite a companion in her. It is a real pleasure to

explain a passage of Scripture to her, she seems to catch your meaning at once, and to grasp the gist of the matter almost instinctively. She had renounced idolatry in its grosser forms before she came to me for instruction, but still retained the ancestral tablets. I pointed out to her that any act of worship performed before these was really idolatry, and it was not long before she returned the tablets to the Buddhist priest, telling him that she had no further use for them, though I am glad to say she thought the matter out for herself, and did not simply take my *ipse dixit* for it. She wished to be baptized some time ago, but I advised her to write to her husband and obtain his permission before taking the step. She acted on my suggestion, but said that she had fully made up her mind to be a Christian whether her husband were favourable or not. Fortunately she was not called upon to act in opposition to her husband's wishes; in due time the reply came, and was all that a fond wife could wish. She told me some time before she heard from Rome that she prayed night and morning that God would dispose the heart of her husband to grant her request, and I need not say that we earnestly united our prayers with hers. Her brother, Mr. Ito (who has been in Tokio for some time on official business) was present when she was baptized, and his presence with us at such a time lent peculiar interest to the service.

Mrs. Ozaki's influence for good was seen shortly after her baptism in the reconciliation of two Church members, whose differences threatened a serious breach in the congregation. She "worked hard to reconcile the offenders. Her social position entitled her to the respect of both, and gave her an advantage which none of the other Christians enjoyed. At no little inconvenience to herself she visited both of them in their own homes, and ultimately they consented to meet each other at her house." The result was a complete reconciliation.

It was also owing to the exertions of Mrs. Ozaki that her friend Mrs. Hada was won to Christ, and before the close of the year—Mr. Ozaki having returned from Rome—these two Christian wives had the joy of seeing their husbands meeting Mr. Williams from time to time to read the Bible, and drawing near to the kingdom of God.

In the following year, 1882, Mr. Williams baptized five adults and two children—two of the former being Mr. Ozaki and Dr. Hada. In their final decision to serve the Lord Jesus, they were much helped by a native pastor of the Presbyterian Church. Mr. Williams thus appropriately refers to this circumstance :—

> For some time doubts about the resurrection of Christ alone prevented them from applying for baptism; but they happened to meet a native pastor of one of the Presbyterian churches in Tokio, and mentioning their difficulties to him, he entered with full sympathy into their case, and put the matter before them in such a way that their doubts were completely dissipated, and they soon after expressed to me their wish to be baptized. I think that purposely to keep His servants humble, God so works that scarcely any one, singly and unaided, can claim to have led a single soul to Christ. There has been some previous work of preparation, or there are a variety of concurring conditions and circumstances, which, if honestly taken into account, would ever lead the successful Christian worker to form a very humble estimate of himself and his work.

The introduction of such men and their wives to the Church tended to raise its tone and character. With intelligence there was spiritual power, and this was specially seen in Dr. Hada's case. From the first he was a great help and comfort to Mr. Williams, and subsequently by his deep spiritual tone, untiring zeal, open-handed liberality, and whole-hearted consecration, he has done much for the cause of Christ in Tokio. In February, 1886, Mr. Fyson wrote of him :—

> Dr. Hada continues to be the most zealous of all, and the most liberal contributor to all Christian objects. He is the only one who can be termed well-to-do, but I do not hesitate to say that his personal zeal and earnestness are of more value for the welfare of the congregation than his pecuniary support. I remember on one occasion when he was exhorting every one to do his or her best for the welfare of the congregation, he said, " If I find I have not time to do my duty to the congregation I will *make* time; make time by curtailing my other business." Professional and business men in England, hear and consider!

In September, 1883, Mr. and Mrs. Williams were compelled to return to England, and Mr. Fyson, who had been residing at Yokohama for more than a year for Old Testament translation work, removed to Tokio to take the oversight of the work. Mr. Makioka, who had worked as a catechist for several years at Niigata, was now transferred to Tokio, and threw himself heartily into the pastoral and evangelistic work of the station. Mrs. Fyson helped in the day and Sunday-schools, and Mr. Fyson's preaching and intercourse with the Christians did much to foster and develop in them the spirit of self-support. In March, 1884, Mr. and Mrs. Fyson left Japan, and it was arranged for Mr. Makioka to continue his work as the Society's agent, under the superintendence of the Rev. C. F. Warren, of Osaka. Bishop Williams, of the American Episcopal Mission, kindly undertook to administer the Sacraments and other rites of the Church between Mr. Warren's visits. It was a critical time. The Society's Tokio work had suffered considerably from the depressing foreboding that the Committee might withdraw their missionaries from the capital, and still its fate was trembling in the balance. A solid foundation of real work had been laid. In spite of some losses, a little congregation of thirty-five souls—most of them full of zeal for Christ—remained, and had a claim on the C.M.S.; and it was for many reasons desirable that their connection with the Society should be maintained. The importance of the capital as a field of labour was emphasised, and it was urged that, in the interests of Christianity in Japan, the C.M.S. ought to be represented there. The leading missionaries of other denominations earnestly deprecated the withdrawal of the Society's missionaries. On the other hand the ecclesiastical position of the clergy of the English Church in Tokio was uncertain and ill-defined, and the C.M.S. Japan Conference all but unanimously recommended the relinquishment of the work there, unless more missionaries could be sent to strengthen the expanding work at Osaka and Nagasaki.

When Mr. Warren visited Tokio in March, 1884, just as Mr. Fyson was leaving, it was evident that the minds of some of the Christians were unsettled, and as Mr. Makioka was a comparative stranger to them, it was by no means certain that he would prove acceptable to the congregation after Mr. Fyson's departure. Trouble was therefore anticipated, and before the next visit, in June, it was rumoured that some of the most zealous members of the congregation contemplated seceding. The outlook was discouraging. "With much prayer for guidance," wrote Mr. Warren, "and supported by the prayers of my colleagues and the native Christians at Osaka, I set out confident that the Lord would make His will plain, and overrule all for His own glory and the advancement of the work of His kingdom." At the first meeting of the Christians on Friday, May 30th, opinions were divided, and Dr. Hada openly declared his intention of leaving the congregation. He explained that this was from no want of desire to co-operate with the Society's missionaries, but because the bulk of the congregation were apparently unwilling to work heartily for the self-support of the Church, and that it would be better for him to join another congregation where a different spirit prevailed. The following Lord's Day, June 1st, was Whit-Sunday. The morning congregation was encouraging. There were thirty present, and eighteen C.M.S. Christians and one stranger partook of the Lord's Supper. The sermon was on the words, "Be filled with the Spirit," and what was said seemed to produce a deep impression. In view of the important questions to be discussed and decided during the week, a special prayer meeting in the evening was suggested, and some fifteen came together to plead earnestly with God for His guidance and blessing. Of this meeting, and the monthly united prayer meeting of Episcopalians, held the day following, Mr. Warren thus wrote :—

There was much in that little meeting of a dozen or fifteen to inspire hope. The earnestness and fervency of the prayers, the simple reliance upon God which they expressed, and the deep conviction that it was by the Spirit of the Lord alone that any good could result from our conferences on the work of the Church, or from that work itself, which seemed to have possession of every heart, were tokens that the Lord was with us; and yet the dark cloud of a possible secession from the congregation still overshadowed us. On the next day there was a united prayer meeting of members of the Episcopal Church, which was held at St. Paul's (the C.M.S. church). Dr. Hada was present, and offered an earnest prayer. As his intended secession from the Episcopal Church was an open secret, allusion was made to it by Mr. Makioka, and all were invited to pray that he might be guided aright. After the meeting I asked Dr. Hada to come into the vestry, and found that he was not without anxiety about the step he was contemplating. I told him that our Church needed every Christian zealous for God and anxious to promote the self-support of the native Church ; and that the efforts of the C.M.S. were intended, with God's blessing, to create and build up congregations of such persons. There would always be much in the Church we should heartily deplore, but instead of leading us to secede from it, this should rather strengthen our determination to remain, so that we might overcome the evil, and help those less conscious of their duty and privileges rightly to estimate them, and so bring glory to our Lord and Master.

The next day, Tuesday, June 3rd, a meeting which lasted nearly three hours was held, and the pastorate of the congregation, the Sunday and other services, the need of a preaching-room in the city, the day-school, and the self-support of the Church, were talked over in succession. After this prolonged meeting the native Christians held another, to discuss the financial position of the congregation. On the following day a second meeting was held, and formal decisions were registered. Dr. Hada declared his intention to remain. The congregation requested that Mr. Makioka might continue to act as their pastoral agent. Arrangements were made for increasing the number of services. The financial question was solved most satisfactorily. The catechist was then receiving yen 15 a month, and it was at first arranged that the congregation should pay fifty-six per cent. of this sum during the remainder of 1884, sixty-seven per cent. during 1885, and eighty-four per cent. during 1886, the balance in each case being paid by the C.M.S. But at a second meeting it was resolved, that instead of asking the Society for a grant to supplement their contributions, any deficiency should be met from their own pastorate fund, which then amounted to some 200 yen. "And thus," wrote Mr. Warren, "with God's blessing we reached the position which the more zealous members of the Church had longed and prayed for, and yet which only a week ago seemed very far distant." When this action had been taken Mr. Makioka, in acknowledgment of God's goodness to the Church, and as a practical proof of his earnest desire for the self-support of the congregation, requested that his salary might be reduced from 15 Yen to 12, thus voluntarily relinquishing twenty per cent. of his moderate income. Well might Mr. Warren conclude the letter communicating these facts with the words, "The Lord hath done great things for us, whereof we are glad."

From that time the little congregation took a fresh start. May we not believe, must we not acknowledge, that with renewed consecration there has been the reception of fresh power to do the Master's will and work? From Whitsuntide, 1884, to the following January, ten adults and seven children were baptized, four of them being members of Dr. Hada's household—his adopted son, his maid-servant, and two of his pupils. There was growth, too, in other respects. For some reason several of the Christians of some standing, amongst whom were Dr. and Mrs. Hada, had not been confirmed.

This was the case, too, with Mr. Makioka, who had recently come from Niigata, where he had had no opportunity of receiving the rite. They were consequently viewed by some of the members of other Episcopal congregations as wanting in fidelity to the Church of their baptism. At Mr. Warren's next visit in September the matter was talked over, and a desire was expressed for Confirmation. Bishop Williams was appealed to, and he kindly offered to hold a Confirmation when a convenient day could be fixed. On January 18th, 1885, he confirmed fifteen candidates, and afterwards administered the Lord's Supper to these and five others. Thus the unsettled feeling in regard to this and other Church questions gave place to a thoroughly loyal and hearty adherence to the edifying order of our Church as embodied in the Book of Common Prayer.

The liberality of the congregation went forward with a bound. In the previous year Bishop Poole, while reporting that the contributions of the C.M.S. and S.P.G. Christians in Japan amounted to £84, or an average of 3s. a head, noted that one congregation was in advance of the rest, having given at the rate of 7s. 9d. a head. This was the C.M.S. Tokio congregation. In 1884 the increase was nearly four-fold, as will be seen from the following list of contributions for the year furnished by Mr. Makioka :—

	Yen Sen		£	s.	d.
Pastorate Fund	120.55	= say	24	0	0
Communion Alms	19.54	,,	3	18	0
Native Missionary Society	27.12	,,	5	8	0
Evangelistic Meetings in Theatre	33.00	,,	6	12	0
Singing Master	4.15	,,	0	18	0
Old Testament Translation	3.00	,,	0	12	0

Yen 207.71 = say £41 8 0

This was at the rate of £1 9s. 6d. for each baptized member of the Church, or £1 14s. 6d. for each adult member.

The congregation were zealous in general evangelistic work. Not only did they contribute to the native Episcopal Church Missionary Society of Tokio—a society which embraces Christians of the C.M.S., S.P.G., and American Episcopal Missions, and which is managed by a representative committee, of which Bishop Williams is chairman—but they took part in a special effort to bring Christianity before the public mind in Tokio. Mr. Warren thus refers to it in his Annual Letter for 1884:—

The congregation took a warm interest in, and liberally subscribed towards the expenses connected with the holding of meetings on two consecutive days in the principal theatre in Tokio. . . . Every difficulty was surmounted, and large audiences listened on each of the two days to definite statements of Christian truth. Dr. Hada was one of the chief promoters of this movement, and he worked hard to make the meetings a success.

From June, 1884, work in the city was resumed, and preaching was held twice a week in a house rented by the Society for the purpose. The burden of this work devolved on Mr. Makioka, but he was constantly assisted by Mr. Fuyeki, and several other members of the congregation.

In March, 1885, after an absence of twelve months, Mr. Fyson returned to Tokio to resume his translational labours, and to take a general oversight of the Tokio congregation. His report for 1885 was full of encouragement, and showed that the hope of further growth and development inspired by the events of 1884 began to be realised. The following causes for thankfulness are especially noted :—

1. The Christians have maintained their position of a *self-supporting* congregation, which as you are aware, they adopted about the middle of 1884. They have paid the salary of their pastor and all Church expenses, and have received no money whatever from the Society's funds. It is

hardly necessary to say that the interest which they take in all that concerns the welfare of the congregation, now that they feel that they have something which belongs to themselves, and for which they are directly responsible, is double and treble of what it used to be. I am glad to say there is an evident determination to maintain this position of entire independence of foreign pecuniary help. I put this cause of thankfulness first, because I think this question of self-support is of the greatest importance.

2. I ought also to mention that in addition to the payment of the pastor's salary and all Church expenses, this little congregation also subscribes liberally to the Episcopal Home Mission, to the support of the Old Testament Translation Committee, and to the erection of a Christian hospital, besides paying about half the salary of an evangelist whom they set to work in the city. Last year they raised altogether about yen 375 : this includes a handsome donation from one member to the Christian hospital just mentioned.

3. I am also very thankful to be able to report a good increase—I may say a large increase—in the numbers of the congregation. During the year twenty-four were baptized, viz., nineteen adults and five children.* The number in connection with this congregation is now fifty-four, a few of whom are in the country. The new converts were brought in, I think I may say entirely, by individual members of the congregation. One of the oldest members, baptized by Mr. Piper, died during the year, and a few withdrew.

4. The weekly prayer-meeting has been well and regularly attended. Indeed there is little doubt that the continued interest and zeal of the congregation may be ascribed mainly to their prayerfulness. To give one or two instances of their earnestness in this particular: last September I found that they were meeting every evening in the church for united prayer, and when I inquired the reason I was told that they felt afraid that they were growing cold and lifeless, and so had arranged for a week of prayer to stir themselves up. I also learned that one member came early every morning to spend an hour by himself in prayer, and that another did the same in the evening, and later on in the year I found that several met in the church every morning for prayer at half-past five. How many congregations in England adopt the same means for reviving themselves?

---

* These probably include several baptized in January, 1885, mentioned on an earlier page.—C. F. W.

The progress still continues, as the following passages from Mr. Fyson's Annual Letter for 1886 shows :—

There were twenty-four baptisms—twenty-three adults and one child—and at the close of the year the number of adherents, including a few not resident in Tokio, and ten candidates for baptism—was about seventy. Number of communicants thirty. Average congregation between forty and fifty. Average number of communicants a little over twenty. Total amount of contributions for Christian work of all kinds about yen 230.

Four names were removed from the register of members, two on account of immorality, and two as having ceased to attend any Church services. But the congregation, as a whole, has grown in strength and spiritual life, and has exhibited a good deal of zeal, both for the spiritual welfare of its own members, and for the evangelization of those without. In addition to defraying all its own Church expenses—no money whatever being received from foreign funds—it has also provided the principal part of the support of two of its number specially engaged in evangelistic work. Perhaps the most encouraging feature is its zeal in prayer. The weekday prayer-meetings are most regularly attended and evidently much enjoyed; and to give a single special instance, after the usual week of prayer at the beginning of the year, held conjointly with other bodies of Christians, this congregation resolved to have a second week of prayer by itself, and the last meeting on the Saturday was the best attended of all, almost an average Sunday congregation being present.

Mr. and Mrs. Williams returned to Tokio in December, 1885. Their presence will, no doubt, do much to strengthen the hands of the Christians, as well to make the day and Sunday-schools more efficient. But their chief work is to break up fresh ground. Mr. Williams has opened two preaching-rooms in the city, and in the evangelistic work he is carrying on there he has received very efficient help from some of the Christians. One of his most zealous helpers is Mr. Fuyeki, who was baptized by Mr. Piper some years ago, and subsequently did excellent work as a colporteur of the British and Foreign Bible Society. For several years he was the most successful colporteur in Japan, and sold thousands of copies of New Testaments and portions. Dragging his well-stocked hand-cart to some open space in the city, or to towns and villages at a distance, he used to stand up and speak of the Book he loved and of the glad tidings it contains. In this way crowds often listened to his statements of Gospel truth, and many were induced to purchase portions of the sacred volume. In 1884 he felt constrained to relinquish this work, which frequently took him away from Tokio, in order that he might work for and with the Tokio congregation. He is now one of the two evangelists employed by the native Church. He is very zealous, " has a fluent tongue, and is specially useful for working amongst the poorer classes."

Thus God is using the gifts, and blessing the efforts of our European missionaries and the native Christian workers, and the little flock is steadily growing, and is being edified in purity and love. With such evidences of a Divine work our brethren may go forward trustfully. "Being confident of this very thing, that He which hath begun a good work in you will perform it until the day of Jesus Christ."

XVI.
THE CHURCH MISSIONARY SOCIETY'S MISSION.
(VII.) *Hakodate.*

"My sheep hear my voice, and I know them, and they follow me."—*John* x. 27.

T this northernmost treaty-port, in the island of Yezo, the Rev. Walter Dening arrived in the summer of 1874. As he was accompanied by Mr. Futagawa, a Nagasaki Christian, he was able to begin services at once; and the first baptism took place on Christmas Day in that year. Two disappointments, however, ensued: Mr. Futagawa left the mission, and the newly baptized person fell back. The second convert, Mr. Ogawa, has proved a valuable helper and active evangelist among his countrymen; and the large numbers that from the first attended the preaching of the Gospel—reckoned by hundreds instead of by tens as at Osaka and elsewhere—seemed to give promise of an abundant harvest hereafter.

A very interesting account of Mr. Ogawa, and of the promising commencement of work in a building in the main street of the town was sent by Mr. Dening, dated June 24th, 1875:—

On the 9th of May I opened a service in what was formerly a large shop, in the main street of the town; about 150 attended in the morning, and 200 in the afternoon. I preached both times on Matt. xxii. 2—13. On the following Sunday (Whit-Sunday) I baptized, in the presence of a large crowd, Ogawa, a young convert of whom I will speak presently. Since their commencement these services have been held regularly twice every Sunday and once in the week. Considering the opposition encountered, I am surprised that the numbers keep up as well as they do. We generally get about seventy or eighty on Sunday morning, and from 100 to 150 in the afternoon; the Wednesday evening service varies very much.

And now for the opposition. The Governor and other local authorities were excessively annoyed that I had obtained the use of a house in the main street. Hitherto all Christian services have been carried on in somewhat obscure quarters of the town—usually in the missionary's house. This is the first time that Christianity has been exposed to public view, as it were, in Hakodate. The young convert Ogawa, who took the house on my behalf, was called up by the authorities, again and again threatened, and charged not to allow any teaching or speaking in the name of Jesus in his house. He informed them he could not obey their commands, that he believed in Christianity himself, and wished it to be made known to others, and he could not interfere with my work. I have reason for believing that the whole matter was referred to Tokio; but no steps have been taken to carry the opposition further. But the Governor forbad the people to attend the service, frequently sent spies, and once came himself to see who were present.

About a month ago, six Buddhist priests came to call on me, and spent most of the morning in arguing about Christianity. I have been visited from time to time by ones and twos, but never had been attacked by six at one time. They evidently came with the idea of proving, if possible, that Buddhism was very similar to Christianity, if only rightly understood. I, seeing this, endeavoured to draw out, as clearly as possible, the difference between the two systems. The Japanese are so excessively polite in argument that it is quite a pleasure to agree with them.

Ogawa (literally "little river") is a young man who commenced attending the Bible-class last September, and since that has rarely missed, and has proved himself a steadfast believer in the Lord Jesus. Since Bible truths apprehended him (to use St. Paul's expression) I have not seen any sign of indecision in him. He has been scoffed at and persecuted in numerous ways. He receives all opposition most bravely, simply smiling at his adversaries. He endeavours to explain Christianity, as far as he understands it, to others. I heard him the other day, much to my delight, telling a dear old grey-headed man of seventy-four about the fall of man and God's anxiety to rescue poor fallen man from hell. The dear old man was struck with wonder at the story of the Cross, and kept uttering expressions of profound surprise at such a salvation. He asked, before he left, what was the name of Him who died upon the cross for sinners.

It is, under God, owing to the boldness and decision of Ogawa that I have succeeded in holding the house in the main street. Please to pray that the waters from "the little river" may flow into thirsty spots, making the desert to blossom as the rose.

HAKODATE, TREATY-PORT IN THE ISLAND OF YEZO.

During the remainder of 1875, and all through the following year, the work was continued with the same vigour as characterised its commencement. Early in 1877 Mr. Dening returned to England, and was absent from his station until May, 1878. During this interval the Rev. J. Williams, who had joined Mr. Dening in 1876, was in charge, and he was ably assisted by Mr. Ogawa and other natives.

In addition to work in the town regular evangelistic efforts were made in several villages near Hakodate. Work was commenced at Ono, a village twelve miles from Hakodate, with a population of about 2,000, in September, 1876. In March, 1877, Mr. Williams procured a house in Arikawa, a village seven miles distant, the centre of a population equal to that of Ono, where a little later weekly preaching was commenced. After Mr. Dening's return to Hakodate, Nanaye, another village, was occupied. Its population was about 400, but it was deemed a place of some importance, as there were some intelligent young men there, connected with a model farm started by the Colonization Department, who were admirers of everything foreign, and who had shown considerable interest in Christianity.

These three preaching out-stations were thus occupied before the close of 1878, and in 1879 a fortnightly meeting was started at Kikiyo, a small village of twenty or thirty houses between Hakodate and Nanaye. This was in response to the invitation of a man who was in charge of the Government branch farm, and who offered the use of his house, and promised to gather the people together. These out-stations were regularly visited from Hakodate, and for some time Mr. Ogawa resided at Ono ; and congregations, smaller or larger —sometimes in the larger villages they numbered 150 or 200 —listened to the preaching of the Gospel from the lips of the European missionary or the native evangelist.

One of the principal events of 1878 was the erection of a commodious Mission Church. The foundation stone was laid by W. J. Eusden, Esq., Her Majesty's consul at Hakodate, on August 14th, and the building, which was a strong framework of timber, with thick walls of mud and plaster, a tiled roof, and windows fitted with iron-sheathed shutters, capable of holding 300 persons, was opened on November 24th. During the erection of the church a convenient place was secured for preaching services, and good congregations—

frequently numbering 200 persons—were addressed three times a week. This work was transferred to the church on its completion. The opening of the church was an occasion of great interest and rejoicing.

In 1879 Mr. Williams was transferred to Tokio. But the year was one of no less abundant labours. In addition to

C.M.S. MISSION HOUSE AT HAKODATE.

the regular work in and around Hakodate two native evangelists spent the month of August in itinerating. One of them visited Matsumaye, a town with a population of some 16,000, about sixty miles from Hakodate, which was formerly the residence of a Daimio; the other went to Yesashi, about the same distance—the whole of their expenses being borne by the native Christians.

Mr. Dening spent much time in translational work. He also made special efforts to reach the better educated classes by preaching courses of sermons on special subjects.

The next two years showed continued progress, and several converts were baptized. One of them was an ex-Government official, well-known and much respected in Hakodate for his scholarship and force of character, and his conversion made

C.M.S. PREACHING PLACE AT HAKODATE.

a great stir in all the neighbourhood. A Shinto priest, introduced by this man as a Chinese teacher, was baptized at the same time. At the close of 1881 the baptized Christians numbered thirty-seven, and there were twelve catechumens under instruction.

But trial was at hand. In October, 1882, Mr. Dening came to England, and in January, 1883, he ceased to be a missionary of the Society. The Society's Annual Report for that year thus referred to this matter :—

> The Society's missionary staff in Japan would have remained the same as last year, but for one circumstance, which has caused the Committee much anxious concern—the disconnection of the Rev. Walter Dening. The work in the Island of Yezo, with which he has been identified from the first, has had its own features of peculiar interest; and the Committee would have rejoiced if they could have looked forward to its being still carried on for many years to come by so energetic a missionary. But being challenged to give their explicit sanction to the public and dogmatic teaching, in Japan, of novel views regarding some of the most profound and solemn theological questions, they felt, while desirous in no way to abridge the reasonable liberty of the Society's missionaries on minor and doubtful points, that they had in this case no alternative but to lose the services of a zealous agent rather than consent to the demand which his letters distinctly made upon them.

This was a severe blow to the Hakodate work, and one from which it has not yet fully recovered. Mr. Dening's disconnection was not only the loss of a laborious and painstaking missionary possessing a good knowledge of the language, and able to use it with fluency and good effect, but it resulted in the temporary secession of the senior catechist and the bulk of the Christians. It was quite providential that Mr. Andrews, whose health had suffered at Nagasaki, had, in the previous May, been transferred to Hakodate, and the changed aspect of the mission cannot be better given than in his words written at the close of 1883 :—

> The Lord has been so good to us this year. As you know, at its commencement there was much to fear, and the clouds were very dark; but all praise be to the great Head of the Church, who has ruled everything for the glory of His name, notwithstanding the imperfection of us, His agents. Our number of Christians stands as it did when Mr. Dening's followers left us. We have also two Christians from Nagasaki in our employ. It does seem a small band, but thank God, there is real life

amongst the members; the adults are earnest readers of their Bibles, and are trying to live consistently before their heathen neighbours. The number all told is ten, including three children.

The second church, which was built in 1880, after a disastrous fire in the previous December, had to be taken down early in March, 1883, owing to a dispute about the title to the land on which it was built, and the reduced band of Christians met at the mission-house for worship, whilst preaching to the heathen was carried on regularly in places secured for the purpose in the native town. During the earlier part of the year twice a week, and during the latter months every evening, except Saturdays, meetings were held, and were well attended, and at the close of the year several promising inquirers were under instruction.

It was at this time that Mr. Terata came more to the front. He had done good service as junior catechist, but more responsibility was now thrust upon him by the changed circumstances of the mission, and Mr. Andrews wrote of him :—

I cannot speak too highly of Terata San. He works most actively, and I feel sure is only actuated by love to the Master. Every day he has people in his house talking about Christianity, and he is of the greatest assistance to me in the work here.

He continued to work with Mr. Andrews as catechist until the autumn of 1884, when he entered the Osaka Divinity School to prepare for Ordination. Besides pursuing his studies he worked zealously both in the neighbourhood of Osaka and in its out-station districts, especially during the vacations. He was ordained to the diaconate on March 6th, 1887, and has now returned to Hakodate for pastoral and evangelistic work.

From the time of the division amongst the Christians already referred to everything was done to minimise its evils, and it augured well for a future reconciliation when Mr. Andrews could write at the close of 1883 :—

> We live on excellent terms with those who have separated themselves from us. Besides our monthly united prayer-meeting we meet together on the second Sunday of each month to partake of the Lord's Supper. On Christmas Day it was most cheering, and made one inwardly rejoice to see them all thus worshipping together.

After his separation from the Society Mr. Dening took up his residence at Tokio, and but little progress was made by his followers in his absence. In December, 1883, Bishop Poole reached Japan, and in the following spring he undertook the responsibility of guiding and supporting the work of the seceding party. When the Bishop visited Hakodate in June, 1884, he arranged that the seceding Christians should unite with the C.M.S. Christians in the same Sunday morning services. A year later, when lying ill at Shrewsbury—it was one of his last acts as Bishop of the English Missions in Japan—he wrote a letter urging them to consider carefully their altered circumstances, and to seek full reconciliation with the Society's Mission. This letter, and another which accompanied it from the Rev. C. F. Warren, who had visited Hakodate in March, 1883, and was therefore known to some of the Hakodate Christians, had the desired effect, and the following letter signed by fourteen of the seceders was subsequently received by the Society :—

> We respectfully write and present this letter to the honourable gentlemen of the English Missionary Society. You have already clearly understood that when in a former year, in firmly guarding our honour, we separated ourselves from the Society, there were circumstances which necessitated our doing so. Subsequently we were indebted to Bishop Poole for his kindness, and as he approached his end he gave us some earnest instruction, and with this Mr. Warren sent us an earnest letter. In advising us they both spoke of our uniting again with the believers connected with your Society. Having fully considered the matter we

feel that it is most fitting that we should again join your Society, and we desire to do so. If you will favourably regard our wish, and put us in the lowest place amongst the believers connected with your Society, we can have no greater joy.

Thus the unhappy division was healed, and the Yezo Mission took a fresh start forward. On Christmas Day, 1885, six weeks after the above letter was written, a small mission church, erected with funds raised by Mr. Andrews, was opened, and the interest of the occasion was deepened as well by the baptism of the first Aino convert in connection with our mission, as by the fact that the Christians met as a united body.

There were two Japanese adults and one child baptized during 1885, making a total of 73 baptisms since the establishment of the mission in 1874. Mr. Andrews gives the following account of this number: "Only 44 remain in Yezo. Of the remaining 29 three have renounced Christianity, four have died, six have gone to other places, eight have joined other Churches, three are in Osaka, and five cannot be traced." Of the 44 in Yezo at the close of 1885 only thirteen (eight men, two women, and three children) were in Hakodate, the rest being distributed as follow: Four at Nemuro, six at Tate, five at Ono, six at Manage, four at Okawa, five at Kamida, and one at Sapporo.

During 1886 four adults and three children were baptized, and through the efforts of Mr. Ogawa, the catechist, two backsliders—one of those baptized seven years ago—have been brought to repentance. Bishop Bickersteth visited Hakodate in the summer and confirmed eight of the Christians. His visit was much appreciated by the little flock. The five families of Christians living in the town have promised to pay the rent of a house for the newly ordained deacon, Mr. Terata, in addition to defraying all the expenses connected with public worship. One of the out-stations, "Kushiro, about 200 miles from Hakodate, promises to be flourishing. There are two families of Christians there and about ten inquirers."

Such then is the present position of the Society's Japanese work in Yezo. Compared with the southern stations exceptional difficulties have had to be encountered. A wide area, with a scattered population, consisting chiefly of immigrants from the south, would hardly be likely, even under the most favourable circumstances, to become so fruitful a field as more settled and populous districts. The division of interests among the Christians for nearly three years, and that just at a time when their united action seemed to be so essential to the growth of the work, checked its progress, and has left it still halting. And, then, whilst the distribution of the Christians, some fifty in number, in several villages may eventually be for the furtherance of the Gospel, for the present it retards united congregational action such as is possible where larger numbers of Christians reside in the same place. But God's ways are manifold, and with patient and earnest labour, carried on in faith and in simple dependence on His Spirit, we may confidently await their development, assured that He will gather a people for His name, to show forth His praise in Yezo.

WORK AT SAPPORO.

In the foregoing narrative no mention has been made of an interesting work done at Sapporo, a town near the west coast of Yezo, and north of Hakodate. This is a place of considerable importance as the centre of the operations of the Colonization Department,* and has now a population of

---

* Since Feb., 1882, Yezo, which was previously altogether under the control of the *Kai-taku-shi*, Colonization Department, has been divided into three *ken*, and its government assimilated to that of the rest of the Empire.

from 10,000 to 12,000. Here among other Government institutions there is an agricultural college, in which a number of young men receive "a good general education, with instruction in the English language and in agriculture and horticulture, civil engineering, chemistry, botany and other subjects." For about a year it was in charge of Mr. Clark, an American Christian gentleman, who had recently entered upon his duties when Mr. Dening first visited Sapporo in July, 1876. Previous to this Mr. Ito, one of the fifty students then in the college, had heard of Christ from Miss Dennis, an English lady who had for a time been in charge of a girls' normal school. On visiting Sapporo Mr. Dening found him leading a humble and simple life of faith quite alone, and on August 2nd he baptized him.

During Mr. Clark's tenure of the Principalship of the college his influence was felt among the students, and when Mr. Dening visited Sapporo in September, 1878, he found that no less than seventeen of them were Christians, brought to the knowledge and profession of Christianity through the quiet influence and holy example of that one man :—

> I found out that most of them were led to embrace the Christian faith through the instrumentality of Mr. Clark, the late Principal of the College, a man whose twelve months' connection with these young men has left an impression on their minds in reference to Christianity, which, I trust, will never be erased. From the time of his arrival to the day of his departure, his daily life and conversation seem to have shown forth the praises of Him who called him out of darkness into His marvellous light ! On being remonstrated with by the Japanese authorities for teaching Christianity, and recommended to teach morality in its stead, he held up the Bible and said, " If I teach morality, here is my textbook !" He then went on to tell them that morality cannot be divorced from religion.
>
> In his secular profession, as a teacher of theoretical and practical agriculture, he was a man of untiring activity, ingenious in devising schemes for improvement and development in all departments of the

work. He took the young men out on exploring tours, and taught them how to endure hardships and overcome difficulties, and, by a thoughtful and economical use of existing means, accomplish the ends they had in view. He took journeys through snow, and put up with all kinds of discomforts, when occasion called for it, in order to show the young men that faint-hearted, ease-loving men will never make good colonists—just the lesson the Japanese need to learn. The Christians of the college seem to have caught his spirit of enterprise and perseverance, for it is said they are always the first to volunteer when any exploring or surveying work involving difficulty and hardship has to be done.

He commenced his teaching with reading the Scripture and prayer, preached on the Sunday, and taught Christian truth during his lectures in many indirect ways. As a result of this life and teaching, added to Ito's influence in the college, by far (according to the testimony of the present professors) the most intelligent portion of the college has become Christian.

A noble example indeed of what, by the blessing of the Most High, a Christian use of secular opportunities may accomplish!

Another was added to the little band of Christians—raising the total number to eighteen—by the baptism of Mr. Arato, who was then teaching in a Government elementary school.

Arato, like his friend Mr. Ito, became and still continues a zealous Christian. When in Hakodate, he frequently assisted in evangelistic work, and was looked upon as likely to prove useful as a Christian worker. When Bishop Poole visited Hakodate in June, 1884, he arranged to have him trained in the Osaka Divinity School. Mr. Arato was then one of the seceding party, but he is now a C.M.S. student, and shows great zeal in such evangelistic work as he takes up under the Osaka missionaries.

The little church in Sapporo is still flourishing, and has about eighty members, but of these only one was baptized by a C.M.S. missionary. In August, 1885, Mr. Batchelor was present at the dedication of a new Church building, which cost

$1,300, the whole of this sum, except $140, having been subscribed by Japanese Christians. Bishop Bickersteth, who visited Sapporo in September, 1886, speaks of their fervent missionary zeal in the past, and now of their exposure to Unitarian error. During his stay he had some pleasant intercourse with them, and administered the Holy Communion to fifty of their number. Although there is no direct connection between the Church at Sapporo and the Society's Hakodate Mission, the Christians there, to whose conversion and growth in knowledge and faith the instruction of C.M.S. missionaries has contributed, and who now "shine as lights in the world, holding forth the Word of Life," may well claim an interest in our prayers, that they may continue in the grace of God and persevere in the work of winning souls to Christ.

XVII.

THE CHURCH MISSIONARY SOCIETY'S MISSION.

(VIII.) *The Aino Mission.*

" Doth He not leave the ninety and nine, and goeth into the mountains, and seeketh that which is gone astray? "—*Matt.* xviii. 12.

N occupying Hakodate the Society had in view the commencement of a mission among the Ainos, the remnant of the aborigines of the Japanese islands, now found only in Yezo. They generally live in small villages in the mountainous regions, and on the sea coasts of the island, and chiefly subsist by hunting and fishing. They are a very hairy race, and their features, expression and aspect are "European rather than Asiatic." They have no written language, and "very few traditions, and have left no impression upon the land from which they have been driven." Although low in the scale of human intelligence, and leading " a life not much raised above the necessities of animal existence," they are said to be "truthful, and on the whole chaste, hospitable, reverent, and kind to the aged."*

Their religion is "the rudest and most primitive form of nature worship," its whole sum being "a few vague fears and hopes, and a suspicion that there are things outside themselves more powerful than themselves, whose good influence may be obtained, and whose evil influence may be averted by libations

---

* *Unbeaten Tracks in Japan,* Vol. II., pp. 10, 73.

of *sake*."* Although they often talk of "the God who made the world," "they deify all the chief objects of nature, such as the sun, sea, fire," and birds, beasts, and fishes, such as "the owl, the salmon, the fox, the wolf, and the hare," whilst the bear, "which is the strongest, fiercest, and most courageous animal known to them," is constantly spoken of "not by one of its numerous proper designations, but as God."† Their great festival is the "sacrifice of the bear," which is thus described by Mr. J. J. Enslie, formerly H.B. Majesty's Consul at Hakodate, in the *Leisure Hour* of April, 1863:—

The savage denizen of the forest destined to be exalted to the position of a god is reared from a cub by the village chief, and the female most distinguished in rank and beauty enjoys the honour of being its wet-nurse. As soon as the bear is two years old, he is carried in a cage to an eminence (previously consecrated for the ceremony), amid shouts of joy and the most inharmonious concert of various noises ever heard; while from time to time, the bereft nurse utters the most piercing and heart-rending cries, expressive of her poignant grief. After this uproar has continued for some time, the chief of the village approaches the bear, and with an arrow gives him the first wound. The animal, previously maddened by the din around him, now becomes furious, the cage is opened, and he springs out into the midst of the assemblage. Then, at a signal given by the children of the nurse, everybody in the crowd wounds him with the various weapons they have brought with them, each one striving to inflict a wound; as all believe that he who fails to wound the bear has no claim to any favour from the new Kami, or god. As soon as the poor animal falls down exhausted from the loss of blood, his head is cut off, and the arrows, spears, knives, sticks, in fact all the weapons by which he has been wounded, are solemnly presented to the headless trunk by the village patriarch, who requests the bear to avenge himself upon the weapons by which he has been insulted and slain. The severed head is then affixed to the trunk, and the dead bear is carried to the altar, where the *Rama Matsouri* (the sacrifice of the bear) commences amid various

---

* *Unbeaten Tracks in Japan*, Vol. II., p. 95.
† Paper by B. H. Chamberlain, Esq., in *Memoirs of the Literature College, Imperial University of Japan*, No. I., pp. 12, 35, 36.

solemnities, such as singing, music, and offerings consisting of everything the Ainos most esteem. The nurse, meanwhile, deals blows with the branch of a tree upon every one who has taken part in the bear's death. The flesh is then distributed among the people, and the head is placed upon a pole opposite the hut of the chief, where it is left to decay.

The Ainos entertain great fear and profound respect for strength and courage; and this is the cause of their veneration for the bear—the strongest and fiercest animal known to them. Their most energetic comparison is the bear. A man is "strong as a bear," "fierce as a bear," &c. The bear is the burden of their national songs, and in a word, this animal is the symbol of everything they think worthy of respect. To compare an Aino with a bear is the surest plan to gain his friendship; and it must be acknowledged that the merit the Ainos attach to the bear is more or less deserved, as the Yezo bear is the finest specimen of his species.

According to one of their traditions, the Japanese hero Yoshitsune, of the twelfth century, came amongst them, and having obtained possession of their treasures and books by a fraud, fled, carrying all with him. To this they attribute their ignorance of the arts of civilised life; and when interrogated on any point they cannot answer, they say, "We do not know, for we have no books. Those that our ancestors had were all stolen by Yoshitsune." According to some writers the Ainos pay special reverence to this Yoshitsune. This however seems to be a mistake. "Mr. Batchelor asserts that the Ainos tell him that they never worship Yoshitsune." On the other hand Mr. Chamberlain "was told that they do worship him, but not often."*

It was during a tour in 1876 that Mr. Dening first visited the Ainos in their villages. He lived for some weeks in an Aino hut, winning the confidence of the people, learning their language, and endeavouring in a simple way to give them

---

* Paper by B. H. Chamberlain, Esq., in *Memoirs of the Literature College, Imperial University of Japan*, p. 37.

The C.M.S. Mission.—(VIII.) The Aino Mission. 263

some notion of the Gospel. Other districts were visited during a second tour in 1878. But although much information was gained and the way prepared for further efforts, not much

AINOS, ABORIGINES OF JAPAN.

was effected in a strictly missionary sense. It was subsequently arranged that Mr. John Batchelor, a lay agent of the Society, should devote himself to work among the Ainos. Mr. Batchelor was originally sent to Hong-Kong to prepare for missionary work in South China under Bishop Burdon, but on his health failing, he was transferred to the Japan Mission, and took up his residence at Hakodate. There, while continuing his other studies, he vigorously applied himself to the acquisition of the Japanese language, in which he made speedy and excellent progress. In 1878 he began to preach occasionally, and later took a regular part in evangelistic work both in Hakodate and at the village out-stations. In this way he rendered much efficient help to the ordained missionaries. In 1880 he accompanied Mr. Dening to Sapporo, and made his first visits to the Aino settlements in that district and began to study the Aino language. During 1881 he paid two visits of two months each to Piratori—the old Aino capital, where Miss Bird spent two or three days in the hut of Chief Penri, in 1878—and, whilst continuing his linguistic studies, made his first attempt to preach the Gospel. Early in 1882 it was arranged for him to return to England to complete his studies at the Islington College, but owing to the difficulties that arose in the mission he returned to Hakodate in the spring of 1883. After some weeks he started for the Aino country and remained there six months. His Aino friends had not forgotten him. They manifested great pleasure at his return, "almost whole villages turning out to welcome" him, and their chiefs expressing the hope that he would remain amongst them for a long time. He located himself with Chief Penri at Piratori, who lent him a corner of his hut. The study of the language was resumed, a vocabulary of about 6,000 words collected, an Aino grammar compiled, and some translational work attempted.* Of his evangelistic work during this visit Mr. Batchelor says :—

In the way preaching the Gospel I hold services at Piratori in chief

* Mr. Batchelor's *Grammar of the Ainu Language* has been published in *Memoirs of the Literature College, Imperial University of Japan*, No. I. 1887.

Penri's hut, and do a good bit of visiting and itinerating. The work is always very encouraging indeed, for it may be literally said that whole villages came together to listen, and sometimes very good questions are asked by the congregations. Penri always accompanies me in my preaching tours, and the services are always held in the hut of the chief who resides at the village where preaching is held. I have visited some ten or twelve villages this summer, where I have always been received with the greatest goodwill.

His visits were evidently much appreciated, for several chiefs of villages which he was then unable to visit came to ask him to visit and preach to their people.

The Ainos, though quiet and gentle, are much addicted to drunkenness. "Beastly drunkenness is the highest happiness to which these poor savages aspire." After careful inquiries in many Aino villages, Mr. Batchelor estimates that ninety per cent. of the men are drunkards, and that the women also drink to excess whenever they have opportunity.

This vice, connected as it is with their worship, is one of the greatest obstacles in the way of their receiving the Gospel. Referring to this, Mr. Batchelor wrote in November, 1883:—

> The chief thing one has to contend against is the supremely inveterate drunkenness of the Aino race. The use of strong drink (Japanese *sake*, *i.e.*, rice wine) forms part of all their religious worship; and in all ceremonies, religious or profane, it is considered indispensable, and the state of drunkenness is regarded by the Aino as a state of supreme earthly joy. Offerings of wine are from time to time placed upon the graves of the dead. How God can be acceptably worshipped without wine is a puzzle to the poor Aino, so intimately connected in his deluded mind are wine and worship. The Christian injunction against intemperance offends him, and I see, even now, the beginnings of a hard struggle between strong drink and religion.

The case of chief Penri sadly illustrates the power which this terrible vice has over the poor Aino. Mr. Batchelor in the same letter thus refers to it :—

> Chief Penri himself takes a very great interest in the religion of Jesus,

and does all he can to assist me. But drunkenness is his great stumbling-block. He has tried twice to give up his drink, but each time he has failed. On the first occasion he was sober for a whole month, and on the second for nearly three. He is now having another try to conquer his old enemy, but this time, however, calling upon the name of Jehovah to help him. I have, therefore, now greater hope of his success than I ever had before, and I earnestly hope and pray strength will be given him from on high, and he will become a conqueror of self and a true follower of Jesus.

So far this hope has not been realised. The Japanese Government seems to be desirous of protecting the Ainos and improving their condition by education. But unscrupulous traders, as in so many similar cases, have done much to hinder Mr. Batchelor's work. Of these he says :—

My next difficulty is with the Japanese merchants who trade with the Ainu. These merchants are all wine-vendors. They come here to buy the skins of animals from the Ainu, and they love to pay for them in wine rather than money. It is to the advantage of these wine-vendors to keep the poor Ainu in a state of ignorance, and that their taste for wine should be encouraged as much as possible. But they begin to see what effects Christian teaching would have upon the Ainu, therefore they are bringing all their forces to bear upon Christianity and myself. Christianity is said to be rotten, therefore useless, and not to be believed in. And as for that "rascal of a hairy Chinaman!" (meaning myself), he has come here to gain the confidence of the Ainu, learn their language, deceive them with a false religion, and, in the end, to seize the country and people.

For some time during 1884, owing to the misrepresentations of these men, Mr. Batchelor was unable to obtain a passport, and consequently could not visit the Aino districts, but he invited chief Penri to Hakodate, and there continued the study of the language. Later in the year he procured a passport, and, accompanied by Mrs. Batchelor, sister of the Rev. W. Andrews, to whom he was married at the beginning of the year, spent some time in the Aino villages. The greatest caution was necessary, lest some technical difficulty should be raised to prevent them from remaining, and they were compelled to lodge at a Japanese inn.

In 1885 they left Hakodate in May, hoping to spend six months among the Ainos. In this, however, they were disappointed, as the state of Mr. Batchelor's health necessitated

AINU WOMAN.

their return to Hakodate in August. During this visit they stayed at Poropet Kotan, of which Mr. Batchelor says :—

> Poropet Kotan is a particularly good centre for our work, for it is nearly mid-way between the Saru and Usu districts. From it, in good health, I could easily keep up close communication between half the Ainu race. In this village there are about 150 Ainu all told.

During the greater part of the time he was confined to the inn by frequent attacks of fever and other ailments, which interfered much with intercourse with the Ainos, as they " can hardly be induced to enter a Japanese house, and the

Japanese do not like them to sit on their mats." Of the gatherings for instruction he wrote :—

We were seldom able to collect more than six Ainu together in the hotel at any one time, but when well enough to preach in an Ainu hut we were generally much crowded, the congregation never numbering less than thirty. All congregations, whether Japanese or Ainu, were always largely attended when it was known that my address was to be illustrated by the magic-lantern (the magic-lantern was kindly lent me by the Rev. W. Andrews for the summer, and I found it of the greatest use).

If the year had its drawbacks and discouragements it had also some features of a cheering character, and before it closed the first Aino convert in connection with the mission was baptized at Hakodate. Mr. Batchelor thus refers to him in his Annual Letter for 1885 :—

At Poropet Kotan we soon became acquainted with a young Ainu named Kannari Taro, son of the village chief. He is a good Japanese scholar, and holds a schoolmaster's certificate. I have engaged him as my teacher of the Ainu language in place of poor old Penri, who has, I am sorry to say, entirely given himself up to strong drink, and is utterly unreliable. Kannari Taro, even before I engaged him as my teacher, early showed a great interest in Christianity. We are perfectly satisfied with him, and are thankfully rejoicing that one Ainu at least has at last been brought to the knowledge of his Saviour, and is about to take the outward sign of baptism.

This man was duly baptized by Mr. Andrews, at Hakodate, on Christmas Day, 1885; and two more—husband and wife— who were then inquirers, were baptized with their adopted Japanese daughter by Bishop Bickersteth on August 29th, 1886, when he was visiting the Aino country. Other inquirers are coming forward. In his Annual Letter, written in November, 1886, Mr. Batchelor mentions two who appear to be very earnest. Of one of them he says :—

The woman is the mother of our female (Christian) servant. She was brought to a saving knowledge of her Redeemer by her daughter and son-in-law. Her age is seventy-five. I often pay her a visit, and have made it a special rule to spend one hour every Sunday afternoon in teaching her of Christ, the Lamb of God. Nothing delights her more than to hear the " Old, old, yet ever new, story of Jesus and the Cross." Her last testimony is: Tane anakne apun no ku mokoro; tane, ratchitara ku shini eashkai ne. " Now I can sleep quietly; now I can rest in peace."

Mr. Batchelor has numerous hearers at the services he holds, and he has found a magic-lantern helpful in "impressing Scripture truths upon the minds of the people." "Mrs. Batchelor has started a singing-class for girls," which is attended by twelve. " These children are also learning to read and write. At present, being able to do neither, they have to be taught the hymns by heart, and almost any day a passer through the village may hear a child singing 'Jesus loves me,' or ' There is a happy land.' "

Several adults are also learning to read. With his Annual Letter for 1885 Mr. Batchelor sent home a copy of the Apostles' Creed, Lord's Prayer, and the hymn, "Jesus loves me "—-"the first things ever printed in the Aino language, and printed with a little press bought with money sent by the children of Jesus' Lane Sunday-school, Cambridge." Since then the translation of St. Matthew's Gospel has been proceeded with, and in November, 1886, seven chapters were ready for the press. Thus a new language is being reduced to writing, and the Word of God is being translated into it.

But the Aino race is dying out. Year by year its members decrease, and in spite of the laudable efforts of the Japanese Government to preserve it, its extinction seems inevitable. But if the race perishes, a precious remnant, won to Christ, will abide for ever. Aboriginal tribes have always had a peculiar share in C.M.S. sympathies, as the Maories of New Zealand, the Red Indians of North America, and the Arrians and Santâls of India, might well testify. And among these races the Gospel has won its greatest triumphs. Again and again has the Church Missionary Society proved the truth of the late Sir Donald Macleod's pregnant words :—

It is highly worthy of attention that in many parts of the world, where the labours of the missionary have been exercised among these primitive races, they have been attended with the most encouraging success. Whether in the Islands of the Pacific Ocean, on the Plains of Africa, or amid the hills and forests of Hindustan, they have been found alike free from those bonds which lay so fatal a hold upon the victims of other idolatries. No venerated literature records the deeds or characters of their deities ; no powerful and sagacious priesthood holds them in a state of mental or moral vassalage ; but led simply by feelings of mysterious awe and dread, which sin has given us as our heritage, to deprecate, by sacrifices and mystic ceremonies, the supposed wrath of an unknown god, they have ever evinced a disposition to listen to the soothing assurances of the Gospel, and to return the most ardent gratitude to those who have turned aside with Christian affection to raise them in the scale of being.*

That the Ainos of Japan may prove a fresh and bright example of the readiness of primitive races to receive Him who has pictured Himself as the Shepherd, leaving the ninety and nine in the wilderness and going after that which is lost until He find it, will surely be the prayer of every reader of these lines.

---

* Lake's *Memoir of Sir D. Macleod*, p. 47.

XVIII.

CONCLUSION.

"Behold, now is the day of salvation."—2 *Cor.* vi. 2.

APAN is fully open to the Gospel. The foundations of the Church are being laid. The leaven of living Christianity has been introduced and is working. Will it leaven the whole lump? Will Christianity spread so far as to affect the whole course of the nation's life? If so, will it be Protestant Christianity, or will some other form be adopted or framed to suit the national taste? These are questions which it is impossible to answer, but it will be well, nevertheless, in this concluding chapter to mark some of the prominent features of the outlook.

Enough has been already said to show that Protestant Christianity is manly, vigorous, and aggressive, and that it is growing rapidly. The words of Mr. Griffis, written more than ten years ago, read like a prophecy in course of fulfilment. He says: "A new Sun is rising upon Japan. Gently but resistlessly Christianity is leavening the nation. In the next century the native word *inaka* (rustic, boor) will mean heathen." If, indeed, the conflict were only between Protestant Christianity and the effete systems of religion which have been hitherto dominant in the country, the progress of the past six years, steadily maintained some thirty years longer, would result in Japan becoming a nominally Christian country. But other forms of Christianity are in the field and have so far registered more converts, though their rate of increase during the last few years appears to have been considerably below that of the Protestant Churches. Thus in July, 1883, the converts of the Russo-Greek Church Mission were 8,863, nearly 2,000 more than the registered Church membership of the Protestant missions at the close of the same year; whereas in 1886 they were only 12,500, or more than 2,000 less than the body of Protestant Christians. The number of Roman Catholic converts in 1881 was 25,633, more than 22,000 being in the southern part of the Empire, where thousands of the descendants of the Christians of the seventeenth century have been received into the Church. If the growth of 1881 and 1882 has been maintained, the number of Roman Catholics in Japan at the close of 1886 was about double that of 1880, whereas the Protestant Christians were twice doubled during the same period. With such rivals in the field, will Protestant Christianity eventually commend itself to the national mind, or will the marvellous changes now in progress result in the adoption of a less pure form of Christianity—a mere name without life?

Whatever answer the future may give to this question, it is a well-attested fact that the current of public opinion is steadily setting in the direction of Christianity of some form. There are multitudes still bent on maintaining the old religions—especially Buddhism—but in spite of the strenuous efforts of the priesthood, Christianity is advancing, and Christian literature is even being studied (no doubt with hostile intentions) in Buddhist Colleges. Some, like the writer of the article quoted in the *C.M. Intelligencer* for January, 1882, may still consider Christianity a national injury, and for various reasons deplore its progress "like a fire sweeping over a plain, which constantly increases in power." Many more, especially among the educated classes, following the Atheists and Agnostics of Europe, may regard Christianity as unnecessary as all religions. But in spite of all the forces hostile to the Gospel, it has become popular to advocate the adoption of Christianity as the national religion. Mr. Evington, in his last Annual Letter (1886), says that there has been "an unmistakable growth of public opinion in favour of the truth and even the necessity of Christianity," and that it is now acknowledged by unbelievers "to be the only religion that can hold its own in the enlightenment of the nineteenth century, and, what is more, the only one that can produce the necessary moral change in the hearts of the people."

But the motives which prompt the advocacy of the adoption of Christianity by the nation in the most influential quarters are mainly political. The Japanese are a high-spirited and patriotic people, and they very naturally chafe under the invasion of their sovereign rights as a nation, by the clauses of the existing treaties which deprive their Courts of Justice of jurisdiction over the subjects and citizens of Treaty Powers. With the advances they have made they claim that the time has come when this extra-territorial jurisdiction should be abolished. They are now anxious to assimilate themselves as much as possible to European nations in every respect, religion included, and hence the advocacy by some of their leading men of the adoption of Christianity as the national religion. Mr. Fukuzawa's article in the *Tokio Times* in 1884 may be quoted to illustrate this. With him it is not a question of the truth or falsity of Buddhism or Christianity. He frankly confesses that he is not a partizan of either system, and that as a personal matter he takes little or no interest in religion. He only discusses the desirableness of making

S

Christianity the national religion as a question affecting the welfare of the country, especially in its international relations. He says :—

> In the eyes of aliens, a people who cherish institutions, customs, religions differing from their own are looked upon with disdain, and as though they could not be treated as civilised nations. It may be due to this fact that international law has never yet been made to apply to Oriental lands. . . .
> If we desire to maintain our intercourse with Western nations on the basis of international law, it is first of all absolutely necessary that we remove completely the stigma from our land of being an anti-Christian country, and obtain the recognition of fellowship by the adoption of their social colour. . . .
> As an absolutely necessary preliminary, however, the Christian religion must be introduced from Europe and America, where it is propagated with the utmost enthusiasm. The adoption of this religion will not fail to bring the feelings of our people and the institutions of our land into harmony with those of the lands of the Occident. We earnestly desire, therefore, for the sake of our national administration, that steps be taken for the introduction of Christianity as the religion of Japan.

Whatever the motive for this change of front on the part of leading politicians in Japan, the fact remains ; and whilst we heartily thank God for it, we must not forget that here, as in all such crises, there is a great element of danger. One leading newspaper, at least, " has openly advocated baptizing the Emperor and a few of the nobles, that Japan may be considered a Christian nation." If this should be resolved on as a political expedient, whatever form of Christianity might be adopted, there would be a large accession of merely nominal converts to the Christian faith. The influence of the Church of Rome would certainly be felt in such a crisis, and if Roman Catholicism should be adopted as the State religion, or religion of the Court, the bulk of Japanese Christianity might become a name and form rather than a power and life.

But the future is in God's hands, and it is for us to recognise the duties and responsibilities of the present. It is the day of Japan's visitation. Most emphatically do the words apply to her, "*Now* is the day of salvation."

The changed attitude of the country towards Christianity— twenty years ago bitterly hostile, then passively neutral, now openly tolerant and friendly—the many open doors, the manifold tokens that God is with His servants in the work He has entrusted to them—all with united voice call us to work while it is day. If to Japan this is a day of salvation, it is for the Church of Christ to strain every nerve to proclaim the word of salvation throughout her Empire. It is a solemn thought that upon our realisation of the greatness of the opportunity and our readiness to seize it prayerfully and vigorously, may, in the mysterious providence of God, depend the future of the Japanese people. God grant that upon the Land of the Rising Sun may speedily arise the Sun of Righteousness, with healing in His wings.

www.ingramcontent.com/pod-product-compliance
Lightning Source LLC
Chambersburg PA
CBHW032122230426
43672CB00009B/1831